'Kate Hardcastle advises some of the world's biggest brands, retailers and, most importantly, shoppers. In this book, her first, she explores the ever-changing retail landscape, the evolution of retail over the years and the impact of technology on consumer behaviour. She concludes that in a fast-moving environment, charged by digitization and AI, that the ultimate differentiator for retail success, is, as it always has been, the human touch.'
Mike Stagg, business adviser and former executive at Unilever, Coca-Cola and Disney

'Nobody understands retail like Kate Hardcastle. This book blends deep consumer psychology with shopping Street Smarts. Add to Basket immediately, whether you're a buyer or a seller.'
Phil Williams, Broadcaster, BBC

'Kate Hardcastle's knowledge of the retail world is second to none. Having worked with some of the biggest brands worldwide, her meticulous research, communication and passion are admirable. We can all learn so much from Kate, whether it's about the consumer-lead world or simply how to shop smarter.'
Hannah Cockroft CBE, Paralympian champion and broadcaster

'Kate Hardcastle MBE is one of the leading voices in retail and consumer engagement of our times. This book is the result of more than 20 years' working in the factories, on the shop floor and in the boardrooms of many of the best-known businesses and brands today. Kate walks the walk and talks the talk and this is a must-read book for anyone wanting to truly understand their customers, improve their business, drive sales and growth.'
Natasha Hatherall Shawe, Founder and CEO, TishTash UAE, brand publicist and writer

'A powerful insight into how we buy, why we're drawn in, and what really drives our choices! Kate Hardcastle blends deep consumer psychology with everyday relevance – it's compelling, clever and a must-read for anyone who shops or sells. I particularly love the key takeaways at the end of each chapter which illustrate the personal USP Kate has for simplifying to amplify!'
Katy Hill, high performance coach and broadcaster

'It's rare that you work with someone who is a strategist but who also pays attention to detail, whilst at the same time thinking big and also being very creative. Kate Hardcastle has a passion for always doing the absolute best for the company, and her need to have meaningful insight into what were the key trends in the marketplace, made it very obvious to me what she would do next. Since then, I have been proud to watch her career progress in the public domain, where she always has valid opinions to share and is still prepared to challenge the norm. This book can become compulsory reading for both marketers and consumers in general.'
Neal Mernock, strategist, mentor and NED, Inmarco Ltd

The Science of Shopping

*How psychology and innovation
create a winning retail strategy*

Kate Hardcastle

KoganPage

First published in Great Britain and the United States in 2025 by Kogan Page Limited

Kogan Page
Kogan Page Ltd, 2nd Floor, 45 Gee Street, London EC1V 3RS, United Kingdom
Kogan Page Inc, 8 W 38th Street, Suite 902, New York, NY 10018, USA
www.koganpage.com

EU Representative (GPSR)
Authorised Rep Compliance Ltd, Ground Floor, 71 Baggot Street Lower, Dublin D02 P593, Ireland
www.arccompliance.com

Kogan Page books are printed on paper from sustainable forests.

ISBNs

Hardback	978 1 3986 2047 6
Paperback	978 1 3986 2046 9
Ebook	978 1 3986 2048 3

British Library Cataloguing-in-Publication Data

A CIP record for this book is available from the British Library.

Library of Congress Control Number

2025009722

Typeset by Integra Software Services, Pondicherry
Print production managed by Jellyfish
Printed and bound by CPI Group (UK) Ltd, Croydon CR0 4YY

To Matt, Nya, Martha and Jude – my purpose

CONTENTS

6 Roll up, roll up! This is retail theatre 129

7 The art of shopping perception 151

8 Goldilocks and the pricing strategy 184

1

The evolution of retail

From high-street store to online marketplace

Born with a passion to shop

When I think about my journey into the world of retail, my fascination with shopping and consumer behaviour has deep roots. All four of my grandparents were involved in the world of retail in some way. From manager of a department store to proprietor of the village store, my grandparents certainly instilled in me a love for this dynamic industry from a young age. Retail was quite literally in my blood. Shopping wasn't just a necessity – it was an experience, a ritual that brought joy and excitement. I vividly remember shopping trips with my grandparents in the late 1970s and 80s, a time when high streets were vibrant, bustling with life and the world seemed obsessed with consumption.

Each Saturday morning would start early with a visit to the local town to find the freshest produce at the butchers, bakers and the fishmonger. These trips weren't just errands – they were also social events. My grandparents knew the shopkeepers by name and there was sense of community and trust that defined their interactions. The conversations with each store vendor were more than business transactions; they were about sharing stories and building relationships. When the butcher set aside a special cut of meat because he knew my grandparents well and respected them, this would be a talking point for the rest of the day: how good service mattered and how respect was both earned and given.

The day would unfold as we moved from store to store, each one offering a unique array of goods. I particularly loved the haberdashers, and those eclectic shops filled with all sorts of curiosities, from cleaning supplies, household goods and greeting cards, to small trinkets and gifts. The vibrant fabrics and clinking curios created an atmosphere that to my child-like eyes was both enchanting and inviting.

As five or six years of age, I found myself captivated by how these stores were laid out, with items placed strategically to catch the eye and entice the shopper. This was my first unconscious exposure to the concept of retail theatre and merchandising.

The notion of retail as an experience has always fascinated me. It is not just about buying and selling – it's about creating an atmosphere, telling a story, connecting with customers on an emotional level. This is what makes retail so special and why it has been such an important part of my life. From the sights and sounds of a bustling market, to the joy of discovering something new, retail has a way of engaging all our senses. It is a constantly evolving industry, driven by the ever-changing desires and behaviours of consumers.

As I grew older, my interest in retail deepened and I took a part-time job on the store floor at the tender age of 11. I began to see the complexities and intricacies of this vibrant business: the art of merchandising, the science of customer psychology, and the ever-changing trends that influence buying decisions. I understood that successful retailing was not just about having the right products but about creating an experience that resonates with the consumer. This understanding has been the foundation of my career, guiding me as I have worked with some of the world's most renowned and beloved brands.

The shift to modern retail

The 1980s and 90s marked a significant shift in the retail industry. The rise of superstores and shopping malls changed the way we shopped. These expansive retail spaces were designed for convenience, offering a vast array of products all under one roof. It was a revolutionary concept at the time and brands like Tesco, Walmart and Carrefour capitalized on it, quickly becoming household names. The appeal of these superstores lay in their ability to cater to a broad range of needs, offering everything from groceries and clothing to electronics and home goods. This era was characterized by the 'big box' retail format, which promised consumers a one-stop shopping experience.

The design of these superstores was strategic. Wide aisles, bright lighting and clearly marked sections made it easy for customers to find what they were looking for, while also encouraging them to explore and make impulse purchases. The layout often included large car parks, food courts and even entertainment options, to make shopping an outing for the family. This shift from small, specialized stores to large, multi-category retailers represented a significant shift in consumer behaviour. People valued the convenience of finding everything they needed in one place, and the concept of the 'mall culture' was born and thriving, particularly in the United States.

However, even as superstores and malls were at their peak, another key shift was quietly taking shape: the digital revolution. The advent of the internet in the late 1990s and early 2000s transformed retail in ways that would have been unimaginable a decade earlier.

With the emergence of online marketplaces such as Amazon and eBay, offering consumers the convenience of shopping from home, a new era of shopping was born. This was a game-changer, as it allowed shoppers to browse, compare and purchase products from the comfort of their own homes, 24/7. The barriers of distance and time were effectively removed, opening a global marketplace to anyone with an internet connection.

I remember vividly the early days of online shopping. The idea of buying something without physically seeing it felt both exciting and slightly risky. Would the product match the picture? Would it arrive on time? Despite these uncertainties, the convenience and novelty of online shopping were somewhat irresistible for me, though certainly not for my parents. They and many of their generation remained resistant to the idea until the Covid-19 pandemic of 2020 offered consumers little other choice.

As use of the internet grew, so did the confidence of consumers. Online shopping quickly became a norm and with it came new challenges and opportunities for retailers. It was no longer enough to simply have a physical presence; businesses needed to be online, accessible and engaging. Websites needed to be user-friendly, payments secure and delivery reliable.

The digital revolution brought with it a more informed and empowered consumer. Today, shoppers can research products, compare prices and read reviews before making a purchase. This level of access to information has made consumers more discerning and demanding. They expect both quality products and a seamless shopping experience. This shift has forced retailers to adapt, to innovate and to constantly find new ways to engage with their customers.

Social media has played a pivotal role in this transformation. Platforms like Instagram, Facebook and TikTok have become essential for many brands, offering a direct line of communication with consumers. Influencers and brand ambassadors have emerged as key players in this space, shaping perceptions and driving trends. This new form of engagement adds depth to the retail experience, one that is personal, immediate and highly influential. Brands can now showcase their products in creative ways, interact with customers in real time, and build communities around their offerings.

As I reflect on these changes, I am reminded of how far we have come. Retail is no longer just about selling products; it is about creating a holistic experience that resonates with the consumer. It is about understanding their needs, desires and behaviours, and using that knowledge to deliver value. This is the new frontier of retail, one that is constantly evolving and challenging us to think in new ways.

What history has taught us about retail

To truly understand the evolution of retail, let us take a journey back to the earliest forms of commerce: the markets and souks. These bustling hubs were the precursors to modern retail stores, offering a colourful mix of goods, services and experiences. For hundreds of years souks and markets were not unique places to buy and sell; they provided a social forum where news was exchanged and relationships were built – an early form of networking if you will. The energy and excitement of these early markets can still be seen in the vibrant bazaars of Marrakech or the grand markets of Istanbul.

The tradition of haggling, still common in many parts of the world, originated in these early marketplaces. Prices were not fixed, and the art of negotiation was a critical skill for both buyers and sellers. This dynamic pricing model was based on demand, quality and the buyer's ability to negotiate, an approach reflected in the pricing strategies of today's retail and e-commerce. Perhaps not such a new 'art' after all. The cut and thrust of this lively bartering process was an integral part of the shopping experience, with a sense of accomplishment and satisfaction when a deal was struck.

Markets and souks have always been vibrant, multifaceted social spaces. In many parts of the world, markets are culinary hubs where street vendors sell everything from your morning coffee to a choice of local delicacies. In the Middle East, for example, it is common to find stalls offering fresh falafel, shawarma and aromatic coffee, making the market not just a shopping destination but a place to enjoy a meal and engage in social interactions. This blending of retail and social activity enriches the market experience, making it a cornerstone of community life.

From the vibrant souks in the UAE to the bustling markets in cities like Bangkok and Hong Kong, I am reminded of my own experiences in various market scenes across the globe. My work has taken me to diverse places such as the UAE, Saudi Arabia and various parts of Asia, where markets and souks are an integral part of daily life. In the UAE, for instance, the souks are a sensory explosion: aromas of spices fill the air, vivid textiles dazzle the eye, and the sound of traders negotiating prices creates its own energy. Each market has its own character and charm, reflecting the local culture and traditions.

In Asia, I have visited bustling markets in cities like Bangkok and Hong Kong, where the pace is frenetic and the diversity of goods on offer can be breathtaking. These markets are cultural experiences in themselves. They offer a window into the daily lives of the people, showcasing local crafts, street food and a myriad of other goods. The experience of walking through these markets, haggling with vendors and discovering unique items is something that modern retail, with all its conveniences, often cannot replicate.

These experiences have helped to influence my understanding of retail. They have shown me the importance of creating an exceptional and engaging shopping experience, whatever the retail setting. The principles of good retail – engaging customers, building trust and providing value – are universal, they transcend specific cultures and time periods. As we continue to explore the evolution of retail, it is essential to remember these roots and the lessons they offer for the future.

When the medicine man rolled into town: Salesmanship

One particularly intriguing aspect of early retail is the concept of the travelling salesman, often portrayed as the 'medicine man'. My first encounter with this sales model was watching old Westerns with my father. I vividly remember the scenes where a charismatic salesman on his wagon would come rolling along the dusty roads and into the settlement, before opening the back of his wagon and setting up a makeshift stage that the locals would gather around. There he would proclaim the efficacy of his 'medicinal compound' promising to cure everything from rheumatism to the common cold. The spectacle was sometimes complete with an assistant feigning illness, only to be 'miraculously cured' after a sip of the tonic. It was captivating and somewhat magical to watch, even via the tiny black-and-white TV screen.

Travelling salesmen were masters of retail theatre, using showmanship and storytelling to captivate audiences and persuade them to buy. The spectacle they created was a crucial part of their sales strategy, designed to draw crowds and create a sense of urgency to buy their products before they moved on to the next town.

These characters would peddle the infamous 'snake oil', a term that has become synonymous with dubious medical remedies. However, not all these products were fraudulent. Many well-known brands today have roots in this era of patent medicines. Coca-Cola, now one of our biggest global brands, began as a medicinal tonic in the late 19th century. Originally formulated by pharmacist John Stith Pemberton, Coca-Cola was advertised as a cure for headaches and fatigue, capitalizing on the era's fascination with patent medicines.[1]

Similarly, Listerine, which started as a surgical antiseptic in 1879, found its niche as a cure for bad breath and a general antiseptic. It successfully transitioned into the consumer market and became a household name.[2] These examples highlight how early retail methods, steeped in performance and persuasion, laid the groundwork for modern marketing techniques.

These early forms of retailing – markets, souks and travelling salesmen – have all influenced contemporary strategies. The emphasis on experience, storytelling and building trust remains central to retail today. Whether through a charismatic salesman of the past or a well-crafted online presence today, the core principles of engaging the customer and providing value have stood the test of time.

In today's complex retail environments, both online and offline strategies are employed to capture and pique consumer interest. The tools and platforms may have changed but the fundamental goal remains the same: to connect with the customer on a meaningful level and create a lasting impression. This historical perspective not only enriches our understanding of retail's past but also provides valuable insights into its future direction.

Bring on the show: Retail as entertainment and experience

Retail theatre today encapsulates the evolution of retail into an immersive experience, where stores transform into stages to create a captivating spectacle and shopping becomes a form of entertainment. Shopping is an event, witness the elaborate window displays of department stores, the allure of interactive pop-up shops and the digital experiences of today.

Retail theatre: creating emotion in action

The concept of 'retail theatre' is designed not just to sell products but to create an immersive experience, as exemplified by the iconic department store Selfridges in London. Founded by Harry Gordon Selfridge in 1909, Selfridges was one of the first to embrace the idea that shopping should be an enjoyable experience. Selfridge famously believed in making the customer experience as delightful and memorable as possible, with his famous 'the customer is always right' mantra. His store was designed to be a place where people could not only shop but also spend time, socialize and be entertained.[3]

Selfridges became known for its extravagant window displays and in-store events, which drew crowds and set trends. These displays were merchandising tools and works of art that told stories and captured the imagination of passers-by. The store's atrium, a grand space often used for fashion shows, exhibitions and events, further enhanced the sense of spectacle. This approach transformed shopping from a mundane activity into a special occasion, making the store itself a destination.

Harry Selfridge's dedication to creating a spectacle in retail was epitomized by the unprecedented decision to leave the lights on in Selfridges' window displays even after the store was closed. This method was revolutionary at the time and transformed the store into a night-time attraction, drawing crowds and keeping the brand in the public eye long after shopping hours, something that had never been done before. This innovation enhanced the visual appeal of the store and positioned Selfridges as a pioneer in the world of retail entertainment and marketing, repeatedly winning Department Store of the Year.

In the United States, popular department store Macy's similarly embraced the concept of experiential retail. Macy's Thanksgiving Day Parade, a beloved annual event, to this day exemplifies how retail can extend beyond the confines of a store to become a cultural phenomenon. The parade, which features elaborate floats, balloons and performances, attracts millions of spectators each year and generates significant media coverage. It is a powerful marketing tool that enhances Macy's brand image and links it with a festive holiday known for fun and togetherness as it draws shoppers into the store during the holiday season.[4]

Today's retail

Modern retail continues to explore new ways to entertain and engage customers. The rise of e-commerce has introduced new challenges, as online shopping lacks the sensory experience of physical stores. Yet retailers are finding innovative solutions to bridge this gap, as virtual reality (VR) and augmented reality (AR) technologies are helping to create immersive online shopping experiences. Companies like IKEA have developed AR apps that allow customers to visualize how furniture will look in their homes before making a purchase. This enhances the shopping experience and helps to reduce returns by ensuring customers are satisfied with their purchases.

Additionally, social media platforms have become key venues for retail entertainment – aka retailtainment. Brands use Instagram, TikTok and other platforms to host live events, showcase products and interact with customers. Influencers play a significant role in this space, as they can create engaging content that resonates with their followers. For example, fashion brands often collaborate with influencers to showcase new collections in creative and authentic ways, thereby reaching a wider audience and generating buzz.

Pop-up shops

Pop-up shops are temporary retail spaces that allow brands to create unique, often thematic, shopping experiences that generate excitement and urgency. This innovative approach can launch new products, celebrate special occasions or simply create a buzz around a brand. Pop-ups offer a way to engage customers in a physical space, even for brands that primarily operate online. For instance, Glossier, a digital-first beauty brand, has successfully used such spaces to build a physical presence and connect with customers through their different senses.[5]

The 1980s and 90s saw the rise of cult TV shopping channels, transforming home retail by bringing the shopping experience directly to viewers. These channels were among the first to turn shoppers into celebrities, featuring live-chats with buyers and making retail an interactive and appointment-to-view event. Channels like QVC and HSN capitalized on the engaging format of live demonstrations and charismatic hosts to showcase products, creating a sense of urgency and exclusivity with limited-time offers. This format made shopping convenient and entertaining. Today, this concept has evolved into new business opportunities, such as TalkShopLive, a Nashville-based retail disruptor. The business blends the interactive nature of social media with the traditional home-shopping model, offering live-streamed product demonstrations and the ability for viewers to purchase items in real time. This modern twist on a classic retail format continues to engage consumers by combining entertainment with convenience. Of course, this is also an area where social media-based retail thrives and has seen a significant success with shoppers in recent years.[6] Expect to see much more in this space.

The integration of entertainment into the retail experience is not limited to luxury or large-scale brands. Local shops and smaller retailers also use creativity to differentiate themselves and attract customers. From themed events and workshops to personalized shopping experiences, smaller retailers often create a sense of community and exclusivity that larger stores may lack. This personal touch can be a significant draw for customers seeking more than just a transaction. A stroll down the streets of an English country village where retailers unite for festivals with store window dressing and events is an enjoyable experience.

Retail has evolved from simple marketplaces to complex, multisensory experiences that entertain, engage and delight customers. As technology continues to advance and consumer expectations rise, the future of retail will likely see even more innovative approaches to creating unforgettable shopping experiences.

The power of great storytelling

As the retail landscape continues to evolve, the power of storytelling and digital transformation has become increasingly vital in capturing consumer attention and fostering loyalty. Of course, the art of telling stories to sell products in retail is not new; it has been an integral part of the industry for hundreds of years. However, the digital age has amplified its importance, providing retailers with new platforms and tools to tell compelling stories that resonate with their audiences.

With the advent of the internet and social media, retailers have access to a broader audience than ever before. This digital transformation has enabled brands to craft intricate narratives around their products and values, reaching consumers through websites, social media, blogs and digital advertisements. The rise of e-commerce has also allowed brands to create immersive online experiences that go beyond simple transactions.

A prime example of storytelling in digital retail is the brand narrative. Global brand leaders such as Apple have mastered the art of weaving a story around their products, emphasizing innovation, quality and a unique life-style as opposed to explaining the sophisticated technology behind the products. Apple's product launches are highly anticipated events, for the unveiling of new technology and for the narrative that frames these products as essential tools for a better life. This approach has created a strong emotional connection between the brand and its customers, turning them into loyal advocates.

REAL-WORLD EXAMPLE
Patagonia: Bringing principles to life

Patagonia, the outdoor-wear retailer has built its brand narrative around environmental activism and sustainable efforts, positioning itself as a leader in ethical retail. The company's story is not just about selling high-quality outdoor gear but also about advocating for the protection of the planet. Patagonia's digital presence, including its website, social media channels and email marketing, consistently highlights stories about environmental issues, conservation efforts and responsible manufacturing methods.

The brand often uses compelling visual storytelling, featuring stunning photography and videos of natural landscapes, as well as content about the environmental impact of its products and the company's initiatives to reduce its carbon footprint. Patagonia's 'Worn Wear' programme, which promotes repairing and reusing clothing rather than buying new items, is another element of its storytelling that emphasizes sustainability and resonates with its environmentally conscious customer base.

Patagonia has effectively used storytelling to strengthen its brand and connect with its audience. Through social media campaigns and user-generated content, such as the #MyPatagonia campaign, the brand empowers its customers to share their personal stories and experiences with the brand's products. This approach not only deepens the emotional connection between the brand and its customers but also amplifies its message through authentic, real-life narratives.

In his memoir, *Let My People Go Surfing: The education of a reluctant businessman*, Yvon Chouinard explains, 'My first principle of mail order argues that "selling" ourselves and our philosophy is equally important to selling product. Telling the Patagonia story and educating the Patagonia customer on layering systems, on environmental issues, and on the business itself are as much the catalogue's mission as is selling the product.' Chouinard further notes, 'Over the years we have come upon a balance between the product content and the message – essays, stories and image photos. Whenever we have edged that content towards increased product presentation, we have experienced a decrease in sales.'[7] This balance has been key to Patagonia's admirable success, demonstrating that storytelling and authenticity can drive both brand loyalty and sales.

The digital transformation of retail and the rise of data-driven storytelling offer retailers access to vast amounts of data on consumer behaviour, preferences and trends. This data allows brands to create ultra-personalized experiences for their customers, tailoring content and recommendations to individual preferences. For example, Netflix uses data to suggest content based on viewing history; Amazon recommends products based on past purchases and browsing behaviour. This level of personalization is intended to enhance the customer experience and make it more relevant and engaging.

The integration of technology in retail has enabled the creation of interactive and immersive experiences as part of a brand's storytelling. Nike, for example, has launched flagship stores that allow customers to customize products, learn about the brand's history and engage with the latest innovations. These stores aren't just retail spaces – they're experiential hubs that tell a story about the brand's values, vision and commitment to innovation.

As we look to the future, the role of storytelling and digital transformation in retail will only continue to grow. The rapid advancement of technology and machine learning, including artificial intelligence (AI), will open new avenues for storytelling and ultra-personalization.

Now that you have read how retail represents a vibrant, complex tapestry of human experience, you can perhaps understand why I am so passionate about it. From my childhood memories of bustling markets to the captivating spectacles of modern retail theatre, the world of shopping is fast-paced and fascinating. We have explored the evolution of retail, from the community-building markets of the past to today's innovative digital landscapes and we have seen how storytelling and experience are at the heart of successful brands.

Together, let's delve deeper into the intricacies of this dynamic industry, uncovering the psychological, technological and strategic elements that make retail the captivating business it is. The future of shopping is being shaped right now and understanding it is more crucial than ever. Read on as we continue to explore the art and science of consumer engagement in this thrilling and ever-changing world.

REAL-WORLD EXAMPLE

Sarah Bianchi and Nick Bianchi, Arighi Bianchi

Arighi Bianchi is a renowned, family-owned furniture and home decor retailer based in Cheshire, UK, with a legacy spanning over 170 years. Founded in 1854 by Italian immigrants, the brand has become a fixture in British retail, celebrated for its quality craftsmanship, timeless style and commitment to customer service. Housed in an iconic, Grade II* listed building, Arighi Bianchi offers a blend of traditional and contemporary furniture, combining classic designs with modern trends. The brand's enduring success is rooted in its dedication to providing beautifully crafted pieces while adapting to changing consumer tastes, making it a trusted destination for home furnishings. I spoke to Managing Director Sarah Bianchi and Partnerships Director Nick Bianchi – brother and sister who are the fourth generation in the family legacy.

170 years of retail transformation

Kate Hardcastle

(KH): Sarah and Nick, Arighi Bianchi has been an integral part of British retail for 170 years – an impressive feat in any industry. Can you share what you think has been key to your longevity in such a competitive market?

Sarah Bianchi

(SB): Absolutely, Kate. We've stayed true to our core values of quality and service, while also embracing change. From the horse-and-cart deliveries of the 19th century to today's digital-first strategies, evolution has always been at the heart of our approach. But it's about more than just adapting – it's about understanding what our customers need and want, and that comes from staying curious and connected to them.

Nick Bianchi

(NB): I agree. It's about constantly learning. In recent years, for instance, we've noticed that customers are seeking more than just products – they want experiences. This is something we've taken to heart, and it's informed our shift from being a traditional interiors store to becoming a lifestyle brand. Our 'Postcards From' campaign is a great example of how we're blending design, culture and trends into one experience. Each quarter, we spotlight a global destination, bringing its lifestyle and interiors trends to our customers, whether that's the music and laid-back style of Los Angeles or the rustic, Mediterranean feel of Sicily.

KH: I love how 'Postcards From' taps into that global influence. Retail has always been about storytelling, hasn't it? From the street markets and souks to grand department stores, it's as much about the experience as the product itself. Do you see that as part of the evolution you're talking about?

SB: Absolutely. Storytelling is integral to the retail experience. We've long understood that people don't just want to buy a sofa – they want to envision how it will look and feel in their homes, how it fits into their lifestyle. Through our campaigns, whether it's 'Postcards From' or our *Giornale* publication, we bring in elements of food, travel and even fashion, so customers feel they're part of a larger narrative, not just making a transaction. It's about creating an emotional connection.

NB: And today's consumers are so much more informed. They're not just looking for a piece of furniture; they want to know its story, where the materials are sourced, and how it aligns with their values – particularly when it comes to sustainability. For us, being transparent about those details is vital, and we've made sustainability a focus in our operations, from sourcing eco-friendly materials to reducing our plastic use and working with local suppliers.

KH: You mentioned transparency and sustainability, which are crucial in today's market. How do you balance that with the need to innovate and stay ahead in a world where trends move so quickly?

SB: It is a delicate balance. While we stay true to our heritage and commitment to quality, we know we must keep moving forward. Our research showed that customers increasingly want a seamless blend of online and in-store experiences, so we've worked on upgrading our digital presence to be as engaging as our showroom. But we also know that people still want that personal, tactile experience – especially when buying furniture. That's why we've invested in areas like our in-store events, which turn shopping into an immersive social experience.

NB: And those events aren't just about selling products; they're about building a community. We host cookery classes, educational events and even reflexology sessions. These in-store experiences give people a reason to visit us, even if they're not ready to make a purchase right away. We're not just a furniture store any more – we're a destination.

KH: It's impressive how you're leaning into this idea of retail as a lifestyle hub. Speaking of innovation, let's touch on your digital strategies. How have you found blending the online and offline worlds?

NB: It's all about creating a seamless experience for the customer. They might start their journey on our website, exploring pieces, then come to the showroom to see their options in person. We've invested heavily in making sure our digital presence is as user-friendly and warm as our physical space. But we're always learning and evolving. For example, AI is becoming a tool we use to enhance the online customer journey – whether it's suggesting complementary pieces or providing personalized recommendations based on their browsing history.

SB: We're also working to ensure that our online content reflects the same sense of discovery people get when they visit the store. 'Postcards From' doesn't just showcase products; it brings in the culture and lifestyle of a different global location, allowing customers to engage with our brand in a more meaningful way. Whether it's the sleek, minimalist vibe of Tokyo or the vibrant energy of Los Angeles, we're offering them a little window into another world.

KH: That's brilliant. The notion of retail storytelling seems to be evolving into something much more fluid and customer driven. You've mentioned how informed today's consumers are – how else have their expectations changed over the years?

SB: There's been a shift. Customers today are more design conscious and value-driven. They care about the origin of products, and they want pieces that reflect their personal style. We've also noticed that people are more willing to invest in quality, especially now that sustainability is such a hot topic. They're thinking long-term rather than following fast-furniture trends. For us, that's encouraging because we've always been about craftsmanship that stands the test of time.

NB: I think another big change is the rise of what's being called the 'experience economy'. People are seeking more than just the product – they want the entire shopping journey to be memorable, from browsing to delivery. That's why we've expanded services like our white-glove delivery, which isn't just about dropping off furniture but about providing a seamless, premium experience, even after the sale.

KH: It sounds like you've managed to blend heritage and modernity beautifully. As you look ahead, what's next for Arighi Bianchi?

SB: Our goal is to continue evolving as a lifestyle brand while staying true to our roots. We're expanding our product lines, bringing in more collaborations with designers, and focusing on that seamless online-offline experience. We also plan to keep building on initiatives like 'Postcards From', which resonate so well with our customers. It's about giving people something new, fresh and exciting while making sure they feel connected to our long history.

NB: We're also excited about deepening our engagement with sustainability. From our suppliers to how we operate, it's something we care about deeply. Our customers are looking for that transparency, and we're committed to delivering it.

KH: Thank you both. It's inspiring to hear how Arighi Bianchi has managed to stay at the forefront of retail for 170 years by blending tradition with innovation.

Key interview takeaways

1 **Embracing change while staying true to core values:** Arighi Bianchi's longevity is rooted in its commitment to quality and service, paired with a willingness to evolve – from 19th-century horse-and-cart deliveries to modern digital-first strategies, they've maintained a strong connection to customer needs.

2 **Retail as storytelling and experience:** Initiatives like the 'Postcards From' campaign highlight the brand's shift from a traditional interiors store to a lifestyle brand, integrating global influences, culture and emotional storytelling into the customer journey to create a richer retail experience.

3 **Transparency and sustainability in focus:** Responding to consumers' demand for eco-consciousness, Arighi Bianchi has prioritized sustainable initiatives, from sourcing materials to minimizing plastic use, ensuring alignment with modern values while maintaining transparency about product origins and impact.

4 **Blending physical and digital:** Arighi Bianchi enhances customer engagement by combining tactile in-store experiences with seamless online journeys. Digital innovations, such as AI-driven recommendations and personalized online content, are paired with immersive in-store events to foster community and connection.

5 **The shift to the 'experience economy':** With consumers seeking memorable experiences beyond mere transactions, Arighi Bianchi's expansion into white-glove delivery and lifestyle events underscores a dedication to delivering a premium, holistic shopping journey that reflects long-term value and quality craftsmanship.

The future of retail: Blending tradition and innovation

As we've journeyed through the evolution of retail, from bustling high streets to the vast expanse of online marketplaces, one thing remains constant: retail reflects the consumer's desires and needs, and it's a sector that must continually adapt to survive.

The essence of retail has always been about experience – whether it's the vibrant markets of ancient times or the immersive digital landscapes of today. Successful retailers understand that the power of storytelling, the creation of emotional connections and the delivery of exceptional service are as crucial now as they were in the early days of market stalls and souks.

As we move forward into a new era, retailers will need to continue blending the best of both worlds – honouring the rich traditions of customer trust and engagement, while embracing the possibilities of digital innovation. The rise of e-commerce, social media and augmented reality is reshaping consumer behaviour, but the fundamental principles remain creating value, building relationships and fostering loyalty.

The future of retail will be shaped by these principles. As we continue to explore the art and science of consumer engagement, we must remember that while the tools may change, the heart of retail remains the same: delivering value through meaningful connections.

KEY TAKEAWAYS

1 **Retail as experience:** Whether in physical stores or online platforms, successful retail hinges on creating memorable experiences that engage all the senses.

2 **The power of storytelling:** Brands that tell compelling stories – through their products, their values or their customer engagement – create deeper emotional connections with consumers.

3 **Adaptation is essential:** From the rise of superstores to the advent of e-commerce, the retail landscape has been in a state of constant change. Those who evolve with consumer behaviour and technological innovation will thrive.

4 **Digital revolution:** The shift from physical stores to online marketplaces has redefined convenience, but it also challenges retailers to innovate with user-friendly, bespoke digital experiences.

5 **Customer-first approach:** Regardless of the medium, the most successful retailers are those that understand and respond to the evolving needs and values of their customers – whether that's sustainability, transparency or personalized service.

References

1   Coca-Cola Company (nd) The birth of a refreshing idea: Coca-Cola history, www.coca-colacompany.com/about-us/history/the-birth-of-a-refreshing-idea (archived at https://perma.cc/Y8B3-U3T7)

2   Fine, Daniel H (2010) Listerine: Past, present and future – a test of thyme, *Journal of Dentistry,* 38 (Suppl.1), S2–S5, https://doi.org/10.1016/S0300-5712(10)70003-8 (archived at https://perma.cc/63G9-5NVP)

3 Morgan, Blake (2021) A global view of 'the customer is always right', *Forbes*, 10 December, www.forbes.com/sites/blakemorgan/2018/09/24/a-global-view-of-the-customer-is-always-right/ (archived at https://perma.cc/92N6-BHP9)

4 Macy's (2024) Macy's Thanksgiving Day Parade: Lineup, www.macys.com/s/parade/lineup (archived at https://perma.cc/ET8Q-EFZN)

5 FashioningLife (nd) Glossier's immersive pop-up is a multisensory exploration of fragrance, *Fashioning Life*, www.fashioninglife.co.uk/post/glossier-s-immersive-pop-up-is-a-multisensory-exploration-of-fragrance (archived at https://perma.cc/2A33-R88B)

6 White, Gemma (2020) What is Talkshoplive? The A-list site where celebrities are shilling their wares, *The National*, 15 December, www.thenationalnews.com/arts-culture/comment/what-is-talkshoplive-the-a-list-site-where-celebrities-are-shilling-their-wares-1.1128505 (archived at https://perma.cc/968S-9YTC)

7 Chouinard, Yvon (2016) *Let My People Go Surfing: The education of a reluctant businessman: Including 10 more years of business unusual*, Penguin Books, New York, NY

2

The psychology of shopping

The Equation of Value and the Buyerarchy of Needs: Why we buy, when we buy

Shopping decisions are rarely linear, nor are they purely rational. Every purchase, from the most functional to the most indulgent, is driven by a complex interplay of needs, desires and perceived worth. To understand how and why consumers make these decisions, I developed two interlinked frameworks: the Equation of Value and the Buyerarchy of Needs.

At its core, shopping is not just about exchanging money for goods – it is about the perception of worth.

This is captured in the Equation of Value:

$$\text{Product/Service} + \text{Perceived Value} = \text{Price Paid}$$

Consumers do not assess value through numbers alone; they assess it through experience, identity and expectation. The same handbag, bottle of wine or gym membership can hold vastly different value depending on context and personal perception. This means that price is not the defining factor in a purchase, perceived value is. Brands that successfully influence this perception can justify higher price points, while those that fail to do so struggle even at a discount.

But if value is subjective, how do we determine what motivates consumers to buy? This is where my Buyerarchy of Needs comes in. Inspired by Maslow's Hierarchy of Needs, but adapted specifically for the fluidity of consumer decision-making, the theory acknowledges that consumers do not always move in a structured sequence from necessity to aspiration, they shift dynamically between financial practicality, emotional pull and social validation.

For example, in uncertain times, a consumer may focus on financial constraints and seek out cost-per-use justification (a functional level of need). Yet the same consumer might also justify a premium purchase based on emotional triggers, nostalgia, self-reward or the psychological reassurance of quality. This fluid movement means that a product or service must meet the consumer at the right level of need at the right time, whether that is functionality, status or deeper self-actualization.

This chapter explores the psychology of shopping through this lens: how brands influence perceived value, how consumers justify purchases beyond necessity, and how decisions are often shaped less by price and more by the emotional and social frameworks in which they sit. Whether we are justifying a high-end coffee machine as a financial investment, choosing a luxury handbag for its brand cachet, or snapping up a discount deal for the thrill of it, every shopping decision exists at the intersection of value, emotion and need, constantly shifting, constantly evolving.

Understanding the Hierarchy and Buyerarchy of Needs

Psychologist Abraham Maslow created the theory of the Hierarchy of Needs in the 1940s, a foundational theory in psychology that outlines a framework for understanding human motivation.[1] Maslow's pyramid begins with the most basic physiological needs, such as food, water and shelter, essential for survival. As these basic needs are met, individuals can focus on higher-level needs: safety, love and belonging, esteem and finally, self-actualization, that is, the pursuit of personal growth and fulfilment.

Maslow's theory posits that higher-level needs become more significant only after lower-level needs are satisfied. In retail, understanding this hierarchy helps businesses recognize why consumers prioritize certain purchases. For example, during economic downturns like the current cost-of-living crisis, consumers may prioritize functional needs over luxury goods.

The Buyerarchy of Needs

Expanding on Maslow's concept, I created my own 'Buyerarchy of Needs', to help my clients and their teams to understand consumer behaviour specifically

FIGURE 2.1 The Buyerarchy of Needs (after Maslow's Hierarchy of Needs)

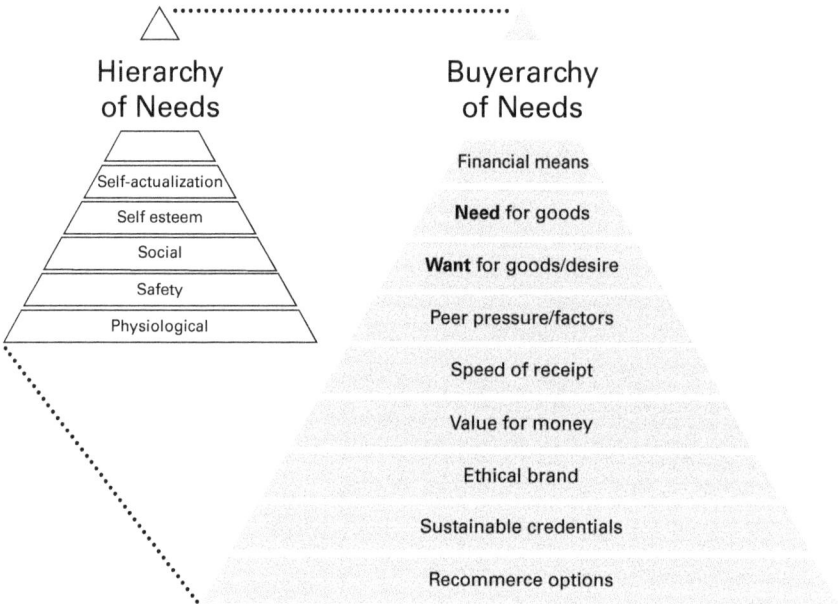

in the retail context. This model acknowledges that shopping decisions are influenced by a complex array of motivations beyond basic needs. The Buyerarchy of Needs is a dynamic model reflecting how consumers' purchasing decisions are often fluid, influenced by emotions, social factors and situational context. Unlike Maslow's static hierarchy, the Buyerarchy allows for movement between levels based on emotional and social triggers, even when financial means or practical needs suggest otherwise.

For instance, even if a consumer cannot afford a high-end product, emotional desires such as the allure of owning a prestigious item can lead them to make purchases that exceed their budget, sometimes resulting in debt. This phenomenon is supported by research highlighting how emotions play a significant role in consumer behaviour, often overriding rational decision-making processes.

AN EXPLANATION OF THE VARIOUS DRIVERS IN MY BUYERARCHY OF NEEDS

Ethical brand: While some consumers prioritize ethical considerations, research shows that emotional appeals or the lure of lower prices can override these values, leading to choices that may not align with their sustainability goals.

Financial means: While typically foundational, this level can be bypassed if the emotional drive is strong enough. For example, consumers may use credit to purchase luxury items they can't afford immediately.

Need for goods: Practical needs are often overshadowed by desires for non-essential items, particularly during emotionally charged events like holidays or sales.

Peer pressure/factors: Social influences can push consumers to make purchases they would not normally consider, such as trendy items promoted by influencers or peers, driven by the desire to fit in or gain social approval.

Recommerce options: The desire for newness or the latest trends can often overshadow sustainable habits like buying refurbished, second-hand products or items with recyclable parts or features.

Speed of receipt: The demand for immediate gratification can lead consumers to prioritize fast delivery options, sometimes paying premium prices for the convenience.

Sustainable credentials: Consumers increasingly prioritize sustainability, particularly after exposure to news stories or impactful media, but this commitment can waver under the influence of emotional advertising or attractive pricing of less-sustainable options.

Value for money: This consideration can be overshadowed by emotional factors or social pressures, such as the perceived prestige of owning a particular brand.

Want for goods/desire: Emotional appeals, such as the desire for new technology or fashion, can elevate the priority of non-essential items, leading consumers to prioritize these wants over practical needs.

Fluid movement across levels demonstrates that consumer behaviour is complex and often guided more by emotions and immediate desires than by rational planning or financial constraints. This insight is crucial for retailers and those aiming to engage consumers effectively by addressing the emotional and social dimensions of their shopping experience.

When I created my 'Buyerarchy of Needs' theory it was clear to me that consumer behaviour, much like Maslow's Hierarchy of Needs, follows a structured set of motivations and desires. From the foundation of financial means to the pinnacle of sustainability and self-actualization, this framework allows us to better understand how brands engage consumers at every level of their journey.

The fluid gearbox of consumer decisions: A look at the Buyerarchy of Needs

In today's consumer landscape, decision making is far from straightforward. Instead, it often resembles a fluid gearbox, where motivations shift dynamically between practical needs, emotional triggers and social influences. The Buyerarchy of Needs provides a valuable framework for understanding this journey, revealing how consumers like Matt navigate different motivational 'gears' – from financial considerations to aspirational desires and social validation – depending on their circumstances and psychological impulses.

Imagine Matt, who begins with a casual interest in purchasing a high-end coffee machine – a non-essential, luxury item. At first, he approaches this potential purchase with practical intentions, focusing on whether the product fits within his budget. However, as he explores the features and sees how it fits into his lifestyle, his motivations shift fluidly, moving up and down through the Buyerarchy. This journey reveals how non-essential products can engage consumers across multiple levels, leveraging a powerful blend of practicality, emotion and social appeal.

Matt's journey: Justifying a luxury purchase through the Buyerarchy of Needs

Financial means: Weighing the cost against daily expenses

Matt's journey begins with financial means, evaluating whether the high cost of a luxury coffee machine can fit within his budget. He's accustomed to buying coffee daily, often spending around £4 per cup. Initially, purchasing a high-end coffee machine feels like a splurge. But as he calculates the cost of his daily coffee habit – approximately £1,450 annually – he realizes that the machine could save him money over time by allowing him to make café-quality coffee at home.

Brands often leverage this insight by framing high-cost items as long-term savings, helping consumers justify an initial expense as a practical investment. For Matt, this shift reframes the coffee machine from a luxury to a financial choice that could ultimately help him reduce his yearly expenses, subtly opening the door for him to consider it seriously.

From practicality to enhanced daily life

As Matt delves into the machine's features – customizable brewing, high-quality filters and a sleek design – he shifts from financial means to the need for goods. This is no ordinary coffee maker; it's designed to create an elevated experience that feels personalized. Matt imagines brewing a perfectly crafted coffee whenever he wants, improving his mornings and reducing the stress of rushing to a café.

This shift highlights how functionality can blend with emotional appeal. What began as a practical consideration starts to feel like a life-enhancing product. Brands that connect functional benefits to lifestyle improvements help consumers like Matt see a product as adding tangible value to their daily lives, transforming a 'nice-to-have' into a 'must-have'.

How lifestyle appeal cultivates desire

With his interest piqued, Matt moves into the realm of desire, focusing not just on the machine's function but on how it complements his lifestyle. He starts picturing it in his own kitchen, alongside curated accessories that complete the look. The coffee machine has become more than a device; it's a lifestyle statement that reflects Matt's taste, attention to detail and appreciation for quality.

Brands use imagery and storytelling to position products as aspirational, helping consumers feel that the item isn't merely functional but an expression of their identity. For Matt, the coffee machine now represents sophistication, transforming his motivation from practicality to a deeper personal desire. He's no longer looking at a coffee maker; he's envisioning an enhanced daily ritual that reflects who he is.

Social validation: Joining a community of like-minded individuals

Matt's journey continues as he encounters online reviews, influencer endorsements and social media posts showcasing the same coffee machine. Suddenly, the product represents more than just personal enjoyment; it's also a way to align with a community of people who share his values and aesthetic. Owning this machine becomes a status symbol, a mark of quality and taste that resonates with others who value similar things.

For brands, cultivating social proof and peer validation can add weight to the purchase decision, making consumers feel that their choice is not just personally rewarding but socially supported. For Matt, seeing this validation reinforces his decision, giving him the sense that by buying this coffee machine, he's joining a like-minded community that values quality, sophistication and attention to detail.

Instant gratification: Capturing the moment of excitement

Another significant factor in Matt's journey is the availability of quick delivery. The option for next-day shipping adds a new layer of appeal, promising that he could be brewing his first coffee the very next morning. Brands that offer rapid delivery or in-store pickup options tap into consumers' desire for instant gratification, reducing the likelihood of second-guessing and capturing the excitement of an immediate reward.

For Matt, the promise of a swift delivery transforms his decision into an experience he can look forward to immediately, helping him commit to the purchase while his enthusiasm is at its peak. By catering to instant gratification, brands allow consumers to act on their excitement without delay, turning purchase anticipation into a source of satisfaction.

Justifying value beyond the price tag

Though excited, Matt still needs to feel that the luxury coffee machine is worth the expense. Here, the perception of value for money becomes key. While the price is high, the product's quality, durability and warranty coverage make it feel like a worthwhile investment. For Matt, the coffee machine is no longer a one-time expense but a long-term addition to his daily routine, offering both functionality and pleasure.

Brands that highlight a product's longevity, quality and customer support help justify the price, creating a sense of value that resonates with consumers on a practical and emotional level. For Matt, the coffee machine has become an investment in his daily life – a choice that feels rewarding both now and in the future.

Ethical appeal: Aligning with personal values

Lastly, Matt considers the brand's sustainability efforts. Knowing the machine is energy-efficient and built with recyclable materials adds an ethical dimension to his decision. While environmental considerations may not have been his initial motivator, aligning the purchase with his values offers an additional layer of satisfaction.

For many consumers today, a brand's ethical and sustainable policies can significantly impact purchase decisions. Brands that promote responsible initiatives allow consumers to feel that their choices are both fulfilling and conscientious, adding depth to the purchase experience. For Matt, this final ethical alignment completes the journey, making his purchase feel like a decision he can feel good about holistically.

The rapid shifts in consumer decision-making: Balancing fast reactions and in-depth reflection

As Matt navigates his decision-making process, he is not only shifting between different needs and desires but doing so at a remarkable speed. Research into consumer psychology shows that decisions about purchases can be made in milliseconds. For instance, a study from Princeton University found that it takes only about 100 milliseconds for individuals to form first impressions.[2] This speed can set an initial tone – positive or negative – that influences the rest of the decision-making journey. In Matt's case, an immediate positive reaction to the coffee machine's aesthetics or features might predispose him to think favourably of the purchase, even as he continues to weigh practical concerns.

Yet, the same rapid processing applies to doubts. Humans are naturally equipped to make fast, intuitive decisions – a phenomenon Nobel laureate Daniel Kahneman describes in his book *Thinking, Fast and Slow* as 'System 1' thinking.[3] This system handles quick, automatic judgements that don't require much conscious effort, such as initial excitement or hesitation about a product. For Matt, moments of guilt over the expense or practical doubts about maintenance might arise just as quickly, as 'System 1' kicks in to warn him of potential downsides.

This fast-thinking process can lead to swift shifts between positive and negative reactions. Matt may be excited about the coffee machine one moment and, within seconds, feel a pang of guilt about the cost or a concern about upkeep. These rapid 'gear shifts' are common in consumer behaviour, as people use cognitive shortcuts, or heuristics, to quickly evaluate options. For example, the 'availability heuristic' – a mental shortcut where people rely on immediate examples that come to mind – might cause Matt to remember a friend who bought an expensive kitchen gadget but rarely uses it. In an instant, he questions whether he'll fall into the same pattern.

Despite these rapid shifts, consumers also have the capacity to engage in more deliberate, rational analysis – what Kahneman calls 'System 2' thinking. This slower, more reflective process allows consumers like Matt to weigh pros and cons, calculate long-term costs and envision how the coffee machine might fit into their lifestyle. This deeper processing can take anywhere from a few seconds to several minutes or longer, depending on how much information the consumer considers relevant. For instance, when Matt thinks about the potential maintenance involved or the logistics of stocking coffee pods, he's using System 2 thinking to assess practical aspects beyond his initial emotional response.

Talking ourselves in and out of purchases: The power of cognitive dissonance

Consumers like Matt often experience cognitive dissonance during their decision-making process – a psychological discomfort that arises when they hold conflicting thoughts or beliefs about a purchase. For Matt, excitement about owning a high-end coffee machine conflicts with guilt over the expense and fear of buyer's remorse. To resolve this discomfort, he might talk himself into or out of the purchase in rapid cycles. This dissonance fuels a pattern of constant reassessment, where he alternates between justifying the purchase ('It will save me money in the long run') and finding reasons to avoid it ('What if I end up not using it?').

Research shows that cognitive dissonance can prompt people to reframe their thinking to reduce discomfort, often leading to self-persuasion. For instance, Matt might remind himself of how much he spends on café coffee to alleviate the guilt of the coffee machine's price, temporarily pushing him back up the Buyerarchy of Needs as he focuses on long-term value rather than immediate cost. However, this shift can be temporary, and another reminder – like the thought of having to clean the machine regularly – can quickly bring him back down, reintroducing doubts.

Emotional and rational processing in rapid shifts

Studies also show that emotional decisions often dominate in the early stages of consumer behaviour. According to research by neuroscientist Antonio Damasio, emotions play a fundamental role in decision making, even when people believe they are being rational.[4] Emotional reactions – like Matt's excitement over owning a stylish, convenient coffee machine – often drive initial interest. However, these feelings can be fleeting, particularly when they compete with practical concerns. This tug-of-war between emotional impulse and rational analysis creates a 'back-and-forth' effect where Matt's motivations shift up and down the Buyerarchy of Needs in rapid succession.

Consumers can also experience 'decision fatigue' when faced with too many shifts in motivation or when they try to process multiple concerns at once. For Matt, constantly weighing the pros and cons – cost versus convenience, desire versus guilt – can lead to decision fatigue, making him more likely to defer the purchase entirely. Brands that understand this dynamic can help simplify decision making by addressing the consumer's primary concerns early on, reducing the mental effort required to justify a purchase.

Inside the consumer's evolving internal dialogue

In essence, Matt's decision-making process is a real-time conversation with himself, where excitement, hesitation and rationalization all compete for dominance. Each thought or feeling acts like a gear shift, propelling him up or down the Buyerarchy of Needs in quick succession. In mere seconds, Matt might move from feeling enthusiastic about the coffee machine's benefits to questioning its practical value, then back to excitement as he imagines enjoying a fresh brew at home.

The speed and complexity of these internal shifts make the consumer journey inherently dynamic. Matt's decision isn't a single moment of choice; it's an evolving dialogue where he balances his emotions with rational concerns, personal values and social influences. Brands that respond to this dynamic, fluctuating state can craft marketing strategies that gently guide consumers through these shifts, acknowledging their hesitations while reinforcing the product's appeal.

Ultimately, Matt's experience encapsulates the intricacies of modern consumer behaviour, where purchases are seldom driven by one clear-cut motivation. Instead, decisions are shaped by a rapid and ongoing interplay of impulses, practicalities and self-reflection, making each consumer journey unique, fluid and fascinating.

And dear reader, after all of that, you may want to know that Matt did indeed buy the coffee machine – and hates to clean it!

How brands like Apple engage consumers across the Buyerarchy of Needs

Matt's journey demonstrates how consumers move fluidly across different layers of motivation within the Buyerarchy of Needs, shifting between practicality, emotional satisfaction and social validation. For brands, recognizing this fluidity allows them to craft strategies that resonate across multiple levels, meeting consumers where they are in their decision-making journey. Apple exemplifies this approach, seamlessly engaging consumers across every level of motivation – from financial flexibility to aspirational branding and social proof – especially during its annual product launches.

FINANCIAL ACCESSIBILITY: MAKING PREMIUM PRODUCTS ATTAINABLE

Despite their premium prices, Apple's products are made accessible through financing options, trade-in programmes and partnerships with telecom providers. By promoting these flexible payment solutions, Apple allows consumers to enjoy high-end devices without the immediate financial burden. For instance, Apple's trade-in initiative enables consumers to offset the cost of a new device by trading in their old model, effectively lowering the price.

This approach empowers consumers who may not otherwise consider a premium device, transforming the financial barrier into a manageable option. Apple combines accessibility with exclusivity, allowing consumers to feel that high-quality products are within reach, which is especially impactful for those who may have initially viewed Apple devices as out of budget.

ASPIRING TO MORE: CREATING DESIRE THROUGH LIFESTYLE MARKETING

Apple takes its appeal to the next level by crafting a narrative around each product, positioning it as an integral part of a sophisticated lifestyle. During its annual launch events, the brand's cinematic presentations highlight how each device seamlessly enhances daily experiences. Apple doesn't just describe product features; it narrates how these features transform moments, from capturing memories in stunning resolution to connecting effortlessly across devices.

This aspirational marketing strategy allows Apple products to transcend functionality, transforming them into lifestyle symbols. The latest iPhone or MacBook becomes more than a device – it's an extension of personal identity. By linking products to lifestyle enhancement, Apple invites consumers to see their devices as a gateway to a refined, high-tech lifestyle.

SOCIAL PROOF AND PEER VALIDATION: CULTIVATING A COMMUNITY OF ENTHUSIASTS

Apple products carry significant social cachet, making ownership a status symbol. Through influencer partnerships, user-generated content and community engagement, Apple builds a network of social proof that reinforces the value of owning its devices. Consumers feel that by purchasing Apple products, they're joining an influential community known for sophistication, creativity and tech-savvy expertise.

Each iPhone release, for example, generates a surge of unboxing videos, influencer posts and consumer reviews that elevate the device as both desirable and socially relevant. This social framework encourages other consumers to buy Apple products not just for functionality but to gain recognition and validation. This sense of community, built around shared admiration for Apple's innovation, reinforces purchase confidence and strengthens brand loyalty.

INSTANT GRATIFICATION: TAPPING INTO IMPULSE AND EXCITEMENT WITH SPEEDY ACCESS

Apple understands the importance of capturing consumer excitement and does so by offering immediate access options. During product launches, pre-orders open the same day, allowing fans to secure the latest products quickly. Apple also offers in-store pickup and fast delivery options, letting consumers experience their new device almost immediately.

The psychological underpinnings of consumer behaviour: Luxury and value

Consumer behaviour is heavily influenced by psychological factors, including emotional triggers, cognitive biases and social influences.

The psychology of shopping for luxury goods

The psychology of shopping for luxury goods delves deep into the emotions, perceptions and social constructs that drive consumers to pay a premium for brands like Louis Vuitton, Hermès and Chanel. While luxury products often boast superior craftsmanship, premium materials and an enhanced shopping experience, a significant portion of their allure – and the justification for their high price tags – lies in the psychological and emotional benefits they offer to consumers.

The allure of luxury: More than just a product

At the heart of luxury shopping lies the emotional experience it offers. Consumers are not merely buying a product – they are buying into a story, an identity and a sense of belonging to an exclusive club. This emotional connection is a key driver of the demand for luxury goods. Psychologically, luxury purchases are often tied to self-esteem, status and identity construction.

For example, when someone purchases a Hermès Birkin bag, they are not just investing in a finely crafted leather product. They are tapping into a narrative of exclusivity, rarity and craftsmanship that has been cultivated over decades. The Birkin, which can sell for tens of thousands of dollars, offers its owner a sense of prestige and social validation. The waiting lists, the rarity of the product and its association with celebrities all enhance the allure, creating a perception that owning one signifies a particular social standing.

This emotional experience is deeply rooted in the psychology of luxury consumption, where status and identity are constantly being negotiated. Consumers are drawn to luxury goods not just for their functional use but for the intangible benefits they provide – elevating one's social standing and reinforcing personal identity.

The role of scarcity and exclusivity

Scarcity is one of the most powerful tools in luxury marketing. Limited-edition collections, rare materials and exclusive in-store experiences all create a sense of urgency and desire. This scarcity principle is grounded in psychological theories, such as reactance theory, which suggests that when individuals perceive their freedom to obtain a product is restricted, they want it even more.

Luxury brands have historically mastered the art of scarcity. For instance, luxury cars like Ferrari or Lamborghini produce a limited number of vehicles each year, and buyers must often wait months or even years to get their hands on one. The brands cultivate an image of exclusivity, and this scarcity makes their cars not just about transportation but symbols of success, status and aspiration.

Over time, the scarcity tactic has evolved. Luxury brands are increasingly creating products with limited availability, not just in terms of volume but in terms of where and how they are offered. Some brands only release certain products to their top clients or at invitation-only events, further driving the emotional desire to belong to an elite group.

This psychological allure of scarcity can be traced back to centuries-old customs among luxury brands, where access to rare goods was reserved for the aristocracy and the elite. Today, luxury goods remain symbols of distinction, and this perception is intentionally fostered by brands.

Luxury in a cost-of-living crisis: Why people still spend

One of the most intriguing aspects of luxury psychology is how resilient the sector can be, even during economic downturns. In a cost-of-living crisis, one might expect consumers to abandon luxury brands in favour of more affordable options. However, the reality is often quite different.

Luxury brands have long offered escapism. In tough times, consumers may turn to them as a form of solace or reward.

Moreover, luxury goods are seen as investments. In times of economic uncertainty, consumers may prefer to buy a high-quality, long-lasting product rather than multiple lower-quality items. A luxury handbag, for example, is often perceived as timeless and can even appreciate over time, as is the case with a rare Birkin.

In the modern era, the perception of luxury goods as investments has been bolstered by the rise of resale platforms like The RealReal or Vestiaire Collective, which offer consumers the opportunity to buy second-hand luxury items. These platforms validate the idea that luxury goods can hold, or even increase, their value, further justifying their high price tags.

The influence of social status and identity

At its core, luxury shopping is also about self-identity and social status. Consumers of luxury brands often view these products as extensions of their personality and as symbols of their success. For many, the allure of luxury lies in its ability to confer a certain social standing.

This is particularly evident in the role of conspicuous consumption, a concept introduced by economist Thorstein Veblen.[5] Conspicuous consumption refers to the act of buying expensive items to display wealth and social status rather than for their intrinsic value. In today's world, this can be seen in the way consumers flaunt their luxury purchases on social media. Platforms like Instagram have amplified the psychological pull of luxury goods, allowing users to showcase their wealth and success to a global audience, be it wearing a luxury watch or indeed boarding a private jet.

Today, luxury brands continue to emphasize this personal touch, offering services like private shopping appointments, personalized products and bespoke experiences. However, the scale and nature of these services have evolved with technology. With advancements in digital personalization, brands can now offer customized recommendations based on purchasing history and preferences, maintaining a sense of exclusivity even as their customer base broadens.

The lure of personalization and customization

Another aspect that makes luxury so appealing is the ability to personalize and customize products. Luxury consumers want to feel that their purchases are unique and tailored to their specific tastes. Brands like Louis Vuitton and Gucci offer personalization options, allowing customers to add their initials to a leather luggage tag or choose custom colours for their bags.

This level of tailor-made detailing enhances the emotional connection between the consumer and the product. It turns the item from a commodity into something inherently personal and unique. The psychology behind this is tied to the endowment effect, which suggests that people place a higher value on things they feel a personal connection to or believe they have a role in creating.[6]

The ability to personalize luxury products taps into deeper psychological needs for self-expression and identity. By offering customization, luxury brands allow consumers to feel that their purchase reflects their individuality, further reinforcing the emotional value of the product.

The dupe market and why luxury still prevails

The rise of dupes (duplications/products that look similar but will be created en masse and to much lower quality) and affordable alternatives has made luxury goods more accessible in terms of design, but not in terms of status

or identity. While high-quality dupes may offer a similar look and functionality, they lack the emotional and psychological cachet that comes with
owning a luxury brand.

This is where signal theory plays a role.[7] Luxury brands act as signals of
wealth, taste and exclusivity. Even though a dupe may look like a designer
item, it does not carry the same social capital. For the consumers that care,
owning a premium item sends a message to the world about who you are,
and for many, that message is worth the premium price.

The future of luxury: Experience over ownership

The future of luxury shopping is increasingly shifting towards experience
rather than ownership. Younger consumers, particularly millennials and
Gen Z, are more interested in the experiential aspect of luxury rather than
just owning a product. This has given rise to concepts like luxury rentals and
luxury subscriptions.

Services like Rent the Runway allow consumers to rent designer clothes
and accessories for a fraction of the price, enabling them to experience
luxury without the long-term commitment.[8] Similarly, high-end concierge
services offer exclusive experiences, such as private shopping sessions, access
to limited-edition items and bespoke travel experiences.

This shift towards experiential luxury reflects a broader psychological
trend. Younger consumers are placing more value on experiences and memories than on material possessions. For luxury brands, this means that the
future may involve creating immersive, memorable experiences that go
beyond the product itself.

At its core, the psychology of luxury shopping is about perceived value.
Consumers are not just paying for the product – they are paying for the
story, the experience and the emotional satisfaction that it brings. Luxury
goods offer a sense of identity, status and exclusivity that is deeply rooted in
human psychology.

Yet psychological drivers behind shopping do not just sit at the luxury
end of life – but indeed the value end too…

The psychology of bargain hunting and the need for a value purchase

The allure of finding a bargain transcends the simple act of saving money; it
taps into deep psychological motivations that drive consumers to seek out

deals, discounts and special offers. Bargain hunting provides not only economic satisfaction but also emotional and psychological rewards, turning shopping into an experience that offers a sense of accomplishment, control and personal validation. What is for some shoppers an absolute necessity for others becomes more of a game and enables 'bragging rights'. For many consumers, the act of finding a discount is just as fulfilling, if not more so, than the product itself. This psychological phenomenon is intricately tied to how we perceive value, manage our emotions and satisfy our need for control over our purchasing decisions.

The thrill of the hunt: More than just savings

At the heart of bargain hunting is the thrill of the search. Consumers are not just seeking out lower prices; they are looking for the rush that comes with finding a good deal. This experience can be likened to a treasure hunt, where each successful bargain provides a sense of accomplishment. The psychological impact of finding a bargain extends far beyond the financial savings – it taps into feelings of triumph and satisfaction.

This phenomenon is connected to the concept of 'dopamine-driven shopping'; when we discover a great deal, the brain releases dopamine, the chemical associated with pleasure and reward. This rush reinforces the behaviour, encouraging consumers to continue seeking out bargains for the emotional pay-off they provide. Over time, this can create a cycle where the pursuit of discounts becomes more important than the actual purchase.

The emotional high of securing a deal

At its core, bargain hunting is driven by the psychological concept of perceived value. Consumers don't just seek out the lowest price; they seek out what they believe is the best value. This perceived value is a combination of the product's utility, the savings achieved and the emotional satisfaction derived from the purchase. In this context, bargain hunting becomes a psychological exercise in maximizing value rather than simply minimizing cost. I always simplify this as *value received for price paid*.

Retailers have long understood the power of perceived value and use it to their advantage. Sales, coupons and flash discounts are designed to create a sense of urgency and heighten the perception that consumers are getting more for less. This tactic taps into prospect theory, which suggests that people are more motivated by the prospect of avoiding losses (in this case, missing out on a deal) than by the potential for equivalent gains.

Loss aversion and the fear of missing out

The psychology of bargain hunting is deeply intertwined with loss aversion, a principle from behavioural economics.[9] Loss aversion suggests that people experience the pain of losing something (or missing out on a deal) more intensely than the pleasure of gaining something of equal value. This principle is key to understanding why consumers are so driven to pursue bargains – failing to take advantage of a deal can feel like a significant loss.

Retailers often capitalize on this with tactics such as limited-time offers, flash sales and countdown clocks, all designed to trigger the consumer's fear of missing out (FOMO). This sense of urgency heightens the emotional stakes of the shopping experience, making the pursuit of a bargain even more compelling.

When a consumer feels they might miss out on a deal, it triggers a sense of anxiety and urgency. This emotional state can push consumers to make quicker purchasing decisions and even buy items they don't necessarily need, simply to avoid the perceived loss of an opportunity.

The need to avoid loss is so powerful that consumers may spend hours searching for the best deal, even if the financial savings are relatively small. This behaviour illustrates how the emotional impact of missing out on a bargain can override logical decision-making processes.

Bargain hunting and control

For many consumers, the act of bargain hunting is about exerting control over their shopping experience. In an economy where prices can feel dictated by corporations, finding a deal provides consumers with a sense of agency. They feel empowered by their ability to navigate the system, uncover discounts and make purchasing decisions that are financially advantageous.

This need for control is particularly important in times of economic uncertainty, where consumers may feel that external factors – like inflation or wage stagnation – limit their financial freedom. Bargain hunting offers a way to regain some of that control by allowing consumers to stretch their budgets and feel more in charge of their spending habits.

Additionally, the abundance of information available to consumers today – through price comparison websites, deal aggregators and review platforms, and the magic of a reverse image search – has made it easier than ever to hunt for bargains. This access to information enhances the consumer's sense of control, as they can easily compare prices across retailers and make informed decisions. The power to choose the best deal provides a psychological boost, reinforcing the feeling that they are making smart, rational choices.

The satisfaction of smart shopping

Bargain hunters take pride in being smart shoppers. This identity is deeply tied to the belief that they are making informed, rational purchasing decisions, rather than being swayed by marketing or brand prestige. For these consumers, finding a deal is not just about saving money – it's about being clever, resourceful and savvy.

In many cases, bargain hunting is a social activity, where consumers share tips, deals and strategies with friends and family. Online forums, social media groups and deal-sharing websites have turned bargain hunting into a communal experience, where like-minded shoppers can connect over their shared pursuit of value.

This social aspect adds another layer to the psychology of bargain hunting. Consumers not only feel validated by their own success but also by the recognition they receive from their peers. Sharing a deal can spark admiration, gratitude and camaraderie, reinforcing the positive emotions associated with the purchase.

Moreover, bargain hunting as a group activity – whether in person or online – can heighten the sense of competition. Shoppers may feel a sense of rivalry as they race to secure the best deals, further increasing the emotional stakes of the hunt.

The dark side of bargain hunting: Compulsive buying

While bargain hunting can provide significant psychological rewards, it also has a darker side. For some consumers, the pursuit of deals can become compulsive, leading to overconsumption and even financial strain. The emotional high of securing a bargain can drive consumers to buy items they don't need, simply because the deal is too good to pass up.

This behaviour is closely tied to the psychological concept of impulse control. The thrill of finding a bargain can override the consumer's ability to make rational decisions, leading to purchases that provide short-term emotional satisfaction but may not be necessary or financially wise in the long run.

Retailers are aware of this tendency and often design sales and promotions to encourage impulse buying. Limited-time offers and flash sales are particularly effective at pushing consumers to make quick decisions, capitalizing on their desire to avoid missing out on a deal.

For some consumers, this compulsive behaviour can lead to bargain fatigue – a state where the constant pursuit of deals becomes overwhelming and exhausting. In these cases, the emotional rewards of bargain hunting may diminish, leaving the consumer feeling stressed or dissatisfied.

In both luxury shopping and bargain hunting, the consumer's psychological motivations play a pivotal role in driving purchasing decisions. While these two types of shopping may seem to cater to vastly different audiences, they share common psychological underpinnings, such as the desire for status, identity formation, emotional satisfaction and control. Luxury shopping leverages exclusivity, scarcity and customization to fulfil consumers' need for self-expression and social validation, while bargain hunting appeals to the desire for value, accomplishment and control over one's financial resources.

In the chapters to come, we will dive deeper into these psychological mechanisms, uncovering how retailers manipulate scarcity, personalization and pricing strategies to trigger emotional responses. Whether it's the rush of finding a deal or the prestige of owning a luxury item, consumers are driven by needs that transcend the act of purchase. Retailers, in turn, are adept at capitalizing on these motivations through targeted marketing, sales tactics and consumer engagement strategies.

We will also explore how modern technology, including AI and Big Data, has revolutionized both the luxury and bargain hunting experiences. Personalization has become more sophisticated, allowing retailers to create one-on-one relationships with consumers that drive loyalty and repeat business. Simultaneously, technology empowers bargain hunters with tools for price comparisons, deal notifications and online communities that fuel the competitive and social aspects of bargain shopping.

From the allure of exclusivity to the satisfaction of a smart purchase, understanding the psychology behind these shopping behaviours gives retailers a road map for shaping consumer experiences. In the following chapters, we will explore these strategies in greater depth, analysing case studies from leading brands, in both the luxury and value sectors, and examining how these psychological principles are applied in real-life situations.

The mechanics of consumer influence: Scarcity and beyond

The scarcity principle is a powerful tool in consumer influence, based on the idea that limited availability enhances an item's perceived value. This principle is widely used in retail to drive urgency and prompt quick decision making. Brands, for example, may release limited-edition products or use countdown timers on e-commerce sites to indicate an offer's impending expiration. This creates FOMO, compelling consumers to act quickly to secure exclusive deals.

For instance, limited-edition sneaker releases from brands like Nike or Adidas often generate significant hype and demand.[10] These products are marketed as exclusive, with a finite number available, often paired with a countdown timer to the release. Fashion brand Supreme exemplifies this by releasing products in limited quantities, creating high demand and urgency.[11] This approach not only drives immediate sales but also elevates the brand's exclusivity and desirability. The 'drop' model, where new products launch on a specific day and time, frequently results in items selling out within minutes, further amplifying their perceived value.

This tactic heightens product desirability and encourages immediate purchases, often resulting in rapid sell-outs, and has in turn created a whole secondary market scene with retailers such as Stock X. The secondary sneaker market has seen explosive growth in recent years, fuelled by the scarcity and exclusivity of certain models. Collectors and enthusiasts are willing to pay premium prices for limited-edition releases, driving up resale values.[12]

StockX is a leading online marketplace for buying and selling sneakers. It offers a platform where prices fluctuate in accordance with demand, acting like a stock market; it has become a go-to destination for sneakerheads looking for rare and sought-after models. The platform's transparent pricing and authentication services have helped legitimize and expand the secondary sneaker market.

Countdown: Time-sensitive discounts

Time-sensitive discounts, such as flash sales or early bird specials, leverage urgency to push consumers towards making faster purchasing decisions. These discounts often come with a ticking timer or a specific expiration date, reinforcing the scarcity of the opportunity. This strategy taps into the psychological desire to avoid regret, or missing out on a perceived bargain or those highly prized concert tickets.

E-commerce platforms like Amazon frequently use time-sensitive deals during events like Black Friday or Prime Day.[13] By displaying a countdown clock next to discounted products, they create a sense of urgency, prompting consumers to buy quickly before the deal ends. This tactic is especially effective in promoting impulse purchases.

Exclusive access and membership programmes also play on the scarcity principle by offering special deals or early access to sales for members only. This not only encourages consumers to join the membership programme but also fosters a sense of exclusivity and privilege; members feel like they are part of an elite group, and many consumers place much value on the red-carpet/VIP treatment.

Engaging consumers through psychology and marketing

Emotional triggers are powerful tools in retail marketing, used to evoke specific feelings that can influence consumer behaviour. These triggers are designed to tap into the psychological and emotional needs of consumers, prompting actions such as purchasing a product or engaging with a brand. They are prevalent across various media, including advertising, online content and in-store experiences. Coca-Cola's advertising campaigns famously focus on themes of happiness, joy and nostalgia, portraying the brand as a staple at family gatherings and celebrations.[14] This emotional appeal strengthens brand loyalty and encourages repeat purchases.

Fear-based marketing, on the other hand, is a strategy that uses the potential negative consequences of inaction to motivate consumer behaviour. By highlighting risks and dangers, this approach aims to create a sense of urgency and compel consumers to act, often by purchasing a product or service that offers protection or a solution. This technique is particularly prevalent in industries where risk mitigation is crucial, such as insurance and pharmaceuticals. It is crucial for marketers to use this approach responsibly, ensuring that the fear element is balanced with informative and reassuring content. Excessive or unethical use can erode consumer trust and trigger backlash. Brands must build confidence through genuine performance, ensuring lasting loyalty.

The beauty industry often exploits emotions related to self-image and confidence. Advertising campaigns frequently promote products that promise to enhance appearance and self-esteem, tapping into the desire to look and feel your best.

Brands like Dove have been notable for their campaigns that challenge conventional beauty standards and promote body positivity. Dove has been at the forefront of promoting body positivity and challenging traditional beauty standards. The brand's Real Beauty campaign has featured women of diverse body types, ages and ethnicities; it has celebrated natural beauty and promoted self-esteem. This campaign resonates emotionally with consumers who often feel excluded by conventional beauty narratives.

Amid the rapid ascent of AI, Dove recently became the first beauty brand to ban AI-generated images of women in its advertising. This decision underscores Dove's commitment to authenticity and representation, aiming to portray real women rather than idealized, digitally created versions. This initiative aligns with Dove's ongoing efforts to combat unrealistic beauty standards and promote a more inclusive and realistic portrayal of beauty in the media.

Dove's approach not only differentiates the brand in a highly competitive market but also builds trust and loyalty via an emotional connection among its key target audience.[15] By focusing on real beauty and banning AI-generated images, Dove strengthens its message of authenticity and inclusivity, further cementing its position as a brand that genuinely cares about its consumers' well-being and self-image. This strategy has been instrumental in creating a powerful emotional connection with the brand, fostering a community of consumers who feel represented and valued.

Luxury brands use emotional triggers tied to aspiration and exclusivity. The marketing strategies of brands like Louis Vuitton, Gucci and Dior focus on the allure of luxury and the status it confers. These brands often use high-quality visuals, celebrity endorsements and limited availability to create a sense of exclusivity and desire. The marketing of luxury cars often emphasizes performance, craftsmanship and the elevated status that comes with ownership. Ads may feature sleek visuals, luxurious settings and testimonials from high-profile individuals to reinforce these messages.[16]

Marketers also use seasonal and cultural triggers to evoke emotions tied to specific times of the year or cultural events. For example, the concept of 'Blue Monday', often cited as the most depressing day of the year, is marketed to promote products and services that offer comfort or escape, such as holidays or self-care products. Travel retailers and airlines may run promotions featuring tropical destinations and sunshine during the winter months, targeting those experiencing winter blues with the promise of a mood-lifting holiday.

Emotional triggers in marketing are highly effective because they connect with consumers on a personal level, influencing decisions through feelings rather than just rational thought. By understanding and leveraging these triggers – whether through fear, well-being, beauty, luxury or cultural cues – marketers can craft compelling narratives that resonate with their target audiences. This not only drives sales but also builds deeper, more meaningful connections with consumers.

Personalization in retail involves tailoring the shopping experience to individual preferences and behaviours. This strategy is increasingly facilitated by advancements in data analytics and artificial intelligence. Curating the approach to each customer enhances the shopping experience by making it more relevant and engaging for the consumer. However, while the practice can enhance the shopping experience, it also raises concerns about privacy and data security. Retailers must navigate these issues carefully, ensuring that they use consumer data responsibly and transparently to maintain trust.

Sensory marketing

Sensory marketing fuels the senses to enhance the shopping experience. For example, the use of scent in stores can significantly affect a customer's perception and behaviour. Lush, known for its handmade cosmetics, uses a strong, pleasant fragrance that's instantly recognizable and can often travel beyond the store to the entrance and indeed the walkway to the store, instantly notifying customers that a Lush is nearby. This scent branding not only makes the shopping experience memorable but also aligns with the brand's image of freshness and natural ingredients.

Nespresso provides another excellent example of sensory marketing. In Nespresso boutiques, the experience often begins with a complimentary cup of coffee, allowing customers to taste and savour the product in a relaxed environment. This ritualistic offering of coffee not only highlights the quality of Nespresso's products but also creates a welcoming atmosphere that encourages customers to linger, explore and make purchases. The in-store design, with its clean lines and elegant decor, further enhances the sensory experience, making it feel like a luxury experience.[17]

The role of body language and non-verbal communication

Body language, a critical component of non-verbal communication, has been shown to account for a significant portion of human interaction – up to 70 per cent in some studies. This figure highlights the powerful role non-verbal cues play in shaping our understanding of interactions, often more than spoken words. In customer-facing roles, especially in high-stakes environments like luxury retail, where every gesture and glance can shape the customer experience, non-verbal communication becomes paramount. Here, customers expect not only attentive service but a level of interaction that feels genuinely tailored and personal, often relying on subtle cues beyond words.

To delve deeper into this, we can look at the work of Dr Albert Mehrabian, whose research in the 1970s sought to quantify the components of effective communication. Through his studies, Dr Mehrabian concluded that when we interpret a message, only a small fraction – 7 per cent – is derived from the actual words spoken (the verbal component). Instead, the tone of voice (vocal) accounts for 38 per cent, and body language (visual cues) represents a substantial 55 per cent. This '7-38-55 rule' suggests that a staggering 93 per cent of communication is non-verbal, underscoring the idea that people tend to focus more on how something is said rather than on the words themselves.[18]

If it helps, think of yourself in a very busy restaurant setting that has the loud chatter of diners, background music and the chinks of crockery and cutlery. Now think of attempting to engage the fast-moving wait staff – and ways in which you might do so – we very quickly become reliant on non-verbal prompts, signals and facial expression.

Mehrabian's formula has relevance in settings like luxury retail, where customers' expectations for a memorable, impactful experience are high. In these settings, sales associates are not merely delivering information about products; they are creating an immersive experience that reinforces brand values. The posture, eye contact and even the positioning of sales associates can communicate warmth, approachability and attentiveness, while subtle facial expressions and hand gestures can convey empathy, understanding and exclusivity. A misaligned or unintentional non-verbal cue, on the other hand, can disrupt this perception, leading to misunderstandings or feelings of alienation.

For example, a customer entering a high-end boutique might subconsciously read a slouched posture or lack of eye contact as disinterest or judgement, while a well-trained associate who stands tall, maintains appropriate eye contact and offers open body language is likely to make the customer feel valued and respected. Non-verbal communication, therefore, becomes an essential tool for associates to communicate inclusivity, warmth and attentiveness – qualities highly valued in luxury retail.

These findings are not limited to luxury settings alone but have broader implications for any customer service environment. In settings where emotions, perceptions and experiences drive customer loyalty, non-verbal cues can make or break relationships. The 7-38-55 principle encourages businesses to train their teams in mastering body language as part of their customer service protocols, equipping associates to 'speak' through their non-verbal behaviours as effectively as they do with words.

To implement these insights, many retail brands now focus on the physicality of customer service training, using techniques to improve posture, gesture and facial expressiveness. As associates become aware of the impact of their body language, they are better able to control the messages they send, even subconsciously. This approach aligns with research showing that individuals who are trained to project positive non-verbal cues tend to generate higher levels of customer satisfaction.

Ultimately, Mehrabian's theory on the weight of non-verbal communication provides a compelling framework for understanding why and how we connect, trust and respond in various contexts, especially within retail. Non-verbal communication, rooted in a deep and often unconscious level of human interaction, is more than an accompaniment to verbal communication – it's a primary vehicle through which we interpret meaning. As customer expectations for personalized service grow, mastering the nuances of body language becomes a valuable skill, elevating interactions from mere exchanges to experiences that foster loyalty and lasting impressions.

In a retail setting, positive body language from staff can significantly enhance the customer experience.

Key indicators of positive body language include:

1 **Smiling:** A genuine smile can make customers feel welcomed and valued, setting a positive tone for the interaction.

2 **Eye contact:** Maintaining eye contact shows attentiveness and sincerity, making customers feel heard and respected.

3 **Open gestures:** Using open hand movements and a relaxed posture can convey openness and willingness to assist.

High-end aspirational brands, for example, emphasize these behaviours in their staff training, understanding that such non-verbal cues are vital in creating an inviting and exclusive shopping experience. These subtle yet powerful gestures help build a rapport with customers, making them feel comfortable and more likely to engage in a purchase.

Negative body language and its impact

Conversely, negative body language can deter customers and negatively impact their shopping experience. Examples include:

1 **Crossed arms:** This can be perceived as defensive or unapproachable, discouraging customers from seeking assistance.

2 **Avoiding eye contact:** This may suggest disinterest or lack of engagement, making customers feel undervalued.

3 **Fidgeting or distracted behaviour:** This can indicate impatience or boredom, leading customers to feel rushed or unwelcome.

Supporting retail colleagues to identify and avoid these behaviours is crucial for maintaining a positive customer experience. Retailers can significantly improve customer satisfaction by ensuring that staff are knowledgeable and skilled in positive non-verbal communication.

While technology can enhance the retail experience, it can also inadvertently create barriers. Devices like tablets and smartphones, used for accessing product information or processing payments, can distract staff and reduce personal engagement. Research indicates that while mobile devices can enhance workplace productivity, their use for business purposes can also lead to unintended consequences. While devices offer flexibility and improved communication, they can also blur the lines between work and personal life, leading to increased stress and potential declines in productivity.

A survey highlighted that 53 per cent of employers think their company loses one to two hours of productivity a day because employees are distracted.[19]

As technology becomes an increasingly more integrated part of retail, business must strike a balance between benefiting from the opportunity of technology and maintaining the personal touch. While tablets can streamline the shopping process, staff should prioritize maintaining eye contact and verbal communication with customers, so that technology enhances rather than detracts from the overall customer experience.

Artificial intelligence and predictive analytics

Artificial intelligence will play an increasingly significant role in modern retail, particularly in predictive analytics. By analysing vast amounts of data, AI can predict consumer behaviours, preferences and trends. Retailers use these insights to tailor marketing strategies, optimize inventory management and enhance the overall customer experience. Stores of the future that are currently being developed have first iterations already in action. These use the movement, heat-mapping, engagement and interaction of consumers in-store to gain better insights and traction that can be converted immediately into real-time data and action, be that store inventory or planning for future product ranges and marketing activities.

Augmented and virtual reality in retail

Augmented reality (AR) and virtual reality (VR) are also making significant inroads into the retail sector. These technologies offer immersive experiences that can bridge the gap between online and in-store shopping. For instance, AR apps allow customers to visualize how products, such as furniture or home decor, will look in their space before making a purchase. This reduces uncertainty and increases confidence in buying decisions.

Sephora uses AR in its mobile app to let customers try on makeup products virtually. This feature, called Sephora Virtual Artist, allows users to see how different shades of lipstick or eye shadow will look on them, enhancing the online shopping experience by providing a level of interactivity typically reserved for in-store visits.[20]

VR, on the other hand, can offer fully immersive shopping experiences. Some high-end fashion brands use VR to provide virtual runway shows or 360-degree views of their flagship stores. These experiences can be accessed from the comfort of home, offering an exclusive glimpse into the brand's world, thereby enhancing customer engagement and loyalty.

A reminder of terms

Conspicuous consumption: A term coined by Thorstein Veblen that refers to the act of purchasing luxury goods to publicly display wealth and social status, rather than for functional value.

Dopamine-driven shopping: The rush or high consumers experience when they secure a deal or make a purchase, driven by the release of dopamine in the brain.

Endowment effect: A cognitive bias where people assign more value to items simply because they own them or have personalized them, increasing emotional attachment to a purchase.

Experience economy: A trend where consumers prioritize experiences, such as luxury travel or personalized services, over the ownership of material goods.

Loss aversion: A psychological principle stating that people prefer to avoid losses rather than acquire equivalent gains. In retail, it manifests in consumers' fear of missing out on deals.

Perceived value: The worth that a product or service has in the mind of the consumer, which may differ from its actual monetary value. It is influenced by factors such as brand reputation, quality and emotional satisfaction.

Reactance theory: A psychological concept that suggests people desire something more when they perceive their freedom to obtain it is being restricted, often leading to heightened interest in scarce or exclusive products.

Scarcity principle: A psychological trigger where limited availability or exclusivity increases the desirability of a product. It's commonly used in luxury marketing and flash sales.

Smart shopping: A consumer identity tied to making informed, resourceful purchasing decisions. It highlights the consumer's ability to find deals and maximize value.

REAL-WORLD EXAMPLE
Thierry Andretta

Thierry Andretta is the Former CEO of Mulberry and Buccellati, and was previously executive chairman/CEO at brands including Lanvin, Moschino, Alexander McQueen, Stella McCartney, Balenciaga, Celine and LVMH Fashion Group.

Luxury retail, sustainability and future trends

Kate Hardcastle

(KH): Thierry, thank you for joining me today. You've had an extraordinary career across luxury fashion, working with some of the most iconic names in the industry. Could you share with us the path that led you through luxury fashion, and how those experiences shaped your leadership style, particularly during your time at Mulberry?

Thierry Andretta

(TA): Thank you, Kate. It's a pleasure to be here and reflect on a career that has certainly taken me through some exciting chapters. I've been fortunate to work with luxury houses such as Gucci, Lanvin, LVMH, and later, Mulberry, each with its own distinctive DNA. Through it all, one common thread has stood out: luxury isn't just about the product, it's about the experience and the story behind it.

Each brand has taught me something invaluable about craftsmanship, consumer expectations and brand identity. At Gucci, for instance, it was about exclusivity and heritage; at LVMH, it was about innovation within tradition. And at Mulberry, what I was able to bring was a sense of how to keep a heritage brand relevant while evolving with the times. Mulberry, with its quintessentially British identity and craftsmanship, gave me the opportunity to focus on sustainability in a way that felt truly integrated into the brand's DNA, not just as a trend.

KH: Reflecting on your career across these major brands, how do you think the definition of 'luxury' has evolved over the years? Has the industry shifted in terms of what consumers expect from high-end brands?

TA: Luxury has certainly evolved, particularly in the past decade. In the earlier part of my career, luxury was very much defined by exclusivity, rarity and status – think limited editions, high price points and an air of untouchability. The focus was on product scarcity and high price signalling.

But today, luxury is about much more than that. It's about experience, personalization, and most importantly, values. Consumers today want to connect with the brands they purchase from – they want to know the story behind the product, they want to feel like they're buying into a set of beliefs. Whether it's craftsmanship, sustainability or a commitment to social causes, consumers now expect high-end brands to offer much more than just beautiful things – they want meaning.

Mulberry was a perfect case study of this evolution. It's a brand rooted in British heritage, known for its leather craftsmanship, but it also has an accessible appeal within the luxury market. I wanted to modernize Mulberry by focusing on sustainability as a core part of our proposition, ensuring that we offered a luxury experience that aligned with the values of our consumers.

KH: Your focus on sustainability at Mulberry really stood out. Can you share more about how sustainability became such a core part of the brand's strategy during your tenure? What does that journey look like for Mulberry now?

TA: Sustainability was a priority for Mulberry long before it became a buzzword. But we knew that to lead in this area, we needed to go further. We began by asking ourselves some fundamental questions: how do we ensure that Mulberry can contribute to a more sustainable future in fashion? What will it take to make this heritage brand a leader in responsible luxury?

From there, we examined every part of the business, from sourcing materials to our production frameworks. We invested in becoming carbon neutral across our UK factories, and we committed to using 100 per cent sustainable leather. These were significant steps, but they were just the beginning. We also introduced repair services, encouraging our customers to invest in pieces that would last a lifetime. A Mulberry bag, after all, is designed to be cherished, not discarded.

In addition, we launched the 'Mulberry Exchange' programme, which allows customers to trade in their old bags for store credit, encouraging a circular economy. This programme reflects a more modern, responsible approach to luxury that resonates with our customers today.

KH: It's impressive how you were able to balance heritage craftsmanship with this modern focus on sustainability. How have consumers responded to these initiatives, particularly the idea of longevity and repair services in an industry that often feels driven by fast fashion and ever-changing trends?

TA: The response has been overwhelmingly positive, especially from younger consumers who are more environmentally conscious. They understand the value of investing in something that will last, rather than being part of a disposable culture. Offering repair services and promoting the longevity of our products has reinforced the message that Mulberry is a brand for life, not just for the season.

The introduction of the Mulberry Exchange programme also taps into this shift in mindset. People are increasingly looking for ways to consume responsibly, and the idea of trading in a beloved bag to give it a second life, while getting credit towards a new piece, appeals to those who value sustainability.

What we've seen is that consumers now appreciate brands that stand for something beyond just aesthetics. They want to feel good about their purchase, knowing that it aligns with their personal values and that it has a positive impact on the environment.

KH: It sounds like Mulberry is embracing a more modern, sustainable take on luxury, but also returning to a time when people truly cherished their belongings. How did you balance the heritage craftsmanship that Mulberry is known for with the need to stay relevant in today's fast-paced market?

TA: It's one of the greatest challenges in luxury – balancing tradition with innovation. Mulberry's craftsmanship is at the heart of everything we do. Many of our artisans have been with the brand for decades, and they take enormous pride in their work. That heritage, that dedication to craft, is something that can't be replicated, and it's something our customers deeply value.

At the same time, the world of luxury is changing. Consumers expect more than just heritage – they want innovation. That's where our focus on sustainability and digital innovation came into play. We wanted to modernize the Mulberry experience without losing sight of what made the brand special. That meant introducing new ways of interacting with customers, such as virtual appointments, personalization and creating a seamless online experience that reflected the luxury you'd expect from walking into one of our stores.

It was about integrating modern needs – sustainability, digital engagement – while always staying true to our craftsmanship and the values that have been at the core of Mulberry since it was founded.

KH: Let's talk more about digital innovation. How did Mulberry adapt to the digital age during your leadership, especially as luxury retail shifted online? How do you maintain that personal touch when so much of luxury is about the tactile experience and the personal connection with a brand?

TA: Digital transformation has been crucial, particularly in recent years. Luxury has always been about the tactile – the feel of the leather, the weight of the bag, the experience of walking into a beautiful store. So, the challenge for us was to translate that into the digital world.

At Mulberry, we focused on creating a seamless, luxurious experience across all platforms. We introduced virtual appointments where customers could speak to our store staff and see products up close, replicating the personalized service we're known for. We also introduced customization options online, allowing customers to design their own bags in real time, which adds a layer of personalization that is essential in luxury.

But beyond that, digital gives us the opportunity to tell the story behind each product. Consumers can now see where their bag was made, learn about the artisans who crafted it, and understand the sustainable materials that were used. It's about creating a narrative and a deeper connection, which is just as important as the physical experience.

KH: As you look back at your time leading Mulberry and forward to the future of luxury, what excites you the most about where the industry is headed?

TA: I'm excited by the possibilities that lie ahead for the industry, particularly in terms of sustainability and digital innovation. I truly believe that sustainability is the future of luxury. Brands that don't embrace it will be left behind. Mulberry was in a strong position to lead that charge, and I'm confident the brand will continue to set an example for the industry.

I'm also fascinated by how technology will continue to evolve the luxury experience. The lines between digital and physical retail are becoming more blurred, and I think we're just scratching the surface of what's possible. Whether it's virtual experiences, personalized services, or even the way we engage with customers on a more emotional level through technology, the future of luxury is going to be about creating an even deeper connection between brand and consumer.

KH: Thierry, thank you for sharing your incredible insights today. It's been fascinating to hear about your journey and the mark you've left on the industry. I look forward to seeing what's next for both you and the world of luxury.

TA: Thank you, Kate. It's been a pleasure to reflect on these experiences, and I'm excited for what the future holds.

Mulberry was awarded the B Corp Certification in 2024, the first company in luxury fashion to do so in the UK – and the second globally, after Celine.

Key interview takeaways

1 **Evolving definition of luxury:** Andretta highlights a shift in luxury from exclusivity and rarity to a focus on experience, personalization and values, with consumers now prioritizing brand stories and shared beliefs over mere aesthetics.

2 **Sustainability as core strategy:** At Mulberry, Andretta emphasized sustainability, integrating carbon neutrality, sustainable materials, repair services and the Mulberry Exchange programme to promote longevity and responsibility in luxury.

3 **Balancing heritage with innovation:** Andretta focused on keeping Mulberry's British heritage and craftsmanship intact while introducing sustainable approaches and digital innovations, thus honouring tradition while staying relevant.

4 **Digital transformation in luxury:** Mulberry adapted to the digital landscape through virtual appointments, customization options and storytelling about craftsmanship, bridging the tactile luxury experience with online consumer engagement.

5 **Future of luxury – sustainability and digital:** Andretta believes sustainability and digital advancements are vital for luxury's future, with technology enabling deeper, more emotional connections between brands and consumers, a trend he sees expanding in the coming years.

Understanding the motivations behind every purchase

In the world of retail, consumer behaviour is never a simple equation. The decisions people make when shopping are deeply rooted in complex psychological principles, such as Maslow's Hierarchy of Needs and the Buyerarchy of Needs. These frameworks help explain the motivations, emotions and social pressures behind the purchase journey – from meeting basic needs to seeking status or self-fulfilment.

Shopping is more than a transaction – it's driven by both rational and emotional triggers. Retailers who succeed are those that can tap into these deeper motivations, appealing to the emotional and psychological needs of their customers. Whether it's creating a sense of urgency through scarcity or fostering a personal connection through storytelling, brands must acknowledge the fluidity of consumer desires and adapt accordingly.

As we continue to explore consumer behaviour, remember that shopping is not simply about acquiring goods – it is about fulfilling emotional, social and psychological needs. Retailers who understand these complexities will be better equipped to connect with their customers and build long-term loyalty in an ever-evolving marketplace.

KEY TAKEAWAYS

1 **Both luxury shopping and bargain hunting fulfil deep psychological needs:** Consumers in both markets seek emotional and social rewards, whether through exclusivity or value, status or accomplishment.

2 **Scarcity and personalization are powerful psychological triggers:** Retailers use these techniques to create urgency and a sense of uniqueness, driving consumers to spend more or act quickly on purchasing decisions.

3 **Technology plays a key role in modern shopping psychology:** AI and digital tools allow retailers to personalize the shopping experience and give consumers more control, particularly in bargain hunting.

4   **Retailers excel at exploiting the fear of missing out (FOMO):** Through
    limited-time offers, flash sales and exclusivity, retailers tap into consumers'
    fear of missing out, pushing them to make quicker purchasing decisions.

5   **The future of shopping will increasingly focus on experiences:** As
    consumers – especially younger generations – place more value on
    experiences, retailers will need to adapt by offering more immersive,
    personalized shopping environments that go beyond the product itself.

References

1   Holzknecht, James (2007) Maslow's Hierarchy of Needs, (video), Castalia
    Media, Austin, TX

2   Willis, A and Todorov, J (2006) First impressions: Making up your mind after a
    100-ms exposure to a face, *Psychological Science*, 17 (7), 592–8, https://doi.
    org/10.1111/j.1467-9280.2006.01750.x (archived at https://perma.cc/SBG2-
    9ZTC)

3   Kahneman, Daniel (2011) *Thinking, Fast and Slow,* Putnam, New York, NY

4   Damasio, Antonio (2008) *Descartes' Error: Emotion, reason and the human
    brain,* Random House, London

5   Veblen, Thorstein (1915) *The Theory of the Leisure Class: An economic study
    of institutions*, MacMillan & Co, London

6   Thaler, Richard (1980) Toward a positive theory of consumer choice, *Journal
    of Economic Behavior & Organization*, 1 (1), pp 39–60, https://doi.org/
    10.1016/0167-2681(80)90051-7 (archived at https://perma.cc/47N5-P5K2)

7   Spence, Michael (1973) Job Market Signaling, *Quarterly Journal of Economics*,
    87 (3), 355–74

8   May, Naomi and Murray, Daisy (2024) The Elle editors' guide to the best
    fashion rental sites in the UK, *Elle UK*, 19 September, www.elle.com/uk/
    fashion/g29187954/rent-dress/ (archived at https://perma.cc/85PT-A7RV)

9   Kahneman, Daniel and Taversky, Amos (1979) Prospect theory: An analysis of
    decision under risk, *Econometrica*, 47 (2), 263–91, www.web.mit.edu/curhan/
    www/docs/Articles/15341_Readings/Behavioral_Decision_Theory/Kahneman_
    Tversky_1979_Prospect_theory.pdf (archived at https://perma.cc/2PVF-YK8S)

10 Bearne, Suzanne (2015) Six lessons in how Nike and Adidas create hype and
    millennial hysteria, *Campaign*, 19 February, www.campaignlive.co.uk/article/
    six-lessons-nike-adidas-create-hype-millennial-hysteria/1334454 (archived at
    https://perma.cc/8NK4-BXZS)

11 Engaged.Social (2024) Mastering the drop: How Supreme utilizes limited releases to drive demand, *Medium*, www.medium.com/@seanglatzer/mastering-the-drop-how-supreme-utilizes-limited-releases-to-drive-demand-cd76289a7838 (archived at https://perma.cc/4DJV-X236)

12 Bearne, Suzanne (2015) Six lessons in how Nike and Adidas create hype and millennial hysteria, *Campaign*, 19 February, www.campaignlive.co.uk/article/six-lessons-nike-adidas-create-hype-millennial-hysteria/1334454 (archived at https://perma.cc/EJW9-22V2)

13 Market Defense (2024) The data behind the hype: How Prime day & big deal days supercharge beauty brands, 8 October, www.marketdefense.com/the-data-behind-the-hype-how-prime-day-big-deal-days-supercharge-beauty-brands (archived at https://perma.cc/8P98-R7C9)

14 Imentiv (2023) The emotional power of Coca-Cola advertising, Imentiv AI, 30 October, www.imentiv.ai/blog/the-emotional-power-of-coca-cola-advertising (archived at https://perma.cc/SE5V-HBNU)

15 Tovar, Virgie (2024) Dove becomes first beauty brand to ban AI-generated women in ads, *Forbes*, 18 April, www.forbes.com/sites/virgietovar/2024/04/18/dove-becomes-first-beauty-brand-to-ban-ai-generated-women-in-ads (archived at https://perma.cc/XXT5-DYG4)

16 Market Defense (2024) The data behind the hype: How Prime day & big deal days supercharge beauty brands, 8 October, www.marketdefense.com/the-data-behind-the-hype-how-prime-day-big-deal-days-supercharge-beauty-brands (archived at https://perma.cc/X6RW-R9K6)

17 Hamacher, Kevin and Buchkremer, Rüdiger (2022) Measuring online sensory consumer experience: Introducing the Online Sensory Marketing Index (OSMI) as a structural modeling approach, *Journal of Theoretical and Applied Electronic Commerce Research*, 17 (2), 751–72, www.mdpi.com/0718-1876/17/2/39 (archived at https://perma.cc/F6E7-DCRH)

18 Mehrabian, Albert (1971) *Silent Messages: Implicit communication of emotions and attitudes*, Wadsworth, Belmont, CA, Penguin

19 CareerBuilder (nd) Are smartphones at work killing productivity in the workplace?

20 Sephora (nd) Virtual Artist, www.sephora.my/pages/virtual-artist (archived at https://perma.cc/AV5D-9E8Q)

3

Mastering the digital landscape
of e-commerce

Living through the evolution of e-commerce

Reflecting on my journey in the digital world, it feels like I'm living through a defining era. From the early, agonizing, clunky dial-up internet process of my youth to the seamless online experiences we have today, the transformation of e-commerce has been nothing short of revolutionary.

Yet not everyone thought this retail channel would become the multi-billion-dollar industry we see today. I vividly remember attending a business conference in London in 1999, where seasoned CEOs laughed at the idea of selling larger luxury items like furniture online. I left that event both frustrated at their short-sightedness and energized, seeing a golden opportunity in a space many doubted.

Learning to code in the early days was another adventure. It wasn't glamorous – just lines of text that felt more like a puzzle than a pathway to a business success. Yet, those early frustrations taught me invaluable lessons.

In 2006, I launched my first e-commerce site. It was a modest venture, ahead of its time, and ultimately not the success I'd hoped for as the demand for my catalogue of offering for an online consumer just wasn't there at that point. But it was a crucial learning experience, helping me understand the nuances of digital retail and the importance of timing and market readiness.

E-commerce is more than just a sales channel; it is a shape-shifter that adapts to consumer needs and technological advancements. The shift from physical stores to online platforms isn't just about convenience; it is about creating a new kind of customer experience. Online shopping lacks the tactile and human interaction of physical stores, but it offers unparalleled convenience and variety. The real challenge now is how to bring the warmth and personal touch of in-store shopping to the digital realm.

REAL-WORLD EXAMPLE

Amazon: The original shape-shifter

Amazon's story isn't just a tale of business success; it is a narrative of transformation and innovation. Jeff Bezos, who started Amazon as an online bookstore in his garage in late 1994, envisioned a place where customers could find and discover anything they might want to buy online. This vision was grounded in a customer-first philosophy; Bezos maintained that they must be stubborn on vision, but flexible in regard to the details.

The introduction of customer reviews was a game-changer, transforming Amazon into a trusted platform where buyers could make informed decisions. This feature not only democratized product information but also built a sense of community and trust. The reviews became a crucial tool for customers to navigate the vast array of products available, making Amazon a reliable go-to for online shopping.

In 2005, Amazon launched Prime, offering free two-day shipping. This wasn't just a logistical achievement – it was a masterstroke in customer loyalty. Prime members, who now number over 200 million worldwide, enjoy benefits that go beyond shipping, including access to streaming services and exclusive deals. This model has fundamentally changed consumer expectations, making fast and reliable delivery a baseline standard in e-commerce.

Moreover, Amazon's use of big data and AI has revolutionized the shopping experience. Its recommendation engine, which suggests products based on browsing history and past purchases, personalizes the shopping experience, making it more relevant and engaging. Bezos believes in the word-of-mouth principle, often citing its importance in the brand strategy. This focus on customer experience, supported by advanced technology, has been key to Amazon's dominance.

Amazon's evolution from a modest online bookstore to a global technology titan exemplifies the virtues of adaptability and unwavering customer focus in the digital era. The company's steadfast commitment to innovation and customer satisfaction has not only propelled its own transformation but has also established new benchmarks across the e-commerce industry. Notably, Amazon Web Services (AWS), its cloud-storage division, is projected to reach a valuation of $3 trillion, nearly tripling the current market capitalization of the entire company.[1]

The transition from catalogue-based retail to e-commerce marked a significant evolution in the retail industry. Catalogues were the pioneers of at-home shopping, offering consumers the convenience of browsing and purchasing products without leaving their homes.

Brands like Sears, JC Penney and Freemans (UK) were trailblazers, mailing thick catalogues filled with a vast array of products. These catalogues were not only practical shopping tools but also sources of inspiration, showcasing the latest trends and products.

During my early career, I had the opportunity to work with several catalogue retailers, and it was an enlightening experience that underscored the importance of visual presentation in selling products. The layout of a catalogue was meticulously planned, with prime real estate given to the right-hand pages, which were more likely to catch a reader's eye first. This positioning was so coveted that brands often paid a premium to feature their products on these pages, ensuring maximum visibility. The stakes were high because these 'books of dreams', as they were often called, were not just shopping tools; they were a primary gateway for introducing new products and brands to consumers.

With the advent of the internet, catalogue retailers faced a new challenge: transitioning to an online format. This was more than just digitizing their catalogue content; it involved rethinking the entire shopping experience to cater to a new generation of digital shoppers. Early adopters of e-commerce, such as Amazon and eBay, demonstrated the immense potential of online retail. These companies capitalized on the convenience and accessibility of the internet, offering a wider range of products than traditional stores could accommodate.

The shift to online retail was not smooth for all. Many catalogue retailers struggled with the digital transformation, facing challenges such as adapting to new marketing strategies, optimizing their websites for search engines, and meeting the logistical demands of online sales. Companies that couldn't adapt, like Sears, found themselves losing ground to more agile competitors. On the other hand, brands that successfully transitioned, such as Lands' End, leveraged their existing customer bases and robust logistics networks to thrive in the online space.

REAL-WORLD EXAMPLE
Next: Catalogue to digital

A prominent British retailer, Next, exemplifies a successful transition from catalogue to an e-commerce giant. The company initially established a strong presence through its catalogue, the Next Directory, which was a staple in many UK households. This foundation provided Next with a solid starting point for its online expansion. The company used its catalogue experience to create a seamless online shopping experience, combining the detailed product information and quality imagery that customers appreciated with the convenience of online shopping.

A crucial aspect of Next's success in e-commerce has been its focus on customer experience, particularly in terms of delivery and logistics. Next set a new industry standard with its next-day delivery service for the majority of orders placed by midnight, which you can read more about in my interview with logistics company Evri at the end of this chapter. This commitment to speedy delivery has been a significant factor in customer satisfaction and loyalty.

Lord Simon Wolfson, Next's CEO said, 'The possibilities of the internet age present the group with far more opportunities than threats. Next product ranges, liberated from the constraints of finite retail space, can offer far more choice to our customers.'

Next's ability to integrate online and offline services further distinguishes it from competitors. The company offers customers the option to return online purchases in-store, a service that not only adds convenience but also drives additional foot traffic to physical stores. This strategy creates opportunities for upselling, as customers often make additional purchases when returning items.

Another strategic move by Next has been its expansion of product offerings through partnerships with other brands like Reiss and MADE.COM. This approach has allowed Next to offer a broader range of products, attracting a diverse customer base.

Wolfson noted, 'Our job is to adapt and serve them [customers] in whatever way they most want. To this end, Next has changed dramatically over the past 15 years. The business has moved from stores to the internet, from UK-only to international, from mono-brand to multi-brand aggregator.'[2]

This diversification not only enhances Next's appeal but also buffers the company against market fluctuations.

The Covid-19 pandemic underscored the importance of a strong online presence. As physical stores faced restrictions and closures, Next's robust e-commerce platform became a critical sales channel. The company reported significant growth in online sales, which offset declines in bricks-and-mortar retail. This resilience highlights the importance of digital readiness in today's retail environment.

Next's successful transition from a catalogue-based retailer to a leading e-commerce player demonstrates the power of adaptability and innovation. By leveraging its strengths, focusing on customer experience and embracing digital opportunities, Next has not only survived but thrived in a rapidly evolving market.

Delivery

While the digital marketplace has transformed how we shop, the delivery and logistics behind these purchases often go overlooked. It is, however, the crucial final step in ensuring customer satisfaction – turning a mere transaction into a positive brand experience.

The logistics of delivering goods has evolved dramatically over the last few decades, moving from a fragmented, slow process to today's streamlined and technology-driven operations. Historically, online shopping began in the 1990s with companies like Amazon pioneering the space, offering books and gradually expanding into a retail behemoth. Back then, delivery was slow, and the process of getting goods from warehouse to consumer was costly, clunky and unreliable. Yet, as e-commerce grew, so did the infrastructure support.

In the early days, the delivery aspect was inefficient, with customers often unsure when or if their packages would arrive, without the tracking tools and service personalization we experience today. This uncertainty created a barrier to the adoption of online shopping, which is why the logistics industry seized the opportunity to catch up rapidly to support this digital growth. Retailers realized that the convenience of shopping from home was only truly successful if the delivery process could match the speed and reliability consumers demanded. By the mid-2000s, the growth of reliable courier services, better technology in tracking and more robust delivery networks began to close the gap, making online shopping more feasible for a broader audience.

Why courier experience is an essential part of the shopping journey

As someone who has worked closely with retail brands and delivery services, I've seen first hand how integral the delivery process is to a brand's identity. It is a fact often overlooked: the courier is not just a means to an end but often the sole human interaction a customer experiences when shopping online. In a world where everything else in the purchase process is digital, the delivery person becomes the physical face of the brand.

In supporting one of the UK's largest logistics companies Evri (formerly Hermes) in an advisory role, I have spent years concentrating on the delivery journey, to partner the brand in creating a better experience. This included spending time out on the road with the couriers on delivery rounds, engaging with the end user and ensuring the swift delivery of parcels.

When Evri was still known as Hermes, it faced significant reputational challenges despite an incredibly healthy success rate on deliveries. Many consumers had stories of lost packages, delayed deliveries, or couriers leaving parcels in inconvenient or insecure places. At the time, this was damaging not only to Hermes's brand but also to the retailers that relied on the company for delivery. If a customer had a bad experience with their delivery, it would negatively impact their view of the entire shopping experience, regardless of how easy or enjoyable the purchasing process had been. It was clear that consumer expectations were high; they expected almost instant delivery and a highly personalized service.

As an independent customer advocate, I advised Evri on a strategy to help shift the perception of delivery services. We focused on understanding that the delivery experience is not an afterthought but a critical touchpoint in the consumer's journey. We worked on ensuring couriers were empowered with better tools and training, emphasizing customer care and satisfaction. After all, couriers don't just transport goods – they deliver the promise a retailer has made to its customer.

In this evolving role, I witnessed the transformation from a logistics provider that was once criticized for inefficiencies to one that now operates at the cutting edge of customer service. Evri embraced technology to improve tracking, communication and efficiency. Today, customers are better informed about their deliveries, with options to reschedule or leave instructions, and they can track their parcel in real time. The difference this has made to customer satisfaction is palpable, and the change in reputation speaks volumes about how vital this 'final touch' in the retail experience truly is. You can read more on this in the interview at the end of this chapter.

The transformation of online delivery: From inception to the present

As online shopping gained popularity, it was not just the retailers that had to adapt – courier services needed to scale up rapidly. Traditional postal services simply weren't designed for the massive influx of individual deliveries that e-commerce would bring. This led to the rise of private delivery services such as DHL, UPS and FedEx, which introduced the now commonplace tracking systems and ensured that delivery windows became narrower and more precise. These courier giants paved the way for more regional and specialized services to enter the market, allowing faster, more flexible delivery options.

Today, the sophistication of the delivery ecosystem is impressive. Machine learning algorithms help predict delivery times, optimize delivery routes and even allocate packages based on warehouse proximity to reduce carbon footprints. Companies like Amazon have perfected their logistics with services like Amazon Prime, promising two-day (and sometimes same-day) deliveries. This has raised the bar for all e-commerce retailers, pushing them to innovate and find ways to speed up their own delivery services.[3]

However, while speed and efficiency are critical, customers also expect a personalized and reliable experience. The rise of gig-economy services like Deliveroo and Uber Eats has further emphasized the importance of hyper-local delivery solutions that cater to the customer's need for immediacy. These services have reshaped expectations, not just for food but for all forms of retail.

Grocery brands are racing to deliver faster than ever, rapidly increasing the speed of their services. Whoosh was introduced by Tesco in 2021 to cater to the rising demand for speedy grocery delivery. With this service, Tesco promises to deliver within 60 minutes, providing convenience-driven customers the option to receive essential items without the need to physically visit a store. This shift reflects the growing consumer preference for rapid, local delivery services, especially in urban areas where time is of the essence. The popularity of such services is largely driven by the pandemic's impact on shopping behaviour and the surge in online grocery orders. Through the Whoosh service, Tesco successfully combines affordability with convenience, reaching a broad customer base in both large cities and suburban areas.[4]

The Co-op's entry into the one-hour delivery space similarly underscores this growing trend in quick delivery. In partnership with several delivery platforms, Co-op offers the option to get groceries and essentials delivered within the hour. By tapping into the 'local' model, the Co-op ensures that nearby customers can quickly access items from their nearest Co-op store without the long wait associated with traditional online deliveries. This method has been instrumental in keeping Co-op competitive in a landscape dominated by larger supermarkets and online giants.[5]

In the United States, quick delivery services have also seen rapid growth, with companies like Gopuff leading the charge. Unlike traditional grocery chains, Gopuff operates its own micro-fulfilment centres, allowing the company to stock a wide range of products and deliver them within a matter of minutes – often as quickly as 30 minutes. This model has proven successful, especially in cities where time-strapped customers are increasingly turning to such services to fulfil last-minute needs. The ability to deliver products ranging from snacks to household items in less than an hour has made Gopuff a major player in the US convenience delivery market, competing alongside the likes of DoorDash and Instacart, which also offer similar rapid delivery options for groceries and essentials.[6]

These innovations in quick delivery demonstrate a significant shift in consumer behaviour, with convenience, speed and accessibility becoming more crucial than ever in the retail space.

As we continue to see advancements in drone deliveries, autonomous vehicles and even predictive deliveries – where systems anticipate what a customer might order before they do – the evolution of delivery will only accelerate. But no matter how advanced the technology gets, the importance of the human element – the delivery person – cannot be overstated.

SEO and website optimization: The lifeblood of e-commerce

In the bustling marketplace of e-commerce, SEO is the charismatic force that draws attention – like a great salesperson who knows *just* what to say. With a blend of keywords and strategic optimization, SEO makes sure a brand stands out, staying top of mind and easily discoverable. It's a bit like being at a party where you're introduced to the most interesting person in the room – someone you wouldn't forget.

Website optimization, on the other hand, is all about seamless functionality and user experience, working quietly yet powerfully in the background. Imagine walking into a beautifully organized store where everything flows effortlessly – from the welcoming layout to the ease of finding exactly what you need. Website optimization is that silent architect, making sure each page loads smoothly, navigation is intuitive, and every interaction feels effortless. It's a behind-the-scenes hero that makes the complex appear simple, so visitors are free to browse, shop and engage without any friction.

By combining the bold allure of SEO with the smooth functionality of a well-optimized website, e-commerce brands can create a powerful presence – one that not only draws customers in but also ensures they stay and have a meaningful, enjoyable experience.

Beyond the technicalities, SEO and website optimization are about understanding and anticipating customer needs. It is about knowing that someone searching for 'best running shoes' might also be interested in fitness apparel or accessories. By optimizing for related keywords and providing comprehensive content, you can cater to broader interests and needs, increasing the likelihood of conversions.

REAL-WORLD EXAMPLE
Warby Parker: A visionary in SEO and website optimization

Warby Parker, the eyewear company known for its innovative approach, has certainly reframed the art of SEO and website optimization. The company was founded with the mission to offer stylish eyewear at affordable prices, disrupting the traditional retail model of having to go through your optician.

Before the advent of digital solutions, purchasing eyewear was a cumbersome and limited experience. Consumers typically had to visit opticians, where the selection was confined to what was in stock, often at premium prices. This process not only restricted choice but also left customers dependent on the optician's recommendations, with little room for comparison shopping or customization.

Warby Parker improved this experience by leveraging SEO and website optimization to provide a comprehensive, customer-centric alternative. The brand offers an extensive range of stylish, affordable eyewear directly through its online platform. With a focus on user-friendly design, Warby Parker's website allows customers to browse a wide array of frames, use virtual try-on features, and even order home try-on kits – all from the comfort of their home.[7] This digital approach seeks to democratize the eyewear market, providing more choices and better pricing transparency.

From the beginning, Warby Parker focused on creating high-quality, informative content that addresses common concerns and questions about eyewear. Its blog features articles on eye health, style tips and behind-the-scenes looks at its design process.

Technical SEO is another area where the business invests significantly. The company's website is designed for speed and ease of use, with a mobile-first approach that ensures a seamless experience across all devices. This is crucial, as a significant portion of its traffic comes from mobile users.

A standout feature of the website is its virtual try-on technology. This feature allows customers to see how different frames will look on their faces using their device's camera. It is a perfect blend of technology and customer-centric design, offering a practical solution to a common online shopping challenge. This feature not only enhances the shopping experience but also reduces the likelihood of returns, as customers can make more informed decisions.

The brand has a strong backlink strategy, with mentions and links from high-authority sites like *The New York Times* and *Vogue*. These backlinks boost the site's domain authority, a critical factor in SEO, and help improve its ranking in search results.

The company's use of social media through customer reviews and testimonials further enhances its online presence and adds a very human side to the strategy. Displaying reviews prominently on product pages builds trust and provides potential customers with valuable insights into the quality and fit of the products.

By focusing on both the technical aspects and the human elements of the shopping experience, businesses can create compelling online environments that attract and retain customers.

The role of AI in personalizing the shopping experience

AI is still in its infancy – a rapidly evolving technology with vast untapped potential. It is a system that learns as we learn, adapting and growing in capability with each new piece of data it processes. It is fascinating to think that just a few years ago, AI was mostly the stuff of science fiction and tech jargon, only coming into the common lexicon recently with the rise of smart assistants like Siri and Alexa. Now, it is everywhere, from our smartphones to our cars, and it is quickly becoming a cornerstone of retail innovation.

Imagine walking into a store where AI-powered systems greet you by name, know your preferences and guide you to products you might love – this is not far off from becoming a reality, and we'll delve deeper into this in Chapter 5.

Online, the vision for AI expands even further. From virtual try-ons to personalized shopping assistants that understand your style and needs better than you do, AI promises to transform the digital shopping experience into something intuitive and personalized. It could revolutionize customer service with chatbots that provide human-like interactions, or dynamically adjust product offerings based on real-time trends and customer feedback.

The future of AI in retail is not just about efficiency; it is about creating a seamless, engaging and highly personalized shopping journey that feels almost magical. This chapter explores how AI is currently shaping the e-commerce landscape and what the future might hold as this technology continues to develop.

AI's impact on e-commerce includes powering recommendation engines that suggest products based on browsing history, past purchases and even social media activity. A prime example is Netflix, whose recommendation system, driven by AI, accounts for over 80 per cent of the content watched on the platform. This illustrates AI's power in retaining customers by providing relevant and personalized content.[8]

In the retail sector, AI-powered chatbots and virtual assistants play a crucial role in customer service. These tools use natural language processing to understand and respond to customer enquiries, creating a smoother shopping experience.

For instance, Sephora's Virtual Artist uses AI to offer personalized beauty recommendations and tutorials, enhancing customer interactions by providing tailored advice and product suggestions – a strategy worth its weight in gold when the Covid-19 pandemic shut down retail as we know it and all elements usually associated with the 'fun' try-on process of cosmetic retail were curtailed.

Dynamic pricing is another significant application of AI, allowing retailers to adjust prices in real time based on demand, inventory levels and market conditions. This strategy maximizes revenue while ensuring competitive pricing. Zalando, a leading online fashion retailer, uses AI to dynamically adjust prices, keeping them competitive and appealing to customers.

REAL-WORLD EXAMPLE
Uber Eats: The power of personalization

Uber Eats, the 'get almost anything' food delivery service, exemplifies the effective use of AI in creating personalized customer experiences. The platform uses AI to provide restaurant recommendations based on a user's past orders, location and even time of day. This level of personalization not only enhances the user experience but also drives engagement and loyalty.

Uber Eats employs machine learning algorithms to optimize delivery routes, predict delivery times, and adjust menu displays based on local trends and individual preferences. This dynamic personalization has been crucial in differentiating Uber Eats from its competitors, leading to significant growth.

In 2023, Uber Eats reported a 35 per cent increase in customer engagement, largely attributed to its advanced personalization features. By leveraging AI, Uber Eats has been able to provide highly tailored experiences, from personalized restaurant recommendations to predictive delivery times. This level of personalization has undoubtedly driven customer loyalty and engagement. However, as with any powerful tool, there is a balance to be struck between effectiveness and overreach.[9]

Looking forward, Uber Eats could continue to innovate by integrating even more advanced AI capabilities. Imagine a future where AI not only suggests restaurants based on your previous orders but also anticipates your cravings before you even realize them. Imagine virtual food trials where customers visualize dishes through augmented reality before ordering, or even developing AI nutritionists that tailor meal suggestions based on dietary needs and health goals? The possibilities are vast and exciting, offering new ways to enhance the customer experience.

However, as we push the boundaries of personalization, there's a growing concern about 'digital distress'. This term refers to the overwhelm and discomfort consumers may feel from constant, hyper-targeted marketing and the feeling of being constantly monitored and pushed to purchase, and I talk about this in an interview on *the mentl space* – the mental health in business podcast.[10]

While AI can optimize user experience, there's a risk of crossing the line from helpful to invasive. The relentless drive to personalize and upsell can sometimes lead to a loss of the human touch in customer interactions, causing fatigue and even resistance among users.

It is crucial for retailers to be mindful of this balance. Just because technology allows for high levels of personalization doesn't mean it should always be used to its fullest extent. There's an ethical consideration in ensuring that customers are not overwhelmed or manipulated into making purchases. The aim should be to enhance the user experience genuinely and thoughtfully, rather than merely maximizing sales.

Creating a seamless online journey: User experience and interface design

Creating a seamless online journey is essential for e-commerce success, ensuring that customers can navigate websites effortlessly, find what they need and complete their purchases without frustration. User experience (UX) and user interface (UI) design are critical components of this process, shaping how users interact with a website and influencing their overall satisfaction.

In the early days of online shopping, websites were often cumbersome and difficult to navigate. However, advancements in UX/UI design have transformed these experiences into intuitive and enjoyable interactions. Today, the goal is to make the online shopping process as seamless as possible, akin to having the most helpful and knowledgeable store associate at hand.

A key aspect of UX design is understanding the target audience. This involves not only demographics but also behaviours, motivations and pain points. For example, younger audiences might prioritize mobile-friendly designs and fast load times, while older demographics may prefer clearer product descriptions and accessible customer service options. This understanding helps tailor the website experience to meet specific customer needs.

The checkout process is a critical phase in creating a seamless retail online journey. A complicated checkout process often leads to cart abandonment – a major challenge for online retailers. To mitigate this, it is essential to streamline the checkout process by minimizing steps, offering multiple payment options and ensuring secure transactions.

REAL-WORLD EXAMPLE
Zara: Fast fashion, faster website

Zara is the golden child brand of the Inditex Group, a global leader in fast fashion. Zara is a good example of a brand that is moving further towards integrated online and physical retail operations to eventually create a seamless shopping experience. The brand's website is a model of efficient UX/UI design, offering an intuitive and visually appealing shopping journey. Its commitment to high-quality imagery and detailed product descriptions helps customers make confident purchasing decisions.

Zara's website integrates AI-driven personalization to recommend products based on users' browsing and purchase history, significantly enhancing the shopping experience. This personalized approach increases the likelihood of customers finding items that match their preferences, thus boosting the probability of a sale. The success of these features is evident in Zara's reported increases in customer engagement and online sales, highlighting the effectiveness of personalized recommendations.

Moreover, Zara's mobile app extends this seamless experience beyond the web, offering functionalities that cater to the modern consumer's on-the-go lifestyle. In-store, the app is used at both standard and self-service checkout points, allowing customers to instantly connect their online accounts with their in-store shopping activities. This integration not only streamlines the checkout process but also provides a holistic view of the customer's shopping journey, enhancing the overall experience.[11]

Zara's commitment to leveraging technology is further underscored by its significant investments in AI and digital infrastructure. According to the latest financial reports, Zara's parent company, Inditex, plans to continue investing heavily in technology, allocating substantial funds to enhance its e-commerce capabilities and digital presence, a clear indication that the significant technology integration is working.[12]

Another standout feature of Zara's online presence is its effective use of responsive design. The website and app are optimized for various devices, ensuring a consistent experience whether customers are shopping on a desktop, tablet or smartphone.

Zara's commitment to refined UX/UI design is a strategic advantage that aligns with its customer-centric approach, ensuring a seamless and engaging online experience. Every aspect of the digital journey – from intuitive navigation and quick-loading images to clear visuals and personalized recommendations – is meticulously crafted to enhance ease and efficiency. This attention to detail reduces common e-commerce friction points, like slow load times or complex layouts, allowing customers to browse with minimal effort and maximum satisfaction. By staying responsive to UX/UI trends and customer feedback, Zara not only enhances user experience but also reinforces brand loyalty, keeping it competitive in the fast-paced fashion industry.

Zara shows how investing into technology to improve the shopping experience can elevate customer ease and market position. As the digital landscape continues to evolve, investing in UX/UI design will remain essential for e-commerce success.

Blending the physical with the digital: Moving towards seamless shopping experiences

The retail landscape has undergone a significant transformation with the advent of omnichannel retailing, which seamlessly integrates physical and digital shopping experiences into a unified journey for consumers. Modern customers expect consistency across all platforms – be it online, in-store or via mobile apps. Omnichannel strategies address these expectations by creating a cohesive customer experience that aligns with the needs of today's connected shoppers.

Historically, shopping was a linear process, confined to either physical stores or online platforms. However, the rise of digital technologies has blurred these boundaries, enabling consumers to move fluidly between online and offline shopping. Consumers now use various devices and platforms to research, compare and purchase products. This shift necessitates a cohesive retail approach, ensuring a consistent customer experience across all channels.

One significant advantage of omnichannel retailing is the flexibility it offers customers. Services like click-and-collect allow shoppers to purchase items online and pick them up in-store, combining the convenience of online shopping with the immediacy of physical stores.

In a Capital One Shopping Research Report in 2024, omnichannel retailers retain 90 per cent more customers than single-channel stores.[13]

Inventory visibility is another critical component of a successful omnichannel strategy. Customers expect real-time information about product availability across all channels. If an item is out of stock online, retailers should provide information about its availability in nearby stores. This transparency not only manages customer expectations but also enhances the shopping experience by offering multiple options for purchasing the desired product.

As we explore the evolution of omnichannel retailing, it's essential to examine how leading retailers are implementing these strategies to meet and exceed customer expectations. The following case study delves into the innovative approaches adopted by the prominent retailer Target, illustrating the practical application and benefits of a robust omnichannel strategy.

REAL-WORLD EXAMPLE
Target: Leading the omnichannel charge

Target has established itself as a leader in omnichannel retailing by seamlessly integrating its online and physical operations to deliver a cohesive shopping experience. The retailer's strategic investments in digital innovations, logistics and inventory management have significantly enhanced its omnichannel capabilities, meeting the evolving expectations of modern consumers.

A standout feature of Target's omnichannel approach is its Drive Up service. This convenient option allows customers to place orders through the Target app and have them delivered directly to their car in a Target parking lot within minutes of arrival. In Q1 2024, Drive Up experienced a remarkable 13 per cent year-over-year growth, contributing over $2 billion in sales. This growth underscores the increasing consumer demand for hybrid shopping options that combine digital convenience with physical accessibility.[14]

Target's commitment to a seamless customer experience is further evident in its approach to inventory management. The retailer utilizes sophisticated technology to synchronize online and in-store inventories, providing customers with accurate, real-time information about product availability. This transparency not only reduces the frustration of stock outs but also enhances the likelihood of completed sales across both digital and physical channels.

To further enhance convenience, Target offers same-day delivery through its partnership with Shipt, catering to shoppers who prioritize speed and ease. This service reflects Target's understanding of today's consumer, who increasingly values flexibility in how, where and when they receive purchases. Same-day delivery has strengthened Target's positioning as a retailer that understands and adapts to the fast-paced lifestyles of its customers.

Under the leadership of CEO Brian Cornell, Target has committed itself to a customer-centric approach that emphasizes competitive pricing, seasonally relevant products and unparalleled convenience. Cornell has emphasized that Target's ongoing investments in strategy and operational efficiency are integral to sustaining long-term growth and profitability. His vision illustrates Target's understanding that omnichannel success depends on more than technological advancements – it requires a comprehensive focus on customer needs and seamless execution.

Through these initiatives, Target has redefined the possibilities of omnichannel retail, setting a benchmark for how retailers can blend the digital with the physical to enhance the consumer experience. By continually innovating and adapting to consumer behaviour, Target not only meets the current expectations of omnichannel shoppers but also positions itself as a forward-thinking leader in the retail landscape, paving the way for what the future of integrated retail could look like.

As we wrap up this chapter on the digital landscape of e-commerce, we're standing at the forefront of a technological revolution, one that could reshape the retail industry more dramatically and rapidly than any other era before it. This chapter, perhaps more than any other in this book, is set to see the most significant changes in technology and strategy in the coming years. The pace at which AI, data analytics and digital tools are advancing means that today's cutting-edge innovation could be tomorrow's standard practice – or even obsolete.

For those navigating these waters, my advice is simple: stay open, stay informed and don't be afraid. The digital world is fast-moving and can be daunting, but it is also full of opportunities. Keep an eye on developments not just within the retail sector but across various industries, from tech to entertainment to healthcare. These sectors often pioneer technologies and strategies that can be adapted and adopted in retail to enhance customer experiences and operational efficiencies.

Shape-shifting is key. Just as e-commerce is the ultimate shape-shifter in retail, being flexible and adaptable is crucial for anyone looking to thrive in this space. The ability to pivot, learn and implement new technologies quickly will set successful brands apart from the rest. Whether it is integrating AI for personalized shopping experiences, optimizing websites for better user experiences, or blending digital and physical retail spaces, the ability to adapt is critical.

However, in this rush towards innovation, it is vital not to lose sight of your core values. Technology should never overshadow the human element that is at the heart of retail. The true north in all of this should always be the consumer. What makes them feel supported? How can we positively impact their lives through our brand? These are the questions that should guide every decision, every experiment and every new initiative.

For me, these values are what guide my own decisions on what I try and trial in the realm of e-commerce and digital retail. I often find myself weighing the potential benefits of a new technology against its ability to genuinely enhance the customer experience. If it doesn't align with these core values or feels too intrusive or impersonal, it is often not the right fit 'right now'. But that doesn't mean it won't be in the future, as both technology and consumer expectations evolve.

Moreover, it is essential to embrace a mindset of continuous learning. The digital landscape is ever-changing, and what works today might not work tomorrow. This means regularly updating your knowledge base, experimenting with new tools and technologies, and, importantly, listening to your customers. They are, after all, the best source of insight into what will resonate and what will not.

Digital transformation is challenging – but also incredibly exciting. The potential to connect with customers in new and meaningful ways, to offer them experiences that are more personalized and convenient than ever before, is truly transformative. And while the technology itself is impressive, it is the human touch – the thought, care and understanding behind it – that makes it truly impactful.

As you navigate the ever-evolving digital landscape, remember that staying true to your brand's values and being consumer-focused is your best strategy. Embrace change, learn continuously and always be guided by the question: How can this technology better serve our customers? With this mindset, you can not only keep up with the rapid pace of change but also thrive in it, offering your customers an experience that is not only modern and efficient but also warm and human.

As we transition to our next segment, it's crucial to understand the pivotal role of logistics in the e-commerce ecosystem. Efficient delivery services are the backbone of a successful omnichannel strategy, ensuring that products reach customers promptly and reliably.

In this context, we turn our attention to Evri, a leading player in the logistics sector. Formerly known as Hermes UK, Evri has undergone significant transformation to become a key partner for retailers aiming to enhance their delivery capabilities. With a robust infrastructure and a customer-centric approach, Evri delivers over 700 million parcels annually, reaching nearly every household in the UK. The company boasts a network of over 20,000 couriers and more than 14,000 ParcelShops and Lockers, providing flexible and convenient delivery options for consumers.

To delve deeper into how Evri is accelerating retail logistics with customers at the heart, we are joined by Chris Ashworth, Chief Information Officer and Chief Customer Officer at Evri. Chris brings a wealth of experience in driving technological innovation and enhancing customer experiences in the logistics industry.

REAL-WORLD EXAMPLE
Chris Ashworth, CIO and CCO, Evri

Accelerating retail logistics with customers at the heart

Kate Hardcastle

(KH): Let's dive straight in – what role do you see delivery partners playing in the evolving e-commerce landscape?

Chris Ashworth

(CA): Delivery partners are pivotal in the success of e-commerce. Today, consumers expect their purchases to arrive quickly, reliably and at a low cost. Delivery is often the only physical interaction customers have with an online retailer, so it's really where the rubber meets the road in terms of customer experience. At Evri, we see ourselves as not just a delivery service, but as an extension of the brands we work with. Our job is to ensure that the consumer's final impression of their purchase is a positive one, which means getting the product to them swiftly, securely and with great communication along the way.

KH: E-commerce is only set to grow further. What do you think the future of last-mile logistics looks like?

CA: The future is all about efficiency and sustainability. Last-mile delivery is the most expensive part of the logistics chain, and it's where many challenges arise, especially with urban congestion and environmental concerns. I believe we'll see increased use of electric vehicles, more automated processes, and even drones or robots for smaller, more compact deliveries. At Evri, we're already investing heavily in AI-driven route optimization to minimize delivery times and reduce emissions. Customer expectations for faster deliveries will likely grow, so meeting that demand sustainably will be key.

KH: Evri recently rebranded from Hermes to further position itself as a leader in innovation. How has technology played a role in that transition?

CA: Technology has been at the core of our transformation. When we became Evri, we didn't just change the name; we overhauled our approach to customer service, transparency and flexibility. We've integrated a lot more AI and machine learning into our systems, from predictive analytics that help us optimize delivery routes, to real-time tracking that keeps customers informed every step of the way. We're also expanding options for customers, like the ability to reschedule deliveries, and introducing more self-service points, which gives consumers greater control over how and when they receive their parcels.

KH: The pressure on delivery partners has been immense, especially post-pandemic. How have you managed these increased volumes and what changes do you expect in consumer behaviour going forward?

CA: That's a great question. The pandemic essentially condensed five years' worth of e-commerce growth into a matter of months. Our volumes increased drastically, and it was a real test of our infrastructure. We managed by scaling up our network quickly, hiring more couriers, and investing in new technology to handle the influx. Post-pandemic, I think consumers have become accustomed to the convenience of home delivery and are unlikely to revert to pre-pandemic habits. We're seeing continued demand for fast, flexible delivery options, so we're constantly looking at ways to enhance the speed and reliability of our services.

KH: Sustainability is a hot topic, particularly in logistics. How is Evri tackling the environmental challenges posed by delivery services?

CA: Sustainability is top of mind for us, and it's one of our key strategic priorities. As I mentioned earlier, we're investing in electric vehicles and trialling low-emission technologies like cargo bikes in city centres.

The biggest accelerator has been our rapid adoption of CNG (compressed natural gas) vehicles in the middle mile. While this may be an interim technology, it touches every parcel we deliver, and therefore this enables ESG (environmental, social and governance) at scale – it's a pragmatic application for a strategy with real focus on the outcome.

We've also implemented a recycling programme for packaging and are working towards making all our deliveries carbon neutral. The challenge is balancing environmental responsibility with the need for speed and affordability. But we're committed to doing both, and I believe the logistics industry is heading in the same direction.

KH: It's interesting to hear about the advancements in technology and sustainability. Can you share what you think the next major innovation will be in logistics?

CA: Absolutely. I think the next frontier will be hyper-personalization in delivery services. Consumers want convenience, but they also want flexibility. Imagine being able to specify not just the day but the exact hour you want your parcel delivered, or being able to have your delivery redirected to wherever you are at that moment. We're also seeing advancements in data analytics that can predict consumer preferences and buying patterns. This will enable us to pre-emptively prepare for peaks in demand, ensuring that we always have the right resources in the right places.

KH: Finally, what advice would you give to retailers when choosing their logistics partners?

CA: My biggest piece of advice is to think of your logistics partner as a key part of your brand, not just a service provider. Your customers' experience with delivery can heavily influence how they perceive your business. Make sure you partner with a provider that shares your values, particularly around customer service and sustainability. Think about agility and fit, we have enabled ecommerce by innovating and improving it regularly – for example we have moved from offering three-day delivery to next day, we offer some retailers a next-day with orders as late as midnight the day before – we are often first to market with our innovations which are focused on giving our retail partners – and indeed the consumer – what they want.

Also, choose a partner that is investing in technology and future-proofing their operations. The retail landscape is changing fast, and you want a partner that can keep up with consumer expectations and innovation.

Key interview takeaways

1 **Customer experience is king:** Delivery partners are often the only physical touchpoint for online shoppers, making them crucial to customer satisfaction.

2 **Sustainability is essential:** Evri is investing heavily in electric vehicles and sustainable practices to reduce its environmental impact.

3 **Technology is transformative:** AI, machine learning and real-time tracking are enabling faster, more reliable and flexible delivery options.

4 **The future is personalized:** Expect hyper-personalization in delivery, with consumers having more control over when and where they receive their goods.

5 **Strategic partnerships matter:** Retailers should view their logistics providers as an extension of their brand, ensuring alignment on values like customer service and sustainability.

KEY TAKEAWAYS

1 **Seamless integration:** The fusion of physical and digital channels is essential. Customers expect a unified experience, whether shopping online, in-store or via mobile apps. Retailers must ensure consistency across all touchpoints to meet these expectations.

2 **Personalization:** Leveraging data analytics allows retailers to tailor experiences to individual customer preferences, enhancing engagement and fostering loyalty.

3 **Flexible fulfilment:** Offering diverse fulfilment options, such as kerbside pickup, same-day delivery, and buy online, pick up in-store (BOPIS), caters to varying customer needs and enhances convenience.

4 **Robust technology infrastructure:** Investing in scalable and secure technology platforms supports seamless operations, real-time inventory management and efficient customer service.

5 **Sustainability:** Incorporating eco-friendly approaches into the supply chain and operations not only meets growing consumer demand for sustainability but also contributes to long-term business viability.

References

1 Business Times (2022) Amazon Cloud Unit on course for US$3 trillion value, Redburn says, *The Business Times*, 29 June, www.businesstimes.com.sg/startups-tech/technology/amazon-cloud-unit-course-us3-trillion-value-redburn-says (archived at https://perma.cc/JE8V-EQN4)

2 Rigby, Chloe (2022) Next says future shape of retail now clearer, as it reports record full-year revenues but scales back future expectations, *InternetRetailing*, 24 March, www.internetretailing.net/next-says-future-shape-of-retail-now-clearer-as-it-reports-record-full-year-revenues-but-scales-back-future-expectations-24578 (archived at https://perma.cc/ZT46-SDAQ)

3 Amazon (nd) Amazon Prime Shipping Benefits, www.amazon.co.uk/gp/help/customer/display.html?nodeId=GRPQFCNVUDYCBG24 (archived at https://perma.cc/7L24-FELK)

4 Tesco (2023) Tesco Rapid Delivery Service Whoosh now available from 1,000 stores as it exceeds rollout target by 25 per cent, Tesco PLC, 24 March, www.tescoplc.com/tesco-rapid-delivery-service-whoosh-now-available-from-1-000-stores-as-it-exceeds-rollout-target-by-25 (archived at https://perma.cc/LV8A-6ZUU)

5 Clarke, Josie and Ballinger, Chris (2024) Co-op announces 24/7 delivery service across London – and it is launching very soon, *My London*, 18 Setptember, www.mylondon.news/whats-on/whats-on-news/co-op-announces-247-delivery-29956297 (archived at https://perma.cc/RV4F-96D7)

6 Gopuff (2021)A peek behind the curtain: Gopuff's unique business model, Gopuff newsroom, 2 September, www.gopuff.com/newsroom/company-news/a-peek-behind-the-curtain-gopuffs-unique-business-model (archived at https://perma.cc/MV6X-6LR7)

7 Miller, Hannah L (2022) How Warby Parker is innovating an age-old industry, *Leaders*, 12 October, www.leaders.com/articles/leaders-stories/warby-parker (archived at https://perma.cc/D9KE-BSUU)

8 Plummer, Libby (2017) This is how Netflix's top-secret recommendation system works, *Wired*, 22 August, www.wired.com/story/how-do-netflixs-algorithms-work-machine-learning-helps-to-predict-what-viewers-will-like (archived at https://perma.cc/8P7Q-X2YD)

9 Malik, Aisha (2023) Uber eats is reportedly developing an AI chatbot that will offer recommendations, speed up ordering, *TechCrunch*, 28 August, www.techcrunch.com/2023/08/28/uber-eats-developing-ai-chatbot-offer-recommendations-speed-up-ordering (archived at https://perma.cc/8PRZ-HZPW)

10 Hardcastle, Kate and Armstrong, Scott (2024) Are we being consumed by digital distress? *the mentl space*, 10 July, www.mentl.space/posts/information-overload-are-we-being-consumed-by-digital-distress (archived at https://perma.cc/5AWQ-5WXT)

11 Wide Eyes (2018) Zara: Technology and customer experience as drivers of business, *Wide Eyes Blog*, 3 May, www.blog.wideeyes.ai/2018/05/03/zara-technology-and-customer-experience (archived at https://perma.cc/ZD3R-Z5QM)

12 Inditex (2023) Inditex Annual Report 2023, https://annualreport2023.inditex.com/en (archived at https://perma.cc/HXY6-7NHN)

13 Capital One Shopping (2024) Omnichannel statistics, 25 October, https://capitaloneshopping.com/research/omnichannel-statistics (archived at https://perma.cc/B952-Q6QT)

14 Target (2024) Target Corporation reports third quarter earnings, press release, 20 November, https://corporate.target.com/press/release/2024/11/target-corporation-reports-third-quarter-earnings (archived at https://perma.cc/QZ77-ZEJZ)

4

Redefining retail in the age of technology

Retail and the evolution of technology

Retail spaces are in the midst of an extraordinary transformation, evolving from traditional shopping venues into dynamic centres of engagement. In an era where digital and physical worlds blur, today's retailers face the challenge of crafting environments that blend convenience with memorable experiences. A retail space is no longer simply a site for transactions – it has become a stage for storytelling, a hub for community engagement, and an experiential journey that bridges online and offline worlds.

To understand this transformation, it's essential to acknowledge the roots of modern retail spaces. Traditional markets and grand department stores historically served as social and cultural centres, where communities gathered and connected. Today's retailers, inspired by this heritage, are building on these functions while using data, technology and consumer insights to meet the expectations of a generation that values both individualism and shared experiences. This chapter examines how retail spaces are being redefined to cater not only to what consumers need but to how they feel, think and interact with the world around them.

A major challenge that retailers face today is achieving clarity in the transactional journey. While some consumers are deeply engaged through apps and digital channels, it remains tricky for retailers to track every interaction. This is crucial not only for gathering data but also for proving ROI on marketing efforts. Research from the Out of Home Advertising Association of America (OAAA) and Solomon Partners reveals that out-of-home (OOH) advertisements yield significantly higher consumer recall compared to other media channels, including television and online ads.[1] Additionally, Newsworks found that print advertisements drive 77 per cent brand recall, surpassing digital's 46 per cent. This difference in recall underscores the need for a multi-channel strategy that tracks every consumer touchpoint.[2] By connecting these dots, retailers can better understand customer behaviour, refine strategies and build a more cohesive, satisfying shopping experience – a vital step for the future success of omnichannel retail.

The role of consumer expectations

Today's consumers are not just looking for products; they are looking for experiences. They expect personalized service, relevant recommendations and a seamless journey regardless of how they choose to shop. We know that consumers use multiple channels during their shopping journey, with recent research by Retail Economics indicating that 73 per cent of UK consumers engage in multichannel shopping. This has pushed retailers to innovate and adopt technologies that provide a consistent and engaging experience across platforms, essential for meeting consumer expectations in today's marketplace.[3]

The rise of mobile technology has further blurred the lines between online and offline shopping. Mobile devices have become a critical part of the shopping journey, used for researching products, comparing prices and even completing purchases. The integration of mobile technology into retail strategies has been crucial for engaging customers and providing a seamless experience. For example, features like mobile wallets and QR codes facilitate quick and easy transactions, enhancing the overall convenience for the customer.

REAL-WORLD EXAMPLE
Walmart's omnichannel strategy

Walmart is a prime example of a retailer that has successfully implemented an omnichannel strategy. As one of the world's largest grocery retailers, Walmart has a massive global presence and an extensive store network. In fact, Walmart is the largest retailer in the world by revenue, serving millions of customers each day across its various platforms. Recognizing the changing landscape, Walmart invested heavily in technology and infrastructure to bridge the gap between its online and physical stores. One of the standout features of Walmart's strategy is its 'buy online, pick up in-store' (BOPIS) service, known as Walmart Pickup. This service allows customers to shop online and pick up their items at a nearby store, often on the same day. It caters to the consumer's desire for convenience while driving foot traffic to physical stores, where customers may make additional purchases.

As Walmart continues to innovate, it is not without competition. Amazon, with its rapid delivery services and expanding grocery offerings, is a formidable competitor. Additionally, other grocery giants like Kroger and international players like Aldi and Lidl are also making significant strides in the omnichannel space. These competitors are leveraging their strengths in various ways, from offering competitive prices to enhancing their own digital platforms. Walmart's ongoing efforts to integrate its physical and digital channels are crucial to maintaining its leading position in this highly competitive market.

Walmart's investment in technology extends to its mobile app, which integrates seamlessly with its in-store and online experiences. The app offers features like mobile checkout, which allows customers to scan items and pay via their phones, skipping the queue at the checkout.

Integrating advanced technologies into retail operations has significantly transformed the customer experience, making shopping faster, more accessible and tailored to individual preferences. In recent years, Walmart has exemplified this approach through its omnichannel strategy, aimed at providing a seamless and cohesive experience across in-store, online and mobile channels. Walmart emphasizes the company's commitment to serving customers through every preferred platform, demonstrating a consumer-centric vision that aligns Walmart's digital investments with its physical presence.[4]

Walmart's commitment to integrated retail delivered results: in fiscal 2024, e-commerce sales grew 21 per cent globally, achieving over $100 billion in online sales alone.[5] This achievement highlights the effectiveness of Walmart's strategy to unify physical and digital spaces in a way that both strengthens customer engagement and maximizes convenience. A critical element of this approach includes utilizing Walmart's extensive network of physical stores to support last-mile delivery solutions, ensuring prompt and efficient order fulfilment.

Innovative initiatives, such as deploying store associates to deliver orders during their commutes home, have further optimized Walmart's delivery processes by reducing times and costs. These solutions exemplify how omnichannel retail, when fully realized, can elevate the customer experience, meeting modern consumer demands for immediacy, flexibility and choice. By harnessing both its digital infrastructure and physical footprint, Walmart is setting a standard for how retailers can effectively leverage omnichannel strategies to stay competitive and relevant in an evolving marketplace.

The evolution from traditional bricks-and-mortar stores to an integrated omnichannel approach underscores the dynamic nature of retail. Retailers like Walmart have demonstrated that a well-executed omnichannel strategy can not only meet but exceed consumer expectations. The key lies in creating a seamless and engaging experience across all platforms, ensuring that every touchpoint reflects the brand's commitment to quality and convenience. As technology continues to advance, the possibilities for enhancing the customer experience are limitless, making omnichannel retail an exciting and ever-evolving field.

The evolution of point of sale: From cash registers to intelligent systems

The point-of-sale (POS) system has long been a cornerstone of retail operations, evolving from simple cash registers to sophisticated, data-driven platforms. This evolution has enabled retailers to enhance the customer experience significantly, making shopping more interactive and personalized. Modern POS systems are not only about processing transactions but also about gathering valuable insights and integrating various business functions. This transformation reflects the broader trend of blending the physical and digital retail worlds, offering a cohesive omnichannel experience.

From basic cash registers to electronic systems

Initially, POS systems were basic devices designed to handle cash transactions. Their primary functions included totalling sales, printing receipts and managing cash storage. However, as retail needs grew, so did the capabilities of these systems. The introduction of electronic cash registers allowed for more complex transactions and better inventory management. Despite these advancements, early POS systems were limited in their ability to provide insights into consumer behaviour or integrate with other business operations.

The digital transformation: Integrated POS systems

The digital revolution transformed POS systems into comprehensive platforms that integrate various aspects of retail operations. Modern POS systems offer real-time data tracking, support for multiple payment methods, and advanced analytics capabilities. These features enable retailers to gain a holistic view of their operations, from sales and inventory to customer relationship management (CRM).

AI and machine learning have further enhanced POS systems, providing deeper insights into consumer behaviour and preferences. For example, these technologies can analyse customer data to offer personalized product recommendations or optimize pricing strategies. This level of personalization helps retailers meet the increasing demand for tailored shopping experiences, both online and in-store.

Enhancing customer experience with intelligent POS

Modern POS systems are not just transactional tools; they are critical for enhancing the customer experience. By gathering and analysing customer data, these systems enable retailers to offer personalized services, such as tailored product recommendations and targeted promotions. For example, POS systems can identify repeat customers and provide them with exclusive discounts or suggestions based on their purchase history.

As technology continues to evolve, POS systems will play an even more integral role in connecting physical and digital retail channels, helping retailers to offer a unified shopping experience.

The evolution of point of purchase: Enhancing in-store experiences

The role and impact of point of purchase (POP) in retail

Point-of-purchase (POP) marketing plays a crucial role in influencing consumer behaviour at the critical moment of decision making. POP marketing uses a range of displays and promotional materials strategically placed within retail environments to engage customers and encourage impulse purchases. This direct engagement at the 'moment of truth' – when consumers are deciding to buy – makes POP an invaluable tool in the retail sector.

What is POP and why is it important?

POP encompasses various marketing strategies, including visual displays, promotional stands and interactive kiosks, all designed to attract customer attention and encourage purchases.

The global market for POP displays is growing steadily, expected to reach $31.1 billion by 2026. With a compound annual growth rate (CAGR) of around 5 per cent from 2021 to 2026 this growth reflects a critical shift in how retailers engage with consumers.[6] As the retail landscape becomes increasingly competitive, brands and retailers are relying on innovative POP displays to capture consumer attention and create memorable in-store experiences. Beyond simply showcasing products, these displays now play a pivotal role in differentiating brands within crowded market spaces and catering to a modern consumer preference for more interactive and engaging shopping environments.

The rise of digital integration within POP displays, from touch screens to augmented reality features, is transforming these fixtures from static presentation tools into dynamic, experience-driven assets. This evolution supports a broader trend in retail where the in-store environment must compete with the convenience and immediacy of online shopping by offering consumers a compelling reason to visit physical locations. As a result, POP displays have become essential in fostering brand loyalty, driving impulse purchases and enhancing the overall shopping experience. The continued investment in this sector underscores the importance of POP displays in an omnichannel strategy, where physical retail spaces provide distinct and immersive experiences that complement digital channels.

The scope of POP in retail

A typical retail store can host numerous POP displays, ranging from basic promotional posters to sophisticated digital setups. These displays can cost from a few hundred to several thousand pounds, depending on their complexity and the duration of the campaign. The strategic placement and design of these displays are crucial for enhancing product visibility and informing customers, which can significantly boost sales.

The impact of POP on consumer behaviour

Research shows that approximately 70 per cent of purchasing decisions are made in-store, highlighting the essential role that POP displays play in shaping consumer choices.[7] This statistic underscores how influential well-designed POP displays can be in capturing attention, directing shopper behaviour, and ultimately driving conversions in a retail environment. Given that so many purchase decisions are made on-site, retailers and brands are increasingly investing in dynamic, visually engaging POP displays to stand out in competitive in-store settings.

Effective POP displays can increase product sales by as much as 20 per cent, a statistic particularly relevant for new or seasonal items where visual attraction and informative content are critical for enticing consumers. Research supports this, showing that strategic use of POP displays not only boosts visibility but also encourages impulse buys, helping products to connect with consumers at the most pivotal moment – just before the purchase decision is made.[8] POP displays are a key retail asset – enhancing engagement, promoting products and reinforcing brand messages. In a market where consumer attention is a finite resource, the ability to influence purchasing decisions directly on the sales floor becomes a valuable competitive advantage.

Evolving consumer expectations and POP

As consumers become more discerning and knowledgeable, they expect more from their shopping experiences, including the POP displays they encounter. Modern consumers look for interactive and engaging displays that offer more than just product information – they seek experiences. This trend has not rendered traditional POP obsolete but rather has driven the evolution of smarter, more responsive POP strategies that meet these elevated expectations and tie in omnichannel experiences.

The cosmetics industry, with its fast-paced and trend-driven marketing, demonstrates effective use of POP displays that resonate strongly with in-store shoppers. One recent campaign from the cosmetic brand Benefit illustrated this approach with a visually compelling POP display featuring bold colours and playful designs that aligned with the brand's aesthetic. Installed in high-traffic locations such as department stores, beauty retailers and speciality cosmetics shops, the display integrated both static and digital elements, including touchscreens and interactive product testers. This multi-sensory set-up allowed customers not only to see the products up close but also to engage with digital tutorials and tips displayed on screens, creating an environment that was both informative and hands-on.

The layout of the display guided customers through different sections, each highlighting various Benefit products, from foundation and concealers to brow enhancers and mascaras. Customers could use the digital screens to access quick beauty tutorials or product demonstrations, encouraging trial and experimentation. These features were particularly effective in department stores, where the POP displays stood out amid competing brands, drawing in customers who might not have initially planned to purchase.

This type of POP display has been shown to effectively increase product visibility and inspire purchases, with reports suggesting that interactive displays in beauty retail can boost sales. By offering added value, such as beauty tips or product recommendations tailored to skin type, these displays enhance the in-store experience, appealing to customers who appreciate personalized advice and the opportunity to test products before committing to a purchase. Through such tailored and interactive POP displays, cosmetic brands like Benefit can more directly engage shoppers, providing an experience that supports their product choices and encourages deeper brand engagement.

Advancing store intelligence through POP

A POP display in-store could feature QR codes that link to product reviews, videos or the retailer's website for more information or purchase options. It enriches the in-store experience and drives traffic to digital channels – creating a seamless shopping journey. The data gathered from these interactions can further enhance personalized marketing efforts, making the shopping experience even more tailored to individual consumer preferences.

In this omnichannel landscape, the role of POP is not limited to influencing in-store purchases but extends to fostering brand engagement across all platforms. By integrating technology with traditional POP strategies, retailers can create a fully cyclical shopping process where in-store experiences drive online engagement and vice versa. This holistic approach ensures that every customer interaction, whether physical or digital, is consistent, engaging and, ultimately, conversion oriented.

As technology continues to advance, the possibilities for POP in omnichannel retail are boundless. From augmented reality (AR) displays that allow customers to 'try on' products virtually, to interactive kiosks that offer personalized recommendations, the future of POP is both exciting and transformative. Retailers that embrace these innovations will not only enhance the shopping experience but also build stronger, more meaningful connections with their customers, driving loyalty and growth in an increasingly competitive market.

Blending the physical and digital worlds

As we've seen, the rise of omnichannel retail has redefined the way businesses interact with their customers. No longer confined to traditional bricks-and-mortar stores or the convenience of e-commerce, modern retail is a seamless fusion of physical and digital experiences. By integrating these channels, retailers can meet consumers' evolving expectations, providing personalized and engaging experiences wherever and however they shop.

At its core, omnichannel retail is about creating a unified and fluid customer journey. Whether through mobile apps, in-store experiences or online platforms, each touchpoint must reflect a consistent brand identity and respond to the shopper's needs. However, achieving true omnichannel integration remains a challenge for many businesses. It requires not only technological investment but also a deep understanding of consumer behaviour and expectations.

As this chapter illustrates, retail spaces are no longer confined to traditional, product-focused layouts; they are evolving into immersive environments that merge physical and digital interactions to meet modern consumer expectations. Omnichannel retail leads this transformation – turning physical stores into vital parts of a seamless, multi-platform experience. These spaces are increasingly designed to go beyond transactions, becoming destinations where customers can connect with brands in meaningful ways through tailored, experience-driven layouts.

In the landscape of physical retail, technology is not just an add-on but an enabler of immersive engagement. Innovations like interactive POP displays, QR code integrations and digital screens are redefining the retail space by creating dynamic environments that encourage exploration and engagement. For instance, stores now incorporate AR and digital kiosks to offer personalized recommendations or virtual try-ons, allowing customers to interact with products in ways that mirror the convenience and customization of online shopping.

POS systems have also advanced beyond simple transaction processing, now acting as essential tools for delivering seamless service and gathering insights that inform store layout, product placement and customer preferences. Retailers like Walmart are blending their extensive physical networks with digital touchpoints, using services like 'buy online, pick up in-store' (BOPIS) to drive traffic to physical stores. This integration reinforces the value of physical spaces as hubs that can offer the immediacy and convenience consumers demand, while also enabling personal, hands-on experiences.

The importance of these evolving retail spaces lies in their ability to foster deeper consumer engagement. Modern shoppers expect experiences that feel bespoke and relevant, and physical stores are uniquely positioned to provide such encounters. As technology continues to advance, retailers will have even more opportunities to enhance their physical spaces, making them adaptable, personalized and interactive. By embracing this shift, retailers are not only redefining the purpose of the retail space but are also creating compelling environments that cater to a diverse array of consumer needs. This is the new frontier of consumer engagement: a retail world where physical spaces play a pivotal role in an integrated, omnichannel strategy that keeps customers connected, engaged and loyal.

KEY TAKEAWAYS

1 **Redefining physical retail spaces:** Today's retail environments are designed to go beyond simple transactions, focusing instead on creating interactive and experience-rich spaces that draw consumers in. This shift is transforming traditional stores into dynamic hubs that blend in-person shopping with digital touchpoints.

2 **Omnichannel integration as a competitive edge:** Retailers like Walmart demonstrate the power of omnichannel strategies in physical spaces, using services like BOPIS to enhance convenience while driving foot traffic. By offering cohesive shopping experiences across in-store, online and mobile channels, retailers are meeting the expectations of today's consumer.

3 **Data-driven personalization in physical stores:** Insights from POS and other digital systems enable retailers to adapt their physical spaces according to consumer preferences, offering personalized recommendations and tailored promotions that enhance the in-store experience and build loyalty.

4 **Engaging customers with interactive POP displays:** Modern POP displays are evolving to include digital and interactive features that attract attention and encourage purchases. These displays, incorporating elements like digital screens and AR, allow consumers to interact with products in ways that bring the convenience of online shopping into the physical store.

5 **The role of physical spaces in omnichannel retail:** In an increasingly digital world, physical retail spaces remain crucial for creating memorable

brand encounters. By integrating technology with traditional layouts, retailers can foster deeper consumer engagement, making the store an essential part of the omnichannel journey that builds lasting customer relationships.

References

1 OAAA (2023) Out of home advertising produces highest levels of consumer recall versus other media channels, according to Solomon Partners 2023 benchmark report estimates for the U.S., 4 January, www.oaaa.org/news/out-of-home-advertising-produces-highest-levels-of-consumer-recall-versus-other-media-channels-according-to-solomon-partners-2023-benchmark-report-estimates-for-the-u-s (archived at https://perma.cc/WL9H-FSW5)

2 Andre, Louie (2022) 26 Relevant print marketing statistics: 2022 AD spending & impact, Gardner Business Media, 28 February, www.gardnerweb.com/blog/post/26-relevant-print-marketing-statistics-2022-ad-spending-impact (archived at https://perma.cc/K4X6-KTPD)

3 Retail Economics (nd) UK Omnichannel Retail 2023: Understanding consumer segmentation for in-store & online markets, www.retaileconomics.co.uk/retail-insights/thought-leadership-reports/uk-omnichannel-retail-2023-report-online-in-store (archived at https://perma.cc/MXZ4-WJ2L)

4 Kumar, S (2022) A buy online and pickup in-store or curbside (BOPIS) experience your customers want, Walmart Commerce Technologies, 25 August, https://commerce.walmart.com/content/walmart-commerce-tech/en_us/articles/a-bopis-experience-your-customers-want.html (archived at https://perma.cc/24WG-PZ8T)

5 Walmart, Inc. (2024) Walmart reports fourth quarter results, 20 February, https://corporate.walmart.com/content/dam/corporate/documents/newsroom/2024/02/20/walmart-releases-q4-and-fy24-earnings/walmart-earnings-release-fy24-q4.pdf (archived at https://perma.cc/RVB5-RLNP)

6 Grand View Research (2021) *Grand View Research*, www.grandviewresearch.com/industry-analysis/point-of-purchase-pop-displays-market (archived at https://perma.cc/Q2EK-WJVV)

7 DisplayMode (nd) 70 percent of purchase decisions are made after customers enter the store, www.displaymode.co.uk/70-percent-of-purchase-decisions-are-made-after-customers-enter-the-store (archived at https://perma.cc/9VMX-RMJD)

8 Rhino Global Solutions (nd) The top driver of retail sales are pop displays, www.rhinoglobalsolutions.com/the-top-driver-of-retail-sales-are-pop-displays (archived at https://perma.cc/2ZVD-YDEV)

5

Retail spaces, evolving places

The evolution of the retail environment
and what the future of stores may entail

In today's world, time has become one of the most valuable commodities for consumers. Paradoxically, although technology has streamlined daily life, many of us feel more time-pressured than ever.

According to research from the Organisation for Economic Co-operation and Development (OECD) a substantial number of individuals across various countries report experiencing a persistent shortage of time. Despite the increasing availability of time-saving tools, digital services and convenience-focused innovations designed to ease daily life, many people continue to feel overwhelmed by time constraints. This trend reflects a paradox within modern society, where the acceleration of technology and accessibility of on-demand services seemingly create more pressure rather than alleviate it. The OECD's Better Life Index indicates that this time scarcity significantly impacts overall well-being, with individuals frequently struggling to balance work, family responsibilities and personal interests. This sense of 'time poverty' not only affects productivity and mental health but also influences consumer behaviour, as people increasingly seek products and services that promise to enhance efficiency and provide greater control over their schedules. In a world where time is perceived as an increasingly valuable and scarce resource, businesses are recognizing the need to create solutions that genuinely address these consumer pressures, offering meaningful convenience rather than superficial time-saving features.[1]

The retail landscape is undergoing a significant transformation, evolving from traditional, transaction-focused spaces to dynamic, multi-experiential environments. This shift is driven by a deeper understanding of consumer needs and preferences, which now prioritize convenience, efficiency and enjoyment. The modern consumer expects more from their shopping experience than just the ability to purchase goods; they seek environments that offer a blend of shopping, leisure and entertainment. This evolution has given rise to the concept of multi-experiential retail spaces, which combine various elements to create destinations worth visiting.

Changing spaces for changing consumers

Shopping malls, once the epitome of retail spaces, are adapting to this new reality. These centres are increasingly incorporating elements beyond retail, such as dining, entertainment and wellness activities. For instance, the Westfield Century City mall in Los Angeles is a prime example of this trend. It features a diverse range of experiences, from high-end shopping and dining options to entertainment venues like cinemas and even an escape room experience called 'The Escape Game LA'. This mix of offerings turns the mall into a vibrant social and entertainment hub, attracting a diverse range of visitors, and widens the opportunity for longer trading hours.

Urban retail environments are also evolving to meet the changing expectations of consumers. Projects like the Regent Street greening initiative in London aim to create more pedestrian-friendly spaces, enhancing the appeal of urban shopping districts. This project, spearheaded by The Crown Estate, aims to transform Regent Street into a more welcoming and vibrant destination, with a strong focus on enhancing both aesthetic appeal and functionality.[2] Key improvements include an increase in green spaces, upgraded pedestrian pathways and the addition of public seating areas, all designed to create an environment where people feel encouraged to pause, relax and enjoy the space. These changes align with a broader trend in urban design, where enhancing the quality of public spaces can have a positive impact on visitor experience, well-being and social interaction.

By incorporating more greenery, such as trees, planters and vertical gardens, the project adds a natural element to the urban landscape, offering respite within the city and contributing to environmental sustainability. Improved pedestrian access and thoughtfully designed seating areas also make Regent Street more accessible and user-friendly, inviting visitors to spend more time exploring the area. This extended dwell time has clear benefits for retail, as studies show that people are more likely to engage with shops, cafés and other amenities when they feel comfortable and welcomed by their surroundings. By investing in these enhancements, The Crown Estate aims not only to elevate the aesthetic and environmental quality of Regent Street but also to support local businesses by fostering a lively, community-oriented atmosphere that attracts a diverse mix of shoppers, tourists and residents.

This evolution in retail spaces goes beyond physical redesigns; it reflects a deep understanding of the modern consumer's psychological and emotional needs. Today's shoppers, especially within younger demographics, are searching for more than a simple transaction – they seek experiences that are enjoyable, memorable and worth sharing. For many consumers, the act of shopping has become an opportunity to connect, explore and discover. This shift is particularly pronounced among millennials and Gen Z, who place higher value on experiential purchases that offer lasting memories over the acquisition of physical goods. According to research by Deloitte, these younger consumers are more inclined to allocate their spending towards activities that enrich their lives and foster social connection, such as dining, travel or immersive retail experiences, rather than accumulating material possessions.[3]

This emphasis on experiences extends across various segments, from luxury shopping to value-driven purchases. Regardless of price point, if a product is seen as non-essential, a heightened retail experience can often be the decisive factor in a purchase. Retailers are responding by creating interactive spaces that go beyond simply displaying products, instead offering elements like immersive installations, in-store events and personalized service options that enhance the shopping journey. These experiences not only differentiate brands in a competitive marketplace but also foster customer loyalty, as consumers are more likely to return to environments that provide meaningful engagement and a sense of belonging.

As the line between retail and entertainment continues to blur, retailers that successfully create spaces that cater to the desire for experience-driven shopping are positioning themselves advantageously. By addressing the psychological motivations behind why people shop, businesses can build deeper connections with consumers and transform their physical spaces into destinations that encourage both repeat visits and organic social sharing.

As consumer demands evolve, retailers are redefining their physical spaces to provide more than just a shopping experience. In today's competitive environment, brands are using immersive, multi-experiential spaces to build loyalty, drive footfall and enhance brand perception.

REAL-WORLD EXAMPLE
Disney and Harrods

Retail spaces with brand activations: Value versus luxury

Primark × Disney

LVMH × Kusama @ Harrods

Primark × Disney: Affordable magic in an everyday space

Primark, widely known for its budget-friendly offerings, has ventured into experiential retail through a strategic partnership with Disney. Located at Primark's flagship Birmingham store, the Disney-themed space serves as a family destination, blending affordability with brand-driven escapism.

What happened?

The Primark × Disney collaboration transformed part of the store into a 'mini-Disneyland' with three key elements:[4,5]

- **Immersive environment:** The Disney-themed area was meticulously designed with character installations, interactive displays and themed decor, making it highly attractive to children and families. This section also featured areas for family photos, creating shareable moments that extended Disney's brand reach to consumers.

- **Disney café experience:** The café offered Disney-themed food and beverages, including Mickey-shaped desserts and character-themed cups, allowing families to enjoy an accessible Disney-themed experience without leaving the UK. By integrating an experiential element like the café, Primark added value to the shopping trip, fostering longer in-store engagement and encouraging families to view the store as a destination.

- **Accessibility to Disney:** By partnering with a beloved global brand, Primark effectively created a space that appeals to Disney enthusiasts who might not typically shop there. This collaboration democratized the Disney experience, enabling a wider demographic to enjoy it affordably without the need to travel to a theme park.

Impact and results

The Disney collaboration demonstrates Primark's ability to leverage accessible, family-friendly experiences to capture a broader audience and engage visitors on multiple levels. This inviting, Disney-themed destination resulted in several clear impacts:

- **Public appeal and social sharing:** The Disney area created a visually appealing space that visitors shared widely on social media. Families and individuals posted their experiences online, generating organic exposure and amplifying Primark's brand visibility within communities that appreciate accessible and enjoyable retail experiences.

- **Memorable customer experience:** The inclusion of a Disney-themed space has provided a memorable experience for visitors, strengthening the emotional connection between Primark and its customers. This family-friendly environment reinforces Primark's position as a destination for more than just affordable shopping, making it a place where families can enjoy shared moments.

- **Broader audience reach:** The collaboration attracted a wider range of customers, including Disney fans and families who may not typically shop at Primark. By appealing to a diverse demographic interested in both value and engaging experiences, Primark expanded its customer base and established itself as a shopping destination that offers both entertainment and affordability.

By creating such experiential spaces, Primark added a new dimension to its value-based offering, supporting the concept of retail spaces as destinations. This has since been followed up with café collaborations with Greggs 'Tasty by Greggs' and Hello Kitty.[6]

This approach highlights how retailers that offer engaging, memorable experiences can attract broader public interest and build lasting connections with customers.

LVMH × Kusama @ Harrods: Art, exclusivity and immersion in luxury retail

In contrast, the LMVH × Kusama collaboration embodies how luxury brands integrate exclusivity into experiential retail. By partnering with LVMH and Yayoi Kusama – a globally renowned artist whose work is celebrated for its avant-garde approach to polka dots and immersive installations – Harrods transformed its space into a high-concept, luxury art experience.

What happened?

The LMVH × Kusama collaboration offered a sensory, visually striking experience that combined luxury, art and exclusivity:[7]

- **Intricate window displays:** The store's famous window displays featured animatronic figures of Kusama 'painting' her signature polka dots in real time, a spectacle designed to captivate both art lovers and luxury shoppers. These displays invited passers-by into the store with a seamless blend of art and retail that embodied the exclusivity of the LVMH x Kusama partnership.[8]

- **Kusama-themed café:** Inside the store, a Kusama-inspired café provided branded food and drink items, including polka-dotted macarons and coffee, which allowed visitors to engage with Kusama's art at an accessible price point. This café offered an 'affordable luxury' moment, giving consumers a memorable, limited-access experience within a luxury setting.

- **Exclusive merchandise:** Limited-edition LVMH items adorned with Kusama's signature polka dots were available, from handbags to smaller accessories. These items, crafted in limited quantities, added an element of scarcity and collectability, appealing particularly to collectors and brand enthusiasts who value the artistry and exclusivity of the collaboration.

Impact and results

The LMVH × Kusama collaboration illustrated the power of luxury retail in creating memorable, art-driven experiences:

- **Extended reach through art and exclusivity:** By merging art and luxury, Harrods attracted a new demographic, extending its appeal beyond traditional high-end shoppers to art aficionados. This likely expanded the customer base by attracting a broader audience while reinforcing the store's status as an iconic luxury destination.

- **Enhanced brand value and consumer loyalty:** The partnership reinforced the exclusivity of Harrods and LVMH, allowing them to create a highly aspirational experience that resonated emotionally with consumers. This blend of luxury and limited-access items was clearly a strategy created to enhance the perceived value of both brands and strengthen loyalty among their core customer base.

How value versus luxury worked in these examples

- **Primark × Disney:** Through accessibility, Primark offered a family-friendly, low-cost experience that appealed to Disney enthusiasts and value-focused shoppers alike. This affordable set-up democratized access to a high-demand brand experience, fostering inclusivity in the store's environment

- **LVMH × Kusama @ Harrods:** Harrods emphasized exclusivity by transforming its space into a high-art environment that captivated affluent consumers. While the café offered an affordable entry point, the overarching experience underscored the aspirational value associated with luxury brands.

Future outlook: The shift towards experiential retail

Both Primark and Harrods showcase the potential of experiential retail to redefine brand–customer interactions, albeit in different ways. As consumers increasingly value experiences over products, retailers must innovate to remain relevant, turning stores into destinations where the journey itself holds value.

For value brands, the future involves:

- **Accessible brand collaborations:** By forming partnerships that make exclusive experiences more affordable, value brands can foster a broader appeal.
- **Creating spaces for family and community:** Value retailers can use experiential spaces to connect with families, offering fun, budget-friendly environments that encourage repeat visits.

For luxury brands, experiential retail will focus on:

- **High-art and high-concept installations:** Integrating art and design can help elevate brand image, attracting both affluent and aspirational consumers.
- **Scarcity and exclusivity:** Limited-edition offerings and exclusive partnerships reinforce the allure of luxury, creating excitement and loyalty through scarcity.

Together, these examples illustrate the importance of evolving retail spaces into destinations, where the experience holds intrinsic value for consumers. As experiential retail continues to grow, brands that prioritize engagement, connection and innovation will remain at the forefront of an increasingly dynamic market.

Retailtainment: Experience shopping and developing trends

One of the key trends in this transformation is the integration of dining and entertainment options within retail spaces. Known as 'retailtainment,' this concept aims to enhance the shopping experience by offering a range of activities that extend beyond traditional retail.

Individual retailers are also embracing this trend, incorporating elements that engage customers on multiple levels. A prime example of this is Nike's flagship stores, which often feature areas where customers can test products, participate in sports activities and receive personalized training sessions. This approach turns the store from a point of sale into a space where customers meaningfully engage with the brand.

The rise of thematic pop-up shops is another significant development in the transformation of traditional retail spaces. These temporary stores are designed to offer unique and immersive experiences centred around specific themes or product launches. For instance, Dior's 'Dioriviera' pop-up shops, located in places like the iconic Beverly Hills Hotel, provide a luxurious and exclusive shopping experience.

REAL-WORLD EXAMPLE
Dioriviera pop-ups at The Beverly Hills Hotel, Los Angeles

The Dioriviera pop-up at The Beverly Hills Hotel is a striking example of how luxury fashion can merge seamlessly with lifestyle and leisure environments.

First introduced in 2023 and expanded in 2024, this collaboration transformed the hotel's iconic pool area into an immersive branded experience, bringing Dior's aspirational Riviera-inspired aesthetic to life in one of Los Angeles's most legendary locations.[9]

This case study explores the elements that made Dioriviera a visually compelling and experiential success.

Transforming space: The Dioriviera aesthetic

Dior's Dioriviera concept was brought to life with meticulous design details that established a Mediterranean ambience against the glamorous backdrop of The Beverly Hills Hotel. Dior's creative team reinterpreted the brand's iconic *Toile de Jouy* pattern in a bold pink hue, which became the defining visual motif of the pop-up. This vibrant print covered almost every aspect of the pool area, creating a cohesive environment that instantly transported guests into a world of Dior luxury, yet did not disrupt the hotel's famous 'Pink Palace' aesthetic.

Elements of the pop-up

- **Cabanas and lounge areas:** Cabanas around the pool were draped in pink *Toile de Jouy*, giving guests an elevated and private space to enjoy the hotel's poolside atmosphere. Each cabana was styled with Dior-branded details, from luxurious sun loungers to towels embroidered with the Dior logo, transforming usual poolside seating into an immersive branded experience.

- **Themed decor and boutique:** The area above the pool housed a boutique that blended seamlessly into the decor, with interior design echoing the same pink motif in everything from wall coverings to seating areas. This boutique displayed exclusive pieces from the Dioriviera collection, including beachwear and accessories specifically curated to align with the resort theme. Visitors were able to move naturally between the poolside and boutique, creating a relaxed browsing experience that was integrated into the leisure setting.

- **Full-environment immersion:** Every aspect of the pop-up was curated to create an experience that extended beyond just visual decor. The set-up included elements such as Dior-branded parasols and plant arrangements, enhancing the Mediterranean vibe and making the entire pool area feel like a cohesive extension of the Dior brand.

Expanding into wellness: The 2024 spa residency

When Dior partnered with the hotel again for 2024, suggesting this was a successful collaboration for them, the brand expanded the experience by introducing a spa residency. This residency offered guests access to Dior's signature face and body treatments within spa spaces decorated to match the Dior *toile* aesthetic.

Social media and public appeal

The visual impact of the Dioriviera pop-up was highly effective in drawing attention from both the public and social media. With each element thoughtfully curated to be photo-ready, the pop-up became a highly shareable experience.

- **Influencer engagement:** The stylish set-up attracted influencers, celebrities and fashion enthusiasts, many of whom documented their experiences online. Every shared photo or video acted as an endorsement, extending Dior's brand presence well beyond the hotel's grounds and reaching audiences worldwide.

- **Organic brand visibility:** The seamless blend of poolside relaxation and luxury shopping attracted organic promotion, showcasing Dior's ability to create memorable, visually engaging experiences that resonate on a global scale.

Broader reach: Dioriviera's expansion to global luxury resorts

Dioriviera at The Beverly Hills Hotel has paved the way for similar pop-ups in high-end locations around the world. In 2024, Dior extended the concept to other exclusive destinations, including Saint-Tropez, Bali, Seoul, Phuket, Kyoto and Capri. These pop-ups allowed Dior to adapt the Dioriviera aesthetic to fit each unique location, while consistently delivering the same Mediterranean-inspired decor and elevated brand experience. Each destination incorporated unique elements that aligned with local aesthetics, while maintaining Dior's signature *Toile de Jouy* motif. For example, sand-sculpted decor, tropical plants and regional artwork were added to enhance the environment's natural beauty and create a sense of place, making each pop-up feel like a unique yet connected part of Dioriviera.

Dioriviera: Experiential luxury retail in aspirational spaces

As the demand for experiential retail continues to grow, Dioriviera offers a model for how luxury brands can turn seasonal events into aspirational destinations. Dior has set a new standard for lifestyle integration in luxury retail, proving that with the right design and strategic placement, a pop-up can leave a lasting impression on guests and global audiences alike.

Transforming technology: Updating retail with interactive experiences

As well as the actual location of stores being part of the transformation, so too is the integration of technology in retail environments, which is increasingly crucial in enhancing customer experiences. Modern consumers expect seamless, interactive and efficient shopping experiences, whether in-store or online. AR and VR are no longer novelties – they're essential tools for enhancing customer experience. These technologies can transform the way customers interact with products, offering a more personalized and engaging experience. It is this shift towards technology-driven experiences that not only enhances customer satisfaction but also can provide retailers with valuable data on consumer preferences and behaviours, helping to tailor offerings more precisely to consumer needs.

One notable example is the use of interactive fitting rooms, such as those introduced by UNIQLO.[10] These fitting rooms are equipped with smart mirrors that allow customers to see how different colours and styles look on them without having to physically change clothes. This not only enhances the shopping experience by providing a more efficient and engaging way to try on products but also offers data insights to retailers on customer preferences and behaviours.

Moreover, retailers are increasingly focusing on creating spaces that encourage social interaction and community engagement. The rise of in-store events, workshops and pop-up cafés exemplifies this trend. Apple's flagship stores are designed not just as retail outlets but as community centres and education zones where people can gather for workshops, tech talks and creative sessions. This approach transforms the store into a hub of activity and learning, fostering a deeper connection between the brand and its customers.

The transformation also extends to creating thematic and aesthetically pleasing environments that resonate with brand identity and customer expectations. Themed stores, like the LEGO flagship store in London, offer immersive experiences that go beyond simple shopping.[11] Visitors can participate in building workshops, explore intricate displays and interact with augmented reality installations. Such experiences not only attract foot traffic but also enhance brand loyalty by creating memorable interactions.

As traditional stores evolve into multi-experiential environments, they are transforming into purposeful destinations that offer far more than a transaction. These spaces are carefully designed to engage customers on multiple levels – visual, sensory and emotional – drawing people in and creating immersive, memorable experiences. This shift is not just a trend but a critical evolution that enables physical stores to maintain relevance in an increasingly digital world. By offering unique experiences that can't be replicated online, traditional stores capture the essence of what makes in-person shopping valuable: a sense of place, community and connection that enhances the customer's journey and strengthens brand loyalty.

In this new era, stores are becoming spaces of discovery and engagement where every element – from lighting and layout to scent and sound – is crafted to deepen the connection between the brand and the consumer. These spaces are about inviting visitors into a curated experience that reflects their lifestyle, aspirations and values, aligning with the growing consumer preference for authenticity and purpose-driven brands. By shifting from purely transactional spaces to environments that celebrate design, culture and community, physical stores are redefining their role in the retail landscape, positioning themselves as essential, dynamic parts of modern life.

This evolution also underscores the importance of 'Place' in retail strategy, where location and atmosphere blend to create a compelling identity that draws people in. It's this focus on creating purposeful spaces that brings us to an insightful perspective on Place curation.

Understanding 'Place' in the retail space

In a world where consumer expectations are high and brand loyalty must be earned, the role of 'Place' has never been more crucial. Leading the way in reimagining iconic retail spaces is The Crown Estate, whose commitment to purposeful placemaking is seen across its prestigious portfolio.

REAL-WORLD EXAMPLE
Richard Ellwood, Head of Customer, Brand and Marketing, The Crown Estate

Kate Hardcastle

(KH): Richard, you've had an incredible career, from Disney to now managing the marketing, commercial leasing and Place curation for some of the most iconic shopping destinations in the world. Could you start by telling us how your past experiences have shaped your approach to retail at The Crown Estate?

Richard Ellwood

(RE): Thank you, Kate. Yes, my time at Disney played a role in shaping how I think about the places people visit, how they make them feel and of course, how that relates to retail experience. Disney taught me the importance of crafting experiences that resonate emotionally with people young and old. However, The Crown Estate is different in that we're working with real-world locations, steeped in history – places like Regent Street and Jermyn Street – where we could blend that legacy with modern expectations.

It's therefore not about creating a fantasy world but more about understanding how people interact with urban spaces. We're focused on using these historical streets to create meaningful, immersive (and sometimes still magical) retail environments that resonate with today's consumer. This still includes the Disney approach of what do people see, hear, smell and touch.

KH: Regent Street and Jermyn Street are so iconic. They're not just places to shop; they're part of London's cultural fabric. How do you keep that balance between preserving their historical significance while ensuring they stay relevant to modern consumers?

RE: Regent Street and Jermyn Street are unique and certainly not just retail destinations – they're part of the cultural identity of London. Regent Street, with its Georgian architecture, has always been a place where grand, flagship stores can flourish next to independent boutiques. But at the same time, we need to stay ahead of the curve. Consumers are looking for more than just a shopping trip. They want a sense of serendipity, a sense of storytelling in what makes the place unique, and that's where our responsibility comes in.

For us, it's about curating the right mix of brands and categories, but also about thinking creatively about how we use the space itself. We've pedestrianized streets for events like 'Summer Streets' and the UEFA Champions League final this year, where Regent Street becomes more of an open-air festival. We're also incorporating public art installations and creating areas where people can simply gather and enjoy the surroundings. It's about making sure that these streets don't just reflect retail, but also culture, creativity and the essence of London.

KH: That brings me to an important point – the physical space. How do you maximize the use of these areas to create an immersive experience that goes beyond traditional retail?

RE: Regent Street is a prime example – its wide pavements and grand facades lend themselves to creating experiences that feel expansive and inviting. We work closely with our retail partners to create flagship experiences – Apple, Burberry and Hamleys, for example, don't just offer products; they invite people into an immersive brand world.

But it's also about the spaces in between. We see the streets as a canvas. Recently, we've worked on public installations and pop-ups that encourage people to stop, interact and engage with the location itself. Jermyn Street, in contrast, is more intimate, but it carries a history of heritage craftsmanship and tradition. Here, we use the architecture and heritage to support experiences that feel personal, such as bespoke tailoring appointments and exclusive events that showcase craftsmanship and the art of making. It's all about bringing these spaces to life in ways that are true to their DNA.

KH: Jermyn Street's history is so rich, particularly in menswear and craftsmanship. How do you ensure that this heritage is not only preserved but also innovated upon for a new generation of consumers?

RE: Jermyn Street is a place where heritage and modernity meet. We're deeply respectful of the history here – after all, this is where British craftsmanship, especially in menswear, really came into its own. But at the same time, we're conscious of the fact that consumer expectations are evolving. Today's shoppers, especially the younger ones, value authenticity, but they also want an experience that feels contemporary.

For example, we've partnered with our retailers to offer more personalized, intimate shopping experiences – bespoke tailoring sessions, fragrance consultations at Floris, and the ability to truly understand the artistry behind each product. We're not just preserving heritage; we're making it relevant. And that's key: people want a story behind their purchase, something that ties them emotionally to the product, and Jermyn Street's legacy allows us to offer that.

KH: It seems like you're creating more than just retail spaces – you're cultivating destinations. How do you see the future of physical retail evolving, especially in the context of such iconic locations?

RE: Physical retail is evolving rapidly, but all data points on footfall, dwell time and spend point to retail having a strong future, particularly in iconic locations like Regent Street and in St James. What we're seeing is that people still crave the physical experience of shopping, but they want more than just products – they want immersion. That's why we're constantly thinking about how we can bring in elements of art, culture and community to these spaces.

We've also seen how our retail partners are integrating technology more seamlessly into the retail environment. Whether it's through augmented reality experiences in stores or apps that guide visitors through the area and highlight events or promotions, we're seeing that the digital complements the physical in a way that feels intuitive.

But most importantly, it's about making these spaces destinations. Regent Street has become known for its seasonal events, like our famous festive lights, which attract people from all over the world. Jermyn Street, on the other hand, offers a more curated, intimate experience. But in both cases, it's about creating a place where people feel connected – whether to the history, the culture, or the innovation of the brands we work with.

KH: Regent Street's events have become almost legendary, like the festive lights. How do you decide what kinds of events or experiences to bring to life in these spaces?

RE: We're always looking at ways to activate our spaces in ways that feel true to their history but also add something new. Regent Street's festive lights are a great example. They've become a huge draw for locals and tourists alike, but they're not just about decoration. Each year, we work to make them a focal point for a season-long experience, with pop-ups, late-night shopping events, and partnerships that extend that festive atmosphere throughout the street.

Similarly, with Jermyn Street, we look at its heritage and think about what experiences would add to that narrative. Recently, we've hosted exclusive events focusing on heritage craftsmanship – bringing in not just fashion brands, but also heritage artisans, to showcase their work in an intimate setting. It's about ensuring that each event, whether it's a public art installation or a private shopping experience, feels connected to the space.

KH: What strikes me about The Crown Estate's approach is how it reflects a deeper understanding of the relationship between place and retail. It's not just about the stores themselves, but about how people move through these spaces and connect with them emotionally. How do you see this evolving in the future?

RE: The future of retail is as much about place as it is about product. In iconic locations like ours, the streets themselves are part of the experience. We see ourselves as custodians of these spaces, and that means thinking beyond just the physical stores. It's about creating environments where people want to spend time, where they feel inspired, and where there's always something new to discover.

Looking ahead, we're focused on how we can continue to integrate elements of sustainability, technology and cultural engagement into these spaces. Regent Street and St James have long been at the forefront of London's retail scene, and our goal is to ensure they remain vibrant, exciting destinations for the next generation of shoppers. We're committed to not just preserving their legacy but ensuring that they continue to evolve in meaningful ways.

KH: Richard, thank you for such an insightful conversation. It's clear that The Crown Estate is setting the standard for the future of experiential, destination-driven retail.

Key interview takeaways

1 **Curating retail through place-making:** The Crown Estate's approach to retail is rooted in understanding how people interact with urban spaces. By blending historical significance with modern consumer expectations, destinations like Regent Street and Jermyn Street offer more than just shopping – they become immersive, cultural experiences.

2 **Retail as an experiential destination:** The focus is on creating environments that go beyond transactions, incorporating flagship brand experiences, pedestrianized events and public art installations. Seasonal activations such as Regent Street's festive lights transform traditional retail spaces into cultural hubs that attract global visitors.

3 **Balancing heritage and innovation:** Jermyn Street's legacy in craftsmanship is being reinterpreted for contemporary consumers through intimate, personalized retail experiences such as bespoke tailoring and fragrance consultations. By ensuring authenticity while embracing new shopping behaviours, The Crown Estate preserves tradition while making it relevant for today's market.

4 **The power of physical retail in the digital age:** Despite the rise of e-commerce, data shows that consumers still crave the tactile and immersive aspects of physical retail. The Crown Estate integrates technology such as augmented reality and app-driven experiences to enhance the in-person shopping journey, bridging the gap between digital convenience and real-world engagement.

5 **The future of destination retail:** Looking ahead, The Crown Estate remains focused on sustainability, cultural integration, and evolving retail environments that foster connection and discovery. With a commitment to ensuring iconic London destinations remain vibrant and relevant, the strategy is to create spaces where history, commerce and experience coalesce to define the future of retail.

The power of physical stores in brand storytelling

Physical stores aren't just points of sale – they're the stages where brands bring stories to life, a good reason why we see so many consumer brands that might not be pure retailers using branded retail stores for storytelling.

Coca-Cola's flagship stores in its headquarters location of Atlanta, and in prime locations like Disney Springs in Orlando, are designed to provide visitors with an immersive experience that celebrates the brand's history and cultural impact. The store features interactive exhibits, a tasting room where visitors can sample different Coca-Cola beverages from around the world, and a fully operational soda fountain that emphasizes the iconic 'Coke pour'. Additionally, the store offers premium Coca-Cola merchandise, creating a unique shopping experience that combines retail with education and entertainment.

Similarly, the Guinness Storehouse in Dublin is a seven-storey attraction that offers visitors an in-depth look at the history and brewing process of Guinness. The experience culminates in the Gravity Bar, where innovative printing technology allows visitors to enjoy a pint of Guinness with their face printed on the foam. This unique touch not only enhances the experience but also creates memorable moments that visitors are likely to share on social media, thereby extending the brand's reach. The store features a vast array of Guinness-branded products, from clothing to glassware, providing a comprehensive retail experience that capitalizes on the brand's rich heritage.[12]

The role of digital marketing in enhancing physical store initiatives

Digital marketing is essential in driving traffic to physical stores and enhancing the in-store experience. For instance, Nike's 'House of Innovation' stores integrate digital and physical channels seamlessly. Customers can use the Nike app to navigate the store, access exclusive content and reserve items to try on in-store. The app offers personalized recommendations based on the customer's purchase history and preferences, creating a seamless and engaging brand experience.

Starbucks also exemplifies how digital marketing can support physical store initiatives. Its mobile app offers promotions and loyalty rewards that encourage customers to visit physical locations. The app's integration with in-store experiences enhances customer engagement and loyalty.

Integrating online and offline marketing efforts

For a cohesive brand experience, it is essential to integrate online and offline marketing efforts. This integration ensures that customers receive a consistent brand experience regardless of the channel they use. Unified messaging, cross-channel promotions and data integration are crucial for this approach.

Hermès is a prime example of a brand that excels in integrating online and offline marketing efforts. With over 14 million followers on Instagram and a highly engaging website, Hermès uses digital platforms to complement its luxurious in-store experience. The brand's social media presence often features artful and cinematic content that mirrors the visual merchandising found in its stores. This cohesive approach ensures that the brand's storytelling is consistent across all channels.

REAL-WORLD EXAMPLE
The magic of the Hermès store experience

Hermès is celebrated for its meticulously crafted in-store experience, which is central to sustaining its elite brand image and drawing customers into a world of unmatched elegance. Entering a Hermès boutique is more than a shopping trip; it's an immersion in refinement. From the finest materials to thoughtfully designed lighting and decor, each element embodies the timeless sophistication and heritage of the brand.

Personalized service is a cornerstone of Hermès's allure. Guests are welcomed warmly, often treated to exclusive refreshments – champagne or specially curated teas served on Hermès's own trays – adding a touch of luxury and personalization that few brands offer. This exceptional hospitality reinforces Hermès's image of exclusivity and care, ensuring customers feel valued and connected to the brand's legacy. To elevate this experience further, certain Hermès items remain exclusive to in-store shoppers, drawing a consistent flow of visitors and creating a unique, tactile experience that cannot be replicated online.[13]

The flagship Hermès store on Rue du Faubourg Saint-Honoré in Paris encapsulates this ethos perfectly. Walking into the store, customers are met with an immaculate display of Hermès creations, each piece curated to highlight its intricate craftsmanship. A dedicated area offers bespoke services, allowing customers to personalize their purchases, whether a monogram on a silk scarf or the selection of materials for a custom handbag, further enhancing the sense of luxury and exclusivity.

Beyond the physical store, Hermès amplifies this story through social media, showcasing moments with personal shoppers, glimpses of bespoke craftsmanship and highlights of new collections. This digital storytelling creates anticipation and enhances the brand experience for consumers worldwide, allowing them to connect with Hermès's heritage even if they're not in-store.

The commitment Hermès places on in-store experience is evident in its consistent financial performance. In 2023, Hermès recorded a remarkable 21 per cent increase in sales at constant exchange rates, reaching €13.4 billion, with all regions contributing to growth of approximately 20 per cent. This success is a testament to the impact of creating a luxury environment that feels both exclusive and welcoming, giving Hermès a distinguished position even in today's digital-driven retail landscape.[14]

In a world where consumer engagement is increasingly fleeting, Hermès has demonstrated that a well-crafted, immersive experience fosters deeper connections, elevates brand loyalty and continues to drive success. Through the art of storytelling, both in-store and online, Hermès has not only preserved its heritage but has also created a modern, memorable journey that resonates globally with a discerning clientele.

The role of non-traditional retail spaces

Non-traditional retail spaces, such as pop-ups, hotel boutiques and mobile units, are transforming the retail landscape. These innovative spaces offer unique opportunities for brands to engage with consumers in novel ways, driving brand perception and consumer behaviour.

The rise of non-traditional retail spaces reflects a broader trend towards creating unique and memorable shopping experiences. Pop-up stores create a sense of urgency and exclusivity, making them ideal for launching new products, testing markets or generating buzz. They can be found in high-traffic areas such as shopping malls, festivals and even vacant storefronts. This temporary nature of pop-ups encourages customers to visit and make purchases before the opportunity is gone, driving immediate sales and increasing brand visibility.

Mobile retail units, such as food trucks and mobile boutiques, offer flexibility and can reach customers in various locations. These units can appear at events, markets and even corporate campuses, providing a novel shopping experience. The mobility of these units allows brands to engage with customers in different environments, creating unique and memorable experiences.

Why Glastonbury? The festival's legacy and appeal

Glastonbury Festival, held annually at Worthy Farm in Somerset, England, is much more than just a music event; it's a cultural phenomenon. Since its inception in 1970, Glastonbury has grown into the world's most famous music and arts festival, renowned for its eclectic mix of live music, art installations, and its commitment to environmental sustainability. With an audience exceeding 200,000 people, Glastonbury has established itself as a space where brands can interact with a diverse and socially conscious crowd eager for unique experiences. It's this blend of music, community and environmental consciousness that attracts forward-thinking brands seeking to engage consumers in ways that resonate beyond traditional advertising.[15]

For brands, Glastonbury offers a rare opportunity: to reach an audience immersed in an environment focused on creativity, sustainability and togetherness. Here, brand engagement transcends standard promotional tactics, offering companies a platform to enhance their brand image through meaningful, purpose-driven interactions. Pop-up experiences at Glastonbury must align with the festival's ethos, reflecting values of environmental awareness, authenticity and community connection. As such, the brands that stand out here are those able to deliver not only relevant products but also experiences that enrich the festival-goers' journey.

In this context, two very different brands – Barbour and The Co-op – have used Glastonbury as a stage to create impactful, memorable interactions. Each brand brings its distinct identity to the festival while enhancing the attendee experience in a way that aligns with Glastonbury's core values.

Barbour's collaboration with Oxfam: Crafting a purposeful experience

At Glastonbury 2024, British heritage brand Barbour teamed up with Oxfam to introduce an innovative, sustainable pop-up experience. Barbour's focus on longevity and craftsmanship made it a natural fit for the festival, where values of environmental responsibility and sustainability resonate deeply. This collaboration brought Barbour's 'Re-Loved' programme to the forefront, allowing festival-goers to rent upcycled wax jackets for £45. The jackets, part of Barbour's broader 'Wax for Life' initiative, were expertly refurbished and featured materials sourced from past Glastonbury collections, giving them a unique, bespoke quality.

Barbour's pop-up was a masterclass in connecting brand values with consumer interests. By offering rental options, the brand introduced a sustainable alternative to fast fashion, inviting festival attendees to embrace circular fashion systems. This rental model, along with the brand's commitment to repairing, re-waxing and customizing jackets, reinforced Barbour's dedication to environmental stewardship. The wax jackets themselves carried an authenticity and history that resonated with Glastonbury's audience, who appreciate quality and heritage as much as sustainability.[16]

The pop-up's impact extended beyond just the products on offer; it fostered a connection with consumers around shared values of durability, quality and environmental care. Barbour's presence at Glastonbury not only highlighted its craftsmanship but also emphasized its alignment with the slow fashion movement – a message that was particularly well-received in the festival's eco-conscious environment. This unique experience allowed Barbour to tap into the festival's culture, creating a lasting impression by combining functionality with purpose-driven retail.

The Co-op: A community-focused retail experience with environmental impact

The Co-op's involvement at Glastonbury demonstrates how a national grocer can resonate with an audience in an unconventional setting by prioritizing sustainability and accessibility. The Co-op is the only national grocery chain with a physical presence at Glastonbury, making it an essential part of the festival's infrastructure. Situated in a 6,000-square-foot wooden barn, the Co-op's pop-up not only provided festival essentials but also reinforced the brand's commitment to eco-friendly practices.

In line with Glastonbury's ethos, the Co-op's entire set-up was designed with sustainability in mind. All packaging, from sandwich bags to food labels, was 100 per cent compostable, a critical detail for an audience that values environmental responsibility. Additionally, the Co-op offered water in refillable aluminium cans, supporting Glastonbury's ban on single-use plastic bottles. This approach demonstrated a practical and impactful commitment to reducing waste, a message that resonated with younger, eco-aware festival-goers.

The Co-op's presence was more than just a grocery stop – it was a carefully curated experience designed to meet the practical needs of attendees while enhancing the festival's community-focused atmosphere. For many festival-goers, this pop-up became an anchor point, providing reliable and convenient access to essentials without compromising environmental standards, and at realistic prices.[17] The Co-op's sustainable set-up not only met a functional need but also demonstrated the brand's alignment with the festival's core values, effectively strengthening its relationship with consumers who share these ideals.

Common themes: Purposeful engagement and brand enhancement

Barbour and the Co-op represent two very different brands with distinct identities, yet both managed to create purpose-driven experiences that enriched the Glastonbury atmosphere. Their approaches were shaped by the festival's values of environmental consciousness, community and authenticity, allowing them to engage the audience in meaningful ways.

Enhancing the festival experience through purposeful pop-ups

The success of Barbour and the Co-op's pop-up experiences at Glastonbury Festival illustrates how brands can elevate their presence by going beyond simple marketing to create meaningful interactions that resonate with festival-goers. Both brands achieved this by aligning with Glastonbury's ethos of environmental consciousness, community focus and authenticity, resulting in experiences that not only served the practical needs of attendees but also left a lasting impression.

Barbour, with its rental model, demonstrated a commitment to sustainability and heritage, creating a direct connection with festival-goers who value craftsmanship and responsible fashion. By inviting people to wear unique, upcycled jackets, Barbour provided a one-of-a-kind experience that felt personal and special within the festival context. The Co-op, meanwhile, transformed its presence into a sustainable grocery hub that aligned perfectly with Glastonbury's values. Its eco-friendly choices – from compostable packaging to refillable cans – highlighted its dedication to reducing waste and catering to the needs of an environmentally aware audience.

In both cases, these brands used the power of experiential retail to foster deeper connections with consumers, offering them memorable experiences that aligned with their values. By taking the time to create spaces that enhanced the Glastonbury experience rather than simply promoting products, Barbour and the Co-op set themselves apart as brands committed to purpose, responsibility and community.

This case study serves as a reminder that experiential retail/retail pop-ups can be more than a marketing opportunity; it's a chance to deepen brand loyalty by engaging consumers in meaningful ways. By creating purpose-driven pop-ups that resonate with festival-goers, brands can enhance their image, build lasting connections, and become part of the unique festival experience that people carry with them long after the event ends.

Future trends in non-traditional retail environments

As the retail landscape continues to evolve, the future of retail is increasingly moving towards non-traditional spaces. Hybrid spaces that combine shopping with other activities, such as cafés, co-working spaces and wellness centres, are becoming more common. These hybrid spaces cater to the modern consumer's desire for multifunctional environments.

Sustainable pop-ups that focus on using eco-friendly materials and promoting environmentally conscious products are also on the rise. This trend aligns with the growing consumer demand for sustainable and ethical brands.

Community-centric retail spaces that focus on community engagement, hosting events, workshops and social gatherings, are becoming more popular. These spaces create a sense of belonging and loyalty among customers.

Personalized experiences, enabled by advanced data analytics and AI, will become more prevalent in non-traditional spaces. These experiences create highly personalized shopping experiences, enhancing customer satisfaction and loyalty.

By leveraging non-traditional retail spaces, brands can create unique and memorable experiences that resonate with consumers. These innovative spaces offer flexibility, exclusivity and a sense of urgency, which drive consumer engagement and brand loyalty.

The impact of layout and store design on consumer behaviour

Have you ever paused to consider how the layout and design of a retail space influence your shopping habits? As you stroll through a store, every element from the entrance to the checkout counter is meticulously designed to trigger certain behaviours and emotions.

The layout of a store plays a critical role in guiding customer behaviour. From the moment you step inside, the store's design sets the stage for your shopping journey. I refer to the entrance as the 'decompression zone' that allows customers to adjust and sets the tone for their experience. An inviting and uncluttered decompression zone can make a significant difference, encouraging customers to explore further.

Product placement is another strategic element. High-demand and high-margin items are often placed in prominent locations to maximize visibility and sales. Supermarkets, for instance, typically place essential items like dairy products at the back of the store. This layout strategy compels customers to walk through various aisles, increasing the chances of additional purchases along the way.

Effective traffic flow within the store ensures a smooth shopping experience. Wide aisles, clear signage and strategically placed displays help direct traffic and reduce congestion, making the shopping journey more pleasant. Research indicates that a well-designed traffic flow can increase the time customers spend in-store and their overall spending.

Impulse zones, typically located near the checkout and high-traffic areas, are designed to encourage last-minute purchases. Impulse purchases, like those sweets at the checkout, can account for a significant portion of a store's revenue, particularly in grocery and convenience stores.

The psychology of space and design in retail

Colour psychology is a powerful tool in retail design. Different colours evoke different emotions and behaviours.

Proper lighting enhances the visual appeal of products and creates a welcoming atmosphere. Bright, well-lit spaces are inviting and make it easier for customers to see products, while dim lighting can create a more intimate and relaxed environment.

Background music can influence the pace of shopping and evoke specific emotions. Slow music can encourage customers to take their time, while faster music can create a sense of urgency.

The arrangement of furniture, fixtures and products can guide customer movement and behaviour. Creating focal points with attractive displays can draw customers deeper into the store. IKEA, for instance, uses a labyrinthine layout that ensures customers pass through the entire store, increasing the likelihood of impulse purchases.

REAL-WORLD EXAMPLE
The design philosophy of Lululemon stores

Lululemon, the athletic apparel retailer, offers a compelling case study in how thoughtful store design can enhance the customer experience and drive brand loyalty. Founded in 1998 in Vancouver, Lululemon has grown into a global brand with a strong emphasis on community and wellness.

Lululemon stores are designed to create a community-focused environment that encourages customers to engage with the brand beyond shopping. Many stores feature dedicated spaces for yoga classes, workshops and community events. These spaces foster a sense of community and position the store as a hub for wellness and fitness activities. By offering these experiences, Lululemon strengthens its relationship with customers and reinforces its brand values.

The product layout in Lululemon stores uses an open design that allows customers to easily browse and interact with products. Clothing racks are strategically placed to create a flow that guides customers through the store, with popular items and new arrivals prominently displayed. This layout encourages exploration and discovery, enhancing the shopping experience.

Interactive elements are another key feature of Lululemon stores. The stores often feature touchpoints where customers can learn about the materials and technology used in the products. Interactive displays provide information on fabric technology and product benefits, educating customers and adding value to their shopping experience.

Visual merchandising in Lululemon stores is designed to highlight the functionality and versatility of its products. Mannequins are posed in active positions, showcasing the apparel in action and helping customers envision how they can wear the products in their own lives. The use of vibrant colours and inspirational imagery further enhances the store's energetic and positive atmosphere.

Conclusion: Lululemon's differentiator throughout store layout and design

Lululemon has long set itself apart in the athleisure market by transforming its stores into community hubs that offer more than just retail transactions. By incorporating in-store yoga studios, event spaces and communal areas, the brand has created immersive environments that foster customer engagement and loyalty. This experiential approach has been instrumental in building a dedicated customer base and establishing Lululemon as a leader in experiential retail.

However, recent developments indicate that Lululemon is facing significant challenges. The company has experienced a slowdown in its women's business, with only a 6 per cent growth in a recent quarter, despite efforts to diversify its product offerings. This deceleration is attributed to increased competition from brands like Alo Yoga and Vuori, as well as consumers opting for more affordable alternatives amid financial constraints. Analysts have noted that a lack of new product options has impacted sales, and the company has undergone a reorganization to better align merchandising with brand and marketing strategies.[18]

Considering these challenges, it may be prudent for Lululemon to revisit and enhance its store layout strategies that were a significant part of its success and legacy. By reinvigorating its focus on community-centric spaces and immersive experiences, the brand can reinforce its unique identity and continue to attract a dedicated consumer base in a crowded market. Doubling down on purpose-driven retail experiences could serve as a significant differentiator, helping Lululemon maintain its edge and ensure future growth amid increasing industry competition online.

Optimizing layout for different retail environments

Optimizing layout involves specific strategies tailored to the unique needs of each retail sector. In grocery stores, focusing on traffic flow and product placement can maximize exposure to high-margin items. Using end caps and aisle displays to highlight promotions and seasonal items can drive impulse purchases.

In clothing stores, creating an inviting entrance and using open layouts can encourage exploration. Placing fitting rooms strategically is crucial, as they are key touchpoints for customer decision-making. Visual merchandising should highlight outfit ideas and accessorizing options to inspire customers.

With electronic and tech stores, highlighting interactive displays and allowing customers to test products can enhance the shopping experience. Clear signage to guide customers to different sections and ensuring that staff are available for assistance can improve customer satisfaction. Creating demo stations where customers can experience the products in action can drive sales.

When it comes to luxury, focusing on creating an opulent and exclusive atmosphere is essential. Using high-quality materials, elegant lighting and personalized service can enhance the shopping experience – the feeling of being in a first-class airport lounge. Offering exclusive in-store items and services can drive foot traffic and reinforce the brand's luxury image.

By understanding and applying these principles, retailers can create environments that not only attract customers but also encourage them to spend more time and money in-store. The future of retail lies in creating spaces that are as dynamic and diverse as the consumers they serve.

The future of retail spaces

What does the shop of the future look like? Imagine stepping into a store where every detail, from the lighting to the layout, is designed to enhance your experience and heighten your emotions positively. A space that feels personalized, engaging and more than just a place to buy things. A very human space yet one powered by the latest technology.

As we move into a new era, the boundaries between shopping, entertainment and community are blurring, creating environments that are more dynamic, immersive and personalized than ever before.

Retail is no longer just about transactions. It is about creating stories, crafting memorable experiences and building connections. The future of retail spaces is being shaped by technological advancements, changing consumer behaviours and the desire for immersive environments. The future of retail spaces is about transforming these places into experiential hubs where shopping is just one part of the overall journey. The landscape is no longer confined to mere transactions; it is about crafting stories, creating memories and building communities.

Think back to the last time you were genuinely excited to be in a retail store. Was it because of the products, or was it the atmosphere, the engagement and the experience? This transformation is reshaping the future of retail spaces. Stores are becoming more than places to buy things – they are evolving into destinations where consumers can explore, interact and feel a deeper connection with brands.

What do consumers want in the future?

Today's consumers are more discerning and demanding than ever, with many now prioritizing experience over mere transactions.[19] They seek convenience, personalization, and seamless integration between online and offline shopping. In addition, technology, sustainability and community engagement rank high in consumer expectations.

CONSUMER DESIRES FOR FUTURE RETAIL SPACES

- **Community-centric spaces:** Stores as hubs for gathering, events and social interaction.

- **Convenience and seamless shopping:** Easy transitions across digital and physical channels.

- **Engaging, immersive experiences:** AR, VR and interactive displays that enhance sensory engagement.

- **Innovative technology integration:** AI, Internet of Things (IoT) and data-driven insights for personalized service and inventory management.

- **Personalized experiences:** Tailored shopping journeys that reflect individual preferences.

- **Sustainable practices:** Eco-conscious choices in materials, operations and product offerings.

Expanding on consumer expectations for future retail spaces

- **Personalized experiences:** Consumers expect interactions that reflect their unique preferences and shopping behaviours. Advanced data analytics, AI and machine learning are critical in making these personalized interactions seamless and intuitive. Imagine a store that dynamically changes product displays or offers recommendations tailored to each visitor. Klarna's findings show that 72 per cent of consumers view personalized experiences as essential, emphasizing the growing demand for retail spaces that can adapt to their needs.

- **Convenience and seamless shopping:** Modern consumers want frictionless movement between online and offline experiences. This means fast delivery, easy returns and consistent service and product availability across all channels. Klarna's research highlights that 84 per cent of shoppers favour retailers with a unified experience across both physical and digital channels. Retailers that invest in synchronizing these elements provide a seamless journey that keeps customers returning.

- **Engaging, immersive experiences:** Immersive retail environments that captivate all of the senses are becoming essential. Consumers are drawn to interactive displays, AR/VR installations and innovative store layouts that transform shopping into a memorable experience. Klarna's data reveals that 68 per cent of shoppers are more inclined to visit stores offering advanced technology, underscoring the demand for innovative shopping spaces that blend digital and physical elements.

- **Sustainable practices:** Sustainability is now a fundamental expectation. Consumers increasingly prefer brands that make eco-friendly choices, from materials to ethical production strategies. Future retail spaces will likely feature environmentally sustainable materials, energy-efficient operations and minimized waste. Instead of temporary displays that require plastic and cardboard, retailers may adopt adaptable digital signage that changes with a simple update, reflecting consumers' values and reducing environmental impact.

- **Community-centric spaces:** As shopping becomes more experience-focused, retail stores are evolving into community hubs. These spaces encourage social interaction, offering more than just products. Consumers are seeking stores that double as gathering spaces for events, local collaborations and educational workshops. This shift adds value to the shopping experience and strengthens a brand's relationship with its customers by fostering a sense of belonging.

- **Innovative technology integration:** The future of retail spaces is inseparable from advanced technology. AI, IoT, AR and VR are no longer optional, but essential tools that can enhance personalization, inventory management and even security. These technologies will also support the development of flexible store layouts, enabling retailers to adapt spaces dynamically for events or seasonal displays. This adaptability not only keeps the experience fresh but also aligns with the need for sustainability by reducing waste from constantly changing physical materials.

The path forward: Creating multifunctional, integrated retail experiences

These future retail spaces are transforming from single-purpose shopping destinations into dynamic, multifunctional hubs that cater to a variety of consumer needs. By integrating retail with complementary experiences like dining, entertainment and wellness, these spaces are evolving to align with modern lifestyles and expectations. Today's consumers value convenience and connection, so creating environments where people can shop, dine, socialize and engage with their communities in meaningful ways has become essential. This transformation supports the notion that retail can be an experience and a lifestyle choice rather than simply a place for transactions.

This shift reflects a broader understanding that consumers seek engaging, purpose-driven environments that resonate with their values and interests. For retail spaces to remain relevant, they must meet customers where they are, offering experiences that blend effortlessly with everyday life. In a single destination, consumers can relax, explore and participate in events, which fosters a lasting connection between them and the brands they interact with. These future-oriented spaces foster local relationships by supporting nearby businesses, hosting community events and creating gathering places that encourage social interaction. Ultimately, this approach enhances both the consumer experience and the retail brand's cultural impact, setting a higher standard for engagement in the industry.

REAL-WORLD EXAMPLE
A vibrant retail space: The Grove, Los Angeles

The Grove in Los Angeles serves as an excellent example of this new direction in retail spaces. Located in the heart of LA, The Grove is an upscale retail and entertainment complex that exemplifies how a shopping destination can evolve into a lively, community-centred environment. It combines premium shopping with dining, entertainment and a steady calendar of community-focused events, creating a vibrant and engaging destination for both locals and visitors. This upmarket complex demonstrates how retail spaces can successfully blend leisure, commerce and community in one location, establishing a multifunctional environment that keeps consumers engaged for longer periods.

The Grove in Los Angeles is owned by Caruso, a prominent real estate development company founded by Rick Caruso. The Grove was designed by David Williams of Elkus Manfredi Architects and opened to the public in 2002. The project, which cost approximately $160 million to build, aimed to create an immersive and engaging retail environment that blended shopping with entertainment and community spaces.

Caruso's vision for The Grove was to establish a destination that offered a unique and memorable experience for visitors, seamlessly integrating high-end retail, dining and entertainment options in a beautifully landscaped, pedestrian-friendly setting.

The Grove's design integrates seamlessly with its surroundings, featuring open-air shopping, beautifully landscaped gardens and a central fountain that serves as a focal point. The complex hosts a variety of events, from brand pop-ups to holiday celebrations, ensuring there's always something new and exciting for visitors. The destination boasts impressive foot traffic and sales figures, highlighting its success as a retail destination attracting over 20 million visitors annually, a testament to its popularity and the effectiveness of its design and offerings.

The blend of high-end retail stores like Gucci and unique offerings like La La Land Kind Cafe contribute to its diverse appeal, drawing both residents and tourists. The success of The Grove underscores the importance of creating engaging, multifaceted environments that cater to a wide range of consumer needs and preferences.

On 10 October 2023, Taylor Swift's 'Eras Tour' film premiere transformed the venue into a star-studded red-carpet venue. Attended by notable celebrities like Beyoncé, Adam Sandler and Julia Garner, the event was a significant occasion for both Swift and her fans. The premiere is just one example of how this is a venue that can transition from a retail and entertainment complex to a premier event location.

The blend of retail and hospitality creates a mix that caters to a diverse audience, ensuring that there's something for everyone and every budget.

La La Land Kind Cafe, for example, provides a unique space where customers can enjoy high-quality coffee in an aesthetically pleasing environment that encourages social media sharing and community engagement.

Founded by Francois Reihani in 2019, aiming to offer more than just a coffee experience; the café's mission is to employ and empower youth who have aged out of the foster care system, providing them with job training and social skills to improve their social mobility. The café's atmosphere is designed to promote kindness and positivity, encouraging customers to engage in acts of kindness. This social mission, combined with its aesthetically pleasing design and quality coffee, has made it a standout in the Los Angeles café scene.

The Grove's success lies in its ability to create a dynamic and immersive shopping experience. It is not just a place to buy goods; it is a place where consumers can spend an entire day, enjoying various activities and creating lasting memories. This holistic approach to retail is what sets The Grove apart and serves as a model for the future of retail spaces. Its ability to offer a special experience, always with something new to see, will keep visitors returning.

The Grove in Los Angeles serves as a live example of how retail spaces can successfully integrate shopping, entertainment and community engagement today. But what could retail spaces look like in the future?

The vision for future retail spaces

As we look to the future, several key trends are emerging that will shape the evolution of retail spaces. These trends are driven by consumer demands for convenience, personalization and unique experiences.

Future retail environments will leverage advanced technologies like augmented reality (AR) and virtual reality (VR) to enhance the shopping experience. Imagine trying on clothes virtually or visualizing how furniture would look in your home without physically being there. These technologies will not only make shopping more convenient but also more engaging and fun.

The Klarna report tells us 62 per cent of consumers are interested in using AR to visualize products before purchasing, indicating a significant trend towards the incorporation of immersive technologies in retail.

The integration of AI will play a significant role in personalizing the shopping experience. AI can analyse customer data to provide tailored recommendations and anticipate customer needs. This level of personalization can create a more seamless shopping experience, both online and offline, ensuring that customers find what they want quickly and easily.

Sustainability will also be a major focus for future retail spaces. Consumers are increasingly aware of the environmental impact of their purchases and expect brands to take responsibility. Retailers will need to design stores that use eco-friendly materials, reduce waste and promote sustainable behaviours. This commitment to sustainability can enhance brand loyalty and attract environmentally conscious consumers.

REAL-WORLD EXAMPLE
Future Stores: Oxford Street, London

The concept of the 'store of the future' is no longer a distant dream but a reality that is soon to be unveiled on one of the world's most iconic shopping streets – Oxford

Street, London. Launched in late 2024, Future Stores is set to redefine retail with its cutting-edge approach, combining technology, flexibility and sustainability in a way that has never been seen before.

This groundbreaking project has been three years in the making and is the brainchild of Ariel Haroush, the visionary leader and retail founder. Haroush's ambition with Future Stores is to create a dynamic retail environment that can evolve continuously, allowing brands to fully realize their potential and vision. 'We wanted to create a space where innovation meets retail, a place where brands can experiment and adapt in real-time,' says Haroush. This vision is set to revolutionize how we think about physical retail spaces.

A dynamic retail space

Future Stores will rely heavily on state-of-the-art screens and advanced technology to bring its vision to life. From the moment customers see the store from bustling Oxford Street, they will be greeted by dynamic advertising and imagery that can be changed with a click of a button. This flexibility allows the store to continuously adapt its facade and interior, presenting new and exciting content that keeps consumers engaged and intrigued.

Imagine walking past the store and seeing an entirely different set-up each time, depending on the brands showcased. The usual set-up for a retail brand involves heavy investment and a consistent display for months, if not years. Future Stores, however, offers a revolutionary approach where the digital screens can be updated instantly to reflect new products, promotions or brand messages. This capability means the store can host a diverse range of brands, from retail giants to emerging technology, hospitality, travel, leisure and beauty companies.

The space inside

Inside, Future Stores offers ample space for traditional product displays, including areas large enough to showcase a brand-new car. However, the real innovation lies in the store's ability to transform its interior dynamically. Whether it is a new fashion collection, the latest tech gadgets, or even a travel agency's immersive display, the possibilities are endless. This adaptability ensures that the store remains fresh and relevant, providing an ever-changing landscape that draws consumers back repeatedly.

One of the standout features of Future Stores is its basement, which functions as a high-tech headquarters reminiscent of a James Bond movie. This area is equipped with advanced analytics and real-time monitoring systems that provide invaluable insights into consumer behaviour. Retailers will be able to track every movement on the floor, from which way a customer turns upon entering the store to which products garner the most attention.

Real-time data and intelligence

The HQ will offer real-time data on footfall, engagement and hotspots within the store, enabling retailers to make immediate adjustments to their displays and product offerings. This intelligence hub will be a game-changer, allowing brands to understand and respond to consumer behaviour like never before. 'The ability to dynamically change what the store looks like based on real-time data is something that will set Future Stores apart,' explains Haroush. This level of adaptability ensures that the store can continuously optimize its layout and offerings to meet consumer demands.

Sustainable and efficient

In addition to its technological advancements, Future Stores also boasts significant sustainability credentials. Traditional retail set-ups often result in considerable waste from plastics, paper, cardboard and other materials used in point-of-sale displays and promotions. Future Stores eliminates this waste by utilizing digital displays that can be updated without physical materials. This approach not only reduces environmental impact but also allows for more frequent and varied promotional changes without the associated costs and logistics.

A glimpse into the future

Future Stores offers a glimpse into the future of retail. It is a pioneering model that other retailers will likely follow, showcasing how technology and innovation can create more engaging, efficient and sustainable shopping experiences. The store's ability to transform rapidly and its real-time data capabilities provide a template for what retail spaces might look like in the coming years.

The launch of Future Stores on Oxford Street is more than just the opening of a new retail space; it represents a significant shift in how we approach physical retail. As Haroush puts it, 'This is not just a store. It is a living, breathing entity that evolves with consumer needs and technological advancements. It is a taste of what's to come in retail, where flexibility, sustainability and consumer engagement are at the forefront.'

As we look towards the future of retail, the innovations presented by Future Stores highlight the direction in which the industry is heading. The blending of physical and digital elements, the focus on sustainability, and the ability to adapt in real time are all critical components of the retail landscape of tomorrow. Future Stores is set to be a beacon of this new era, providing a space where brands can experiment, innovate and thrive. The anticipation of its opening is a testament to the retail industry's excitement for this revolutionary concept and the endless possibilities it holds.

By embracing such forward-thinking approaches, Future Stores not only meets the expectations of today's tech-savvy consumers but also sets the stage for a more sustainable and dynamic future in retail. This project underscores the importance of innovation and adaptability in the ever-evolving retail sector, promising an exciting new chapter for both brands and consumers alike.

In this ever-evolving industry, staying ahead of trends and continuously innovating will be crucial. The journey of retail transformation is just beginning, and the future holds endless possibilities for those willing to embrace change and push the boundaries of what retail spaces can be.

By looking to trailblazing examples like The Grove and the Future Stores concept, we can glimpse the exciting possibilities ahead. These spaces show that with the right blend of creativity, technology and customer focus, the future of retail is not just bright – it is brilliant.

REAL-WORLD EXAMPLE
Ariel Haroush, CEO of OUTFORM and founder of Future Stores

Kate Hardcastle

(KH): Ariel, thank you so much for taking the time to talk with me today. Your work at OUTFORM has positioned you as a key player in the fusion of retail and technology, and now with Future Stores, it seems like you're pushing the boundaries even further. Could you start by telling us about your journey with OUTFORM and how it led you to where you are today?

Ariel Haroush

(AH): Thanks, Kate. OUTFORM was born out of a desire to revolutionize how brands interact with customers in physical spaces. When we started, it was clear that traditional retail displays – your standard point-of-purchase (POP) and point-of-sale (POS) systems – were stuck in a kind of static mode. They weren't evolving in a way that kept pace with customer expectations, which were increasingly shaped by digital experiences.

At OUTFORM, our mission was to inject creativity and technology into these spaces to bridge the gap between digital and physical retail. We pioneered interactive displays, digital signage and retail interiors that didn't just look good, but enhanced the shopping experience. We wanted to make it engaging, almost like walking into a live conversation between the brand and the consumer.

KH: That's such an interesting perspective, to see the physical space as part of the dialogue between brand and consumer. How have you found retailers responding to this idea of blending digital elements into physical spaces?

AH: It's been an interesting journey. In the early days, there was a lot of hesitation – retailers were still very focused on the traditional in-store set-up. But as online shopping grew, the need to make physical stores more interactive became clear. Retailers began to realize that it wasn't just about selling products any more; it was about creating experiences.

Digital elements – whether it's interactive mirrors, touchscreens or smart shelving – don't just add novelty; they add functionality. They provide customers with real-time information, product recommendations and customization options, making the store feel much more dynamic. And that's what today's consumer expects: a seamless blend of technology and human interaction.

KH: That brings us to Future Stores. You've created a vision for the future of retail that goes beyond the technology itself and focuses on the entire customer experience. How did Future Stores come to be, and what's your vision for it?

AH: Future Stores was born out of a realization that while retail technology was advancing, many retailers still weren't fully grasping how to use it to create an ecosystem. Too often, we saw brands introducing technology in silos – an in-store app here, a smart shelf there – but not integrating these elements in a way that truly enhanced the entire customer journey.

With Future Stores, the idea is to create environments where every touchpoint – whether it's digital or physical – feeds into a unified experience. For example, a customer could start their journey online, customize a product, and then visit the store to see it in person, where additional personalization options are available through interactive kiosks. The store isn't just a place to buy things any more – it's an extension of the brand's digital presence, and vice versa.

What excites me about Future Stores is that it's not just about creating cool tech experiences. It's about building spaces that understand the customer's needs on an emotional level. If a customer is coming into a store, they're not just looking for products – they're looking for inspiration, for connection and for a sense of belonging. Technology should enhance those emotions, not replace them.

KH: That emotional intelligence in retail is such an important point. Especially as we see the rise of e-commerce, the physical store has to offer something different, something that can't be replicated online. How do you see the balance between physical and digital evolving?

AH: The balance is key. Physical stores aren't going anywhere, but their role is changing. The store of the future will be less about the transaction and more about the brand experience. We're already seeing this with flagship stores that are designed more like immersive brand showcases rather than just places to buy things.

At Future Stores, we're focusing on how technology can create that seamless blend. It might be something as simple as using data from a customer's online behaviour to personalize their in-store experience, or something more complex, like creating immersive environments where customers can interact with products in ways that aren't possible online.

One of the concepts we're working on is the idea of 'invisible technology' – where the tech is so integrated into the space that it doesn't feel like technology at all. It's just part of the environment, enhancing the experience in subtle ways. The goal is to create spaces where customers don't just shop; they explore, discover and engage in ways that feel both personal and effortless.

KH: Invisible technology sounds fascinating, especially in a world where we're so used to flashy screens and devices demanding our attention. How do you think this approach changes the customer's relationship with the brand?

AH: It changes everything. When technology becomes invisible, it allows the customer to focus on the experience, not the tools facilitating it. We want the customer to leave the store thinking about how amazing their experience was, not how many screens or gadgets they interacted with. The technology should serve the story, not be the story.

For example, in some of our concept stores, we've integrated digital platforms that allow customers to scan items with their phones to learn more or see how they're made, but these features aren't front and centre. They're there if the customer needs them, but they don't overwhelm the space. The technology fades into the background, allowing the focus to remain on the product and the customer's emotional connection to the brand.

KH: That emotional connection is what keeps customers coming back, isn't it? In an increasingly digital world, how do you maintain that human touch while leveraging technology?

AH: That's exactly the challenge we're solving at Future Stores. Technology can't replace the human touch, but it can enhance it. One of the things we're working on is using data to empower store associates. Imagine a scenario where a customer walks into a store, and the associate already knows their preferences based on past purchases or online behaviour. That associate can then offer a much more personalized experience, guiding the customer toward products they'll love and even suggesting new things they might not have considered.

It's about using technology to make the human interaction more meaningful. We're not trying to replace the associate with a robot – we're giving them tools to be more intuitive, more connected and more responsive to the customer's needs.

KH: Ariel, thank you for sharing these incredible insights. It's clear that the work you're doing with OUTFORM and Future Stores is shaping the future of retail in ways that we're only just beginning to understand. What excites you most about the future?

AH: What excites me most is that we're just scratching the surface of what's possible. Retail is evolving faster than ever, and with technology, we have the tools to create experiences that are not only more engaging but also more human. At the end of the day, retail is about people – it's about creating connections, telling stories and inspiring discovery. The future of retail will be about using technology to deepen those connections, and I can't wait to see where that takes us.

Key interview takeaways

1 **Seamless integration of digital and physical:** Haroush's vision centres around creating environments where digital and physical touchpoints blend to enhance the customer journey.

2 **Dynamic store design:** The store of the future will constantly evolve, with technology allowing for instant updates to the store's interior and exterior, creating fresh experiences.

3 **Real-time data intelligence:** Future Stores will feature a high-tech HQ that gathers real-time data on consumer behaviour, allowing retailers to adapt quickly to customer needs.

4 **Invisible technology:** Technology should enhance the shopping experience without overwhelming it. The goal is for tech to blend into the background, allowing customers to focus on the brand and products.

5 Emotional intelligence in retail: Future Stores will prioritize the emotional connection between the brand and the consumer, using technology to make human interactions more meaningful.

As we close this chapter on the evolution of retail spaces and the creation of multi-experiential destinations, it's time to delve into the next level of retail's transformation: the magic of retail theatre. If designing meaningful spaces is about setting the stage, then retail theatre is about bringing that stage to life, captivating customers with immersive, memorable experiences that elevate shopping from a simple transaction to a dynamic, engaging spectacle.

Retail spaces: Evolving to captivate and connect

Retail spaces today are undergoing profound change, moving far beyond traditional layouts focused on product displays and checkout counters. Consumers are no longer content with purely functional shopping experiences; they want environments that spark joy, inspire connection and create lasting memories. This shift to multi-experiential retail spaces reflects the growing consumer appetite for convenience, entertainment and meaningful engagement – a mix that is redefining what a store can and should be. It's not just about providing products; it's about creating places where people can experience a brand's identity and values first-hand.

This evolution calls on retailers to rethink their spaces as dynamic environments that blend physical and digital experiences, inviting consumers into something more akin to a lifestyle journey than a conventional store visit. In the future, retailers must embrace innovative design, emerging technologies and a deep understanding of customer behaviour to remain relevant. It's about setting a stage that invites discovery, fosters community and meets consumers' growing desire for unique and impactful moments.

KEY TAKEAWAYS

1 From transactions to experiences: Retail spaces are no longer just about selling products – they are becoming destinations that blend shopping with dining, entertainment and wellness, offering unique experiences that encourage longer visits and deeper brand engagement.

2 **Technology-driven personalization:** Advanced technologies such as augmented reality, virtual reality and artificial intelligence are becoming essential tools for creating personalized, interactive experiences. These technologies enhance customer satisfaction and help retailers better understand consumer preferences.

3 **Sustainability at the core:** As consumer awareness around sustainability grows, retail spaces must prioritize eco-friendly materials, reduce waste and adopt sustainable commitments that align with consumers' values.

4 **Non-traditional retail spaces:** Pop-up shops, hotel boutiques and hybrid spaces that combine shopping with social and cultural activities are increasingly popular. These spaces provide brands with flexible, innovative ways to engage with consumers.

5 **The role of sensory marketing:** Engaging the senses – sight, sound, smell, taste and touch – remains a powerful tool in retail. Sensory elements enhance the shopping experience, helping retailers create emotional connections with consumers and build brand loyalty.

References

1 OECD (2020) How's Life? 2020: Measuring well-being, OECD Better Life Index, www.oecdbetterlifeindex.org/#/11111111111 (archived at https://perma.cc/GEM3-ZRTA)

2 The Crown Estate (nd) The future of Regent Street, Haymarket and Piccadilly Circus public realm, www.thecrownestate.co.uk/our-business/property-and-places/regent-street (archived at https://perma.cc/R7TD-3PH2)

3 Deloitte (2019) Global Powers of Luxury Goods 2019: Bridging the gap between the old and the new, www2.deloitte.com/content/dam/Deloitte/ar/Documents/Consumer_and_Industrial_Products/Global-Powers-of-Luxury-Goods-abril-2019.pdf (archived at https://perma.cc/G9PH-PNL8)

4 Esposito, Alicia (2024) The house of mouse: Inside Primark's mecca for all things Disney and marvel, *Retail TouchPoints*, 11 November, www.retailtouchpoints.com/topics/store-operations/the-house-of-mouse-inside-primarks-mecca-for-all-things-disney-and-marvel (archived at https://perma.cc/H9X9-WBKF)

5 Hoeijmans, Nico (2019) Primark and Disney collaborate to bring experiential retail, *Cross-Border Magazine*, 9 April, www.cross-border-magazine.com/primark-and-disney-collaborate-to-bring-experiential-retail (archived at https://perma.cc/9VJU-U997)

6 Marketing Week Reporters (nd) How Greggs and Primark joined forces to go viral, *Marketing Week*, www.marketingweek.com/greggs-primark-joining-forces (archived at https://perma.cc/U8PF-EQCA)

7 Adegeest, Don-Alvin (2023) Harrods is painted in dots in latest Louis Vuitton x Kusama collaboration, *FashionUnited*, 18 January, www.fashionunited.uk/news/retail/harrods-is-painted-in-dots-in-latest-louis-vuitton-x-kusama-collaboration/2023011867353 (archived at https://perma.cc/PR7X-798C)

8 Carter, D (2023) Yayoi Kusama turns Harrods into a canvas for new Louis Vuitton collaboration, Creative Boom, 25 January, www.creativeboom.com/news/yayoi-kusama-vuitton (https://perma.cc/A5TF-MF7L)

9 Faurote, Adrienne (2024) Dior takes over the Beverly Hills Hotel – an inside look, *Haute Living*, 29 May, www.hauteliving.com/2024/05/dior-takes-beverly-hills-hotel-inside-look/751983 (archived at https://perma.cc/W69C-Q582)

10 Holition (2012) Uniqlo: World's first magic mirror, www.holition.com/work/uniqlo-world-s-first-magic-mirror (archived at https://perma.cc/C2CL-AULY)

11 Ldn-Post (2024) The LEGO Group launches FREE interactive workshops in London, *London Post*, 5 March, www.london-post.co.uk/the-lego-group-launches-free-interactive-workshops-in-london (archived at https://perma.cc/DU4L-ZRR6)

12 Guinness Storehouse (nd) The Gravity Bar: A milestone in the Guinness Storehouse history, www.guinness-storehouse.com/en/whats-hoppening/the-gravity-bar (archived at https://perma.cc/B5H5-SZRP)

13 Hypebeast (2024) Behind the hype: How Hermès ushered in the era of fashion exclusivity with the coveted Birkin handbag, www.hypebeast.com/2024/4/behind-the-hype-hermes-birkin-handbag-video (archived at https://perma.cc/Y9UE-DBFB)

14 Hermès Paris (2024) 2023 Full-year results, 9 February, https://assets-finance.hermes.com/s3fs-public/node/pdf_file/2024-02/1707422069/hermes_20240209_pr_2023fullyearresults_va.pdf (archived at https://perma.cc/CWA4-MG3B)

15 Hicar, Stuart (2025) Glastonbury Festival, *Britannica*, 25 January, www.britannica.com/art/Glastonbury-Festival (archived at https://perma.cc/66QR-ECUG)

16 Barbour (2024) Our Re-Loved jackets in partnership with Oxfam, 13 June, www.barbour.com/uk/blog/re-loved-jackets-oxfam (archived at https://perma.cc/YS4B-RWU9)

17 Battison, Jess (2023) Co-op at Glastonbury Festival praised for decent prices, *LADbible*, 23 June, www.ladbible.com/entertainment/glastonbury-coop-shop-worthy-farm-prices-302734-20230623 (archived at https://perma.cc/5ALY-L4MB)

18 Graham, Megan (2024) Lululemon is seeing a slowdown in its women's business. Has it reached its ceiling? *Wall Street Journal*, 11 September, www.wsj.com/articles/lululemon-is-seeing-a-slowdown-in-its-womens-business-has-it-reached-its-ceiling-f99a48a8 (archived at https://perma.cc/R5KE-E4ML)

19 Klarna (2023) Retail revolution: New data reveals next generation of shoppers ready for AI, AR and robots! 16 May, www.klarna.com/international/press/retail-revolution-new-data-reveals-next-generation-of-shoppers-ready-for-ai-ar-and-robots (archived at https://perma.cc/9GN6-NNKW)

6

Roll up, roll up! This is retail theatre

Now that we've explored the importance of place and the role of location, let's turn our attention to the artistry that brings these spaces to life: retail theatre. Retail theatre is where storytelling, design and interactive elements converge, creating experiences that go beyond aesthetics to touch consumers on an emotional level. It's the art of crafting environments that engage all the senses, transport visitors to new worlds and deepen their connection with a brand. In a marketplace saturated with options, it's this 'magic' – the immersive and theatrical elements – that makes a retail experience stand out.

The role of retail theatre in modern shopping

Retail theatre taps into the essence of consumer psychology, drawing on the power of narrative and spectacle to create memorable experiences. It turns the act of shopping into a performance, with customers as active participants rather than passive observers. When done well, retail theatre can evoke the kind of excitement and curiosity that keeps people coming back, offering them more than products – it offers an escape, a story and a reason to remember the brand long after they've left the store.

In this next chapter, we'll explore how retailers are using theatrical techniques to enhance the shopping journey, creating spaces that surprise, delight and resonate deeply with their audiences. From flagship stores that transport visitors to another world to pop-ups that capture the spirit of a brand in a fleeting, unforgettable way, retail theatre is all about making shopping feel magical and meaningful.

Retailers are finding inventive ways to use lighting, sound, scent and even texture to engage the senses. They're introducing immersive technologies, like augmented reality and virtual reality, to add layers of interaction and excitement. These techniques invite customers to become part of the brand story, turning ordinary store visits into engaging, sensory-rich experiences that can't be replicated online.

Setting the stage for memorable brand experiences

Retail theatre is more than just decoration; it's about creating spaces that are as emotionally engaging as they are visually compelling. Imagine entering a store that feels like stepping into a film set or a carefully crafted scene that embodies a brand's values and story. This approach transforms shopping into something memorable and emotive, encouraging people to spend time, explore and immerse themselves fully in the experience. Through curated atmospheres and thoughtful design, retail theatre has the power to foster emotional connections that go beyond the transaction.

Sensory marketing: Engaging the senses

The moment I stepped into Disney's Christmas shop, it felt like entering another world. The soundtrack of a crackling fire with a very soothing Christmas-style playlist humming softly in the background, while the smell of cinnamon and pine filled the air, instantly transporting me to the holiday season. The room shimmered with delicate glass ornaments, their surfaces reflecting the soft glow of twinkling lights strung across every corner.

As I walked through the displays, I found myself picking up a small bauble, beautifully hand-painted, and as I examined it, an artisan in the store offered to personalize it with our family name for an extra $7. In that moment, I didn't think twice. The experience was so immersive, so perfectly crafted to evoke the feelings of warmth, nostalgia and holiday cheer, that I happily spent $40 on a Christmas ornament being beautifully personalized and wrapped – something I hadn't even been looking to buy.

With the bauble now ready to go, I stepped back outside into the blazing Floridian sun and headed for a cooling drink, the sharp contrast bringing me back to reality. It was a reminder that, when done well, retail emotion can take hold of you at any time, in any place. The setting, the smells, the sounds – it all came together to create a connection that overrode practicality or logic – and I know these tricks of the trade better than many!

This is the power of emotional retail. While data and analytics can tell us a lot about consumer habits and preferences, it's the experiences that engage our senses and emotions that often drive the most impactful purchasing decisions.

This experience serves as a reminder that while data is essential in understanding consumer behaviour, the emotional response a brand can evoke is what creates lasting memories and drives spontaneous decisions. Retailers need to harness the power of both – leveraging data to tailor experiences, while ensuring that the emotional connection remains at the heart of their strategy.

The concept of sensory marketing has become increasingly important in the retail world. Engaging the senses – sight, sound, smell, taste and touch – can significantly enhance the shopping experience, making it more memorable and enjoyable. Retailers are now leveraging these sensory elements to create environments that captivate and retain customers, differentiating their brands in a crowded market.

This is the essence of retail theatre – an orchestrated experience that touches the senses and influences behaviour far more deeply than any promotional email or digital ad could. In today's competitive market, it is not enough to sell a product; brands must immerse consumers in an experience that awakens their emotions and triggers sensory connections.

The power of sight

Visual merchandising has long been a cornerstone of retail strategy, but its importance has only grown in the digital age. Stores are not just places to shop; they are brand showrooms where visual elements like colour, lighting and display design play a crucial role in shaping the customer experience. The right visual elements can create an inviting atmosphere, highlight key products and guide customer behaviour.

Strategic product placement and visual hierarchy

Strategic product placement leverages visual hierarchy to guide customers' attention and enhance their shopping experience. For example, the placement of fresh produce at the entrance of a grocery store serves as an inviting visual cue that emphasizes freshness and quality. This strategy is not arbitrary; research indicates that shoppers are more inclined to make healthier choices when they encounter fresh produce first, which can increase overall sales in the fresh food category.

In retail, the positioning of beauty sections plays a pivotal role in shaping customer experience and driving store traffic. Research and industry insights suggest that visually appealing, strategically placed beauty displays not only draw shoppers into the store but also encourage deeper engagement throughout their visit. Beauty products, known for their attractive packaging and sensory appeal, act as a gateway that entices customers to explore other areas of the store. This layout strategy leverages the natural allure of cosmetics to create a flow that guides customers through various sections, increasing the likelihood of additional purchases and enhancing the overall shopping experience.

A well-designed beauty section positioned near store entrances or high-traffic areas can act as a focal point, capturing attention immediately and setting a positive, inviting tone for the visit. This set-up encourages customers to linger, sample products and even participate in interactive elements such as try-on stations or product demonstrations. Such engagement transforms what might be a quick visit into a more immersive experience, heightening the emotional connection between the consumer and the brand.

In addition, strategically placed beauty displays can influence shopping patterns, encouraging shoppers to move through other key product areas. By integrating beauty and wellness sections thoughtfully into the store's layout, retailers can increase dwell time and encourage cross-category purchases, as customers who come in to browse cosmetics may feel inclined to explore apparel, accessories or lifestyle products nearby.

This approach aligns with findings on consumer behaviour, which indicate that shoppers are more likely to make multiple purchases when visually appealing products are showcased prominently and interwoven with other retail categories. Such strategies demonstrate how effective store layouts can transform beauty sections into anchors that drive traffic and increase overall sales.

Impact of window displays and entry points

Effective window displays are instrumental in attracting customers and boosting in-store foot traffic. A study by NPD Group found that 24 per cent of consumers were enticed into stores by eye-catching window displays, highlighting their significant role in drawing potential shoppers.

By crafting visually appealing and strategically designed window displays, retailers can capture the attention of passers-by, encouraging them to enter the store and explore further. This approach not only increases foot traffic but also enhances the overall shopping experience, potentially leading to higher sales and customer satisfaction.[1]

The design of store entry points is equally critical. High-end retailers like Harrods and Saks Fifth Avenue invest heavily in creating opulent entryways that reflect their brand's luxury image. These entry points often use sophisticated lighting, high-quality materials and elaborate visual elements to set an aspirational tone for the shopping experience. Such visual cues can influence consumer perception and justify premium pricing by enhancing the perceived value of the products offered.

Colour psychology in visual merchandising

The colour yellow is widely recognized for its ability to enhance visibility and recognition, making it an excellent choice for retail signage that aims to stand out in crowded environments. Its high luminance and association with warmth and positivity create a welcoming atmosphere, positively influencing customer perceptions and behaviours. Research indicates that yellow's brightness and attention-grabbing qualities make it highly effective in capturing consumer attention, which is crucial in competitive retail settings.

Incorporating yellow into retail signage not only improves visibility but also leverages its psychological associations to enhance the overall shopping experience. The colour's connection to warmth and positivity can make customers feel more comfortable and welcome, potentially increasing their likelihood of engaging with the store and making purchases. Therefore, strategically using yellow in retail environments can be a powerful tool for attracting customers and fostering a positive shopping atmosphere.

Red is traditionally associated with sales and clearance events, a colour choice that signals excitement and urgency. Research into colour psychology suggests that red has a strong psychological impact, creating a sense of scarcity and prompting consumers to act quickly. This effect can be particularly effective in retail environments, where urgency often translates to higher conversion rates as consumers feel encouraged to make quicker purchasing decisions.[2]

Additionally, red is commonly linked to energy and excitement, helping to foster a lively and dynamic atmosphere that enhances the overall shopping experience. Retailers use red strategically to drive attention to promotions, creating visual cues that guide customers towards specific areas in the store. This approach not only supports quick turnover and high-volume sales but also reinforces red's effectiveness in amplifying the impact of marketing messages in a retail setting.

Green, on the other hand, is increasingly used to highlight natural, eco-friendly and sustainable products. It evokes feelings of tranquillity and health, aligning well with the values of environmentally conscious consumers.

The increasing use of green in branding and store design reflects a broader trend towards sustainability in retail, with many companies highlighting their environmental initiatives through green-themed marketing and store layouts. The colour green is commonly associated with nature, health and environmental consciousness, and incorporating it into branding can signal a company's commitment to sustainability and eco-friendly efforts. This strategic use of colour can positively influence consumer perceptions and behaviours, as shoppers may be more inclined to support brands that align with their values regarding environmental responsibility.[3]

A prime example of this approach is The Body Shop, a global cosmetics and skincare retailer known for its dedication to sustainability and ethical sourcing. The Body Shop extensively uses green in its branding and store design to reinforce its eco-friendly image. This consistent use of green communicates The Body Shop's commitment to environmental causes and appeals to consumers who prioritize sustainability in their purchasing decisions.

Sound: A retail marketing strategy that can play well

Background music plays a pivotal role in shaping customer behaviour within retail environments. Research indicates that the tempo of in-store music can significantly influence the pace at which shoppers move through a store, and their overall mood. Slower-tempo music tends to encourage customers to take their time, leading to a more relaxed shopping experience and poten-tially higher sales. Conversely, faster-tempo music can create a sense of urgency, prompting quicker decisions and shorter store visits.

A study examined the effects of music tempo on supermarket shoppers. The findings revealed that slower music resulted in a 38 per cent increase in sales volume compared to faster music, as customers spent more time in the store and purchased more items. This research underscores the importance of carefully selecting background music to align with desired customer behaviours and sales objectives.[4]

By strategically choosing music that complements the intended shopping atmosphere, retailers can enhance the customer experience and influence purchasing patterns. For instance, luxury boutiques may opt for slower, soothing music to encourage leisurely browsing, while fast-paced retailers might select upbeat tunes to energize shoppers and facilitate quick transactions.

Starbucks, for example, carefully curates its playlists to create a soothing atmosphere that encourages customers to linger. This strategy not only enhances the customer experience but also increases the likelihood of additional purchases, such as a second cup of coffee or a snack. The consistent, calming music helps to establish a brand identity that aligns with the idea of Starbucks as a 'third place' between home and work.

However, not all retailers manage to get their sound strategy right. One of the most common mistakes is playing music that does not align with the brand's identity or the shopping environment. For instance, loud, fast-paced music in a high-end store can create a jarring experience, detracting from the luxurious atmosphere the brand aims to project.

Another issue is the use of generic or poorly curated playlists that fail to engage the customer or, worse, annoy them. This can lead to a disconnect between the shopper and the brand, potentially driving customers away. The holiday season often exacerbates this issue, with some stores overplaying Christmas music to the point of fatigue, which can deter shoppers rather than attract them.

Looking forward, the role of sound in retail environments is poised to become more sophisticated. Retailers are increasingly using data and technology to customize soundscapes that adapt to the time of day, the types of customers in the store, and even the weather. For example, a store might play more upbeat music during peak hours to energize shoppers and switch to a softer playlist during quieter times to create a more relaxed atmosphere.

Sound is a powerful, yet I feel generally underutilized tool in retail marketing. When used thoughtfully, it can enhance the shopping experience, reinforce brand identity and influence consumer behaviour. As retailers continue to innovate, we can expect to see more sophisticated and tailored use of sound, creating environments that are not just places to shop but immersive experiences that resonate with customers on a deeper level.

The power of scent: Aroma appeal in retail

Scent is a subtle yet powerful component of the shopping experience. It can evoke memories, create emotional connections and influence customer behaviour.

Retailers like Lush have mastered the use of scent to enhance the in-store experience. The moment customers step into a Lush store, they are greeted by a distinctive blend of fragrances from its handmade cosmetics. This olfactory experience is not just pleasant; it is strategic. The scents are carefully crafted to create an immersive experience that aligns with the brand's identity and products.[5]

Research has shown that scent can have a profound impact on shopping behaviour, influencing both the amount of time customers spend in a store and their willingness to make purchases. This phenomenon, sometimes referred to as the 'Proustian effect', highlights how specific scents can evoke positive memories and emotions, enriching the shopping experience and creating a sense of familiarity and comfort. The use of scent can thus be a powerful tool for retailers, allowing them to craft an atmosphere that resonates emotionally with shoppers, encouraging them to linger and ultimately boosting sales.

A well-chosen scent can align with a brand's identity and enhance the atmosphere of a store. For example, a calming lavender scent in a wellness or beauty store can encourage relaxation and exploration, while fresher scents like citrus may create a vibrant, energizing mood that feels dynamic and engaging. Research has found that scents congruent with the store environment – meaning they match the store's design and product type – can have the strongest impact, enhancing customers' perception of products and increasing the likelihood of purchase.

When applied strategically, scent marketing can transform retail environments, creating memorable and sensory-rich spaces that encourage repeat visits and foster a deeper connection with the brand.

REAL-WORLD EXAMPLE

Lush: Scent as a brand signature

In the health and beauty industry, one retailer has set itself apart by transforming the traditional shopping experience into a rich, sensory journey that fully immerses customers. Embracing an aesthetic reminiscent of a greengrocer's market, the brand displays its vibrant, handmade products in crates and baskets, fostering a fresh, welcoming atmosphere. This approach goes beyond the conventional cosmetics retailer set-up, aligning with the founders' vision of creating a space that engages customers in a meaningful way rather than simply offering products for sale. As co-founder Mark Constantine has regularly highlighted, the brand has a determination to create a meaningful shopping experience, beyond just selling products.

A hallmark of the retailer's identity is its masterful use of scent. Its stores are recognized by a distinctive fragrance that often wafts into nearby spaces, capturing the attention of passers-by before the store itself is even visible. This powerful olfactory signature is crafted from natural ingredients like essential oils, herbs and fresh fruits, creating an environment that feels both vibrant and authentic. The strategic use of scent is far more than an aesthetic choice; it embodies the brand's commitment to natural, ethical and environmentally friendly practices, reinforcing its values and distinguishing it within the crowded beauty market.

The impact of scent on customer behaviour is profound. Research has demonstrated that sensory elements like scent can create positive associations, and for this retailer, the unique fragrance in each store evokes emotions and memories that bring customers back time and time again. The welcoming scent creates an inviting atmosphere, prompting shoppers to linger, explore and experience the products in a relaxed, immersive environment. This sensory appeal contributes to an increase in time spent in-store and encourages customers to engage with a wide range of products, boosting the likelihood of purchase.

This olfactory strategy aligns with a growing consumer preference for brands that prioritize transparency, sustainability and authenticity. By using high-quality, natural ingredients, the retailer resonates deeply with a segment of shoppers who seek eco-conscious choices in their beauty and wellness products. The result is a store environment that not only invites exploration but also strengthens the brand's reputation for ethical practices and high-quality, natural offerings.

The effectiveness of this sensory-driven approach is evident in the retailer's strong customer loyalty and continued financial success. For example, in the fiscal year ending June 2023, the company reported a brand turnover of £816.8 million – a testament to the success of its unique in-store experience.[6] This iconic scent is not just a pleasant addition; it is a core element of the retailer's holistic approach to creating a memorable and engaging shopping experience.

In addition to its powerful fragrance, the retailer has crafted an open, vibrant layout that enhances the sensory appeal of the store. The colourful product displays, accessible shelves and inviting sample stations encourage customers to touch, smell and even test products, creating a multilayered experience. This design fosters a high level of engagement, allowing customers to connect with the products and the brand in an interactive, personal way. Such a tactile, immersive environment not only attracts new visitors but also deepens the loyalty of existing customers, creating a community of shoppers who are invested in the brand's values and quality.

In sum, this retailer's innovative use of scent, combined with its distinctive store design and dedication to natural ingredients, has redefined what a beauty and wellness retail experience can be. By embracing sensory engagement as a key part of its brand identity, the company has succeeded in creating spaces that not only capture attention but also cultivate lasting connections with customers. As consumer expectations evolve, this brand continues to lead by example, illustrating the powerful impact that thoughtful, sensory-rich environments can have on customer loyalty and overall brand strength.

Tantalizing with taste: Food for thought in retail

Taste is a powerful yet often underestimated sensory element in retail, particularly within the food and beverage sectors. The practice of offering product samples has been a staple in grocery stores and speciality food retailers for decades, providing customers with the opportunity to engage directly with products before making a purchase decision. Sampling activates the senses in a way that few other marketing techniques can, offering an immediate experience that builds trust and encourages exploration. Research suggests that a significant percentage of consumers who try a product sample go on to make a purchase, underscoring the effectiveness of taste-based engagement as a sales driver. According to research in 2022, 78 per cent of sampled consumers who purchased the product said the opportunity to try it prompted the purchase.[7]

Beyond driving immediate sales, sampling creates a sensory connection that lingers in the consumer's mind, making the shopping experience more memorable. In many cases, sampling is one of the few opportunities for a brand to directly influence taste perception, which can be especially impactful with new or unfamiliar products. By allowing customers to taste items, brands can bypass scepticism and reduce the hesitation that often accompanies trying something new. The impact is twofold: customers gain confidence in their purchase, and brands strengthen their reputation by offering high-quality, desirable products.

Retailers like Trader Joe's, Costco and luxury Los Angeles-based Erewhon have become widely known for their sampling stations, offering customers the chance to taste a range of products, from artisan cheeses to seasonal snacks. This strategy goes beyond simply promoting specific items; it creates a friendly, inviting atmosphere that enhances the customer's overall experience.

These sampling areas are often positioned in high-traffic areas to encourage customers to pause, taste and engage with staff, who can provide product insights and suggestions. This approach makes customers feel personally attended to and valued, enhancing their experience and building loyalty. The friendly interaction that accompanies sampling creates a low-pressure environment where customers can freely explore without feeling obligated to purchase, which, paradoxically, can make them more likely to buy.

Sampling also serves as a bridge between the retailer and the customer, promoting deeper engagement through conversation and feedback. Customers who try samples often engage with store employees, seeking more information about the products or discussing flavour preferences. This interaction not only educates customers but also provides the retailer with valuable insights into consumer preferences and potential best-sellers. By actively listening to customer feedback during sampling, stores can adjust their stock and promotions to better align with shopper desires, creating a more responsive and customer-centric retail environment.

In a competitive market where consumers have endless choices, providing a tangible experience like sampling allows brands to stand out and make a lasting impression. This approach aligns with modern consumer desires for transparency and authenticity; by allowing customers to taste before they buy, retailers demonstrate confidence in their offerings, making them more appealing to quality-conscious shoppers.

By creating an interactive and welcoming environment, retailers aim to create long-term loyalty and turn one-time visitors into regular customers. Sampling, when done thoughtfully, transforms a retail space into a place of discovery and enjoyment, where customers feel valued and are more likely to return, creating a win–win for both consumers and retailers.

REAL-WORLD EXAMPLE
Erewhon

Erewhon, an upscale organic grocery chain based in Los Angeles, demonstrates how taste can be a powerful driver in the retail experience. Known for its meticulously curated selection of organic, fresh and high-quality foods, Erewhon has established itself as a destination for health-conscious consumers seeking more than just groceries. From the store layout to the product offerings, Erewhon's approach transforms shopping into a sensory journey that engages customers on multiple levels.

Since Tony Antoci acquired Erewhon in 2011, he has shaped it into a wellness hub where taste, quality and sustainability are paramount. Under Antoci's leadership, the market has adopted a philosophy that emphasizes transparency and authenticity, making it more than a standard grocery store. This vision is reflected in every aspect of Erewhon's operations, from a 100 per cent organic produce selection to speciality offerings at its tonic and juice bar. Here, customers can sample unique elixirs like hot tonic Jing City and Reishi Cappuccino, products that align with the store's health and wellness ethos and that encourage exploration and engagement. This emphasis on quality and the unique nature of Erewhon's products attracts a dedicated clientele, including celebrities and wellness enthusiasts, who view Erewhon as both a status symbol and a trusted source for holistic nourishment.[8]

Sampling is a core part of Erewhon's strategy, giving customers the opportunity to taste fresh foods made from scratch and high-quality products that might be unfamiliar to them. This practice drives immediate sales and establishes trust, as customers experience first-hand the quality of what they are purchasing. The interactive nature of sampling also fosters a community atmosphere in the store, where knowledgeable staff engage with shoppers to explain the ingredients, benefits and origins of each product. This immersive, educational approach transforms the typical grocery shopping trip into an experience that feels personalized and enriching.

The impact of the retailer's commitment to taste and quality is clear in its financial success. In recent years, the market has seen impressive growth, reporting annual revenue close to $100 million. This success is not merely due to product pricing or exclusive items; rather, it is the result of a carefully cultivated in-store experience that resonates with customers seeking premium, health-focused products. The taste-driven strategy and the commitment to creating a welcoming, educational environment have helped Erewhon build a loyal customer base that values the brand's dedication to health and authenticity.

This is a retail brand that exemplifies how taste, when strategically integrated into the retail experience, can elevate a brand's identity and build long-term customer loyalty. By creating an environment where sampling and customer education are central, Erewhon not only enhances the shopping experience but also strengthens its reputation as a leader in the organic and wellness-focused grocery sector. This approach positions Erewhon as a place that nourishes the body and mind, embodying a brand philosophy that has become a benchmark for success in experiential retail.

Touch: A key driver in physical shopping

Touch is a powerful sensory element in retail, influencing consumer behaviour and drawing shoppers into physical stores to interact directly with products. Over the past four decades, retail environments have evolved dramatically, yet one shopping habit remains consistent: customers' reliance on touch to evaluate and connect with products. Whether it's assessing the ripeness of produce in a grocery store or feeling the fabric of a garment, touching products provides essential information that online images or descriptions cannot fully convey.

Touch creates a sense of personal connection and perceived ownership of an item. This tactile experience often reassures shoppers, enhancing their confidence in purchase decisions. Research indicates that when customers can physically engage with products, they develop a stronger attachment, leading to more favourable evaluations and a higher likelihood of purchase.[9] This relationship between touch and consumer satisfaction underscores why touch remains a cornerstone of the in-store shopping experience.

Many shoppers instinctively reach out to touch items as part of their evaluation process, reinforcing the unique value that physical engagement brings to retail. The sensory feedback customers receive – whether it's the firmness of an apple, the softness of a sweater, or the weight of a kitchen appliance – supports informed decision-making and enhances customer satisfaction.

Retailers that prioritize touch in their store layouts often see increased engagement and higher sales. For instance, beauty stores with open displays that allow customers to feel product textures and try colours directly on their skin tend to perform better than those with limited accessibility. The same principle applies to other sectors, from electronics to home goods, where touch remains essential in assessing product quality and suitability.

Touch extends beyond merely using hands; it encompasses the whole sensory experience, including how a product feels when tried on or handled. This tactile interaction not only shapes immediate purchase decisions but also strengthens emotional connections to products, encouraging repeat visits and long-term loyalty.

In summary, touch is a crucial component of the retail experience, offering unique benefits that digital shopping cannot replicate. By facilitating hands-on interaction, retailers can build trust, increase customer satisfaction and drive sales, demonstrating the lasting importance of touch in the evolving retail landscape.

Reducing returns: The potential of touch in retail

As highlighted in Chapter 3 and the evolution of e-commerce, returns are a significant concern for retailers, often leading to substantial financial losses.

One key advantage of tactile engagement in physical retail is its potential to reduce product returns, addressing a significant financial challenge for many retailers. By providing shoppers with the opportunity to interact physically with products before purchasing, retailers may increase customer satisfaction, potentially decreasing return rates – a strategy that enhances the customer experience while safeguarding the business's bottom line.

Returns have become a major concern for retailers, particularly with the rapid growth of e-commerce. In 2020 alone, U.S. retailers faced $428 billion in returned merchandise, representing approximately 10.6 per cent of total retail sales.[10] This staggering figure underscores the financial impact of returns, which not only affect revenue but also add costs related to restocking, inspection, repackaging and potential markdowns when returned items cannot be sold at full price.

For many retailers, the true cost of returns extends beyond these logistical expenses. The resources required to process returns – from reverse logistics to labour and warehouse space – place strain on operational efficiency and profitability. Some returned items, particularly those that are seasonal or trend-driven, may require heavy discounts or even disposal, resulting in a total loss. Given these financial challenges, retailers are increasingly interested in proactive ways to reduce return rates, with in-store tactile engagement viewed as one potential approach.

In physical stores, the ability to touch and interact with products could help lower return rates by encouraging more informed purchasing decisions. When shoppers have the chance to try on clothing, for instance, they can assess fit, comfort and style suitability on the spot, potentially reducing the likelihood of returns due to unmet expectations. Similarly, in electronics or home goods stores, the ability to hold, test and engage with products gives customers valuable insights into weight, durability and functionality – factors that can be difficult to gauge accurately through online images or descriptions alone.

Theoretical models of consumer behaviour suggest that tactile interaction may help reassure customers and increase confidence in their purchasing decisions. By meeting shoppers' needs for sensory feedback, physical stores can facilitate more satisfactory shopping experiences, possibly reducing the occurrence of 'post-purchase regret' or unmet expectations, both of which are common causes of returns.

Building customer satisfaction and loyalty through tactile engagement

Beyond financial implications, high return rates can impact customer satisfaction and loyalty. A shopper who frequently returns items due to mismatched expectations may become frustrated with the brand or retailer, potentially reducing their long-term engagement. Allowing shoppers to experience products in-store, where they can verify quality and suitability, could help to minimize such frustrations and cultivate trust and loyalty.

In sectors such as beauty and skincare, stores that allow customers to test product textures or try samples tend to achieve higher satisfaction rates, as customers feel more confident in their choices. Similarly, furniture stores that encourage customers to try products, such as seating or bedding, enable them to make well-informed decisions, which may lower the likelihood of returns. These positive in-store experiences foster loyalty, as shoppers are more likely to trust brands that enable well-informed decisions.

Touch as a potential investment for retailers

Encouraging tactile engagement in-store is more than a benefit for consumers; it represents a potential investment for retailers. While conclusive data on the relationship between touch and reduced returns may be limited, the theory suggests that by enhancing customer satisfaction and minimizing purchasing mistakes, retailers could reduce the operational strain and financial costs associated with returns. This strategy may optimize resources and allow stores to focus on growth opportunities rather than managing frequent returns.

In summary, the golden power of touch remains a cornerstone of effective retail strategy, offering customers a richer, more satisfying shopping experience. For retailers facing rising return rates – particularly in e-commerce – tactile engagement in physical stores presents a potential tool for fostering loyalty and improving the overall shopping experience. As the retail landscape continues to evolve, the role of touch could become an increasingly important consideration for retailers seeking to align customer satisfaction with financial sustainability.

REAL-WORLD EXAMPLE
Apple: The power of touch in retail

Apple Inc. has transformed retail by making touch the focus for in-store experience, redefining how customers interact with technology products. Apple Stores are purposefully designed to immerse customers in an environment where interactivity and tactile engagement are encouraged at every step. Unlike many traditional electronics stores, which often feature rows of boxed items, locked cases and security barriers, Apple's stores create an open, hands-on space that makes products readily accessible. The emphasis here is not on packaging, but on allowing customers to feel, explore and experience the products as they would use them in their everyday lives.

When customers walk into an Apple Store, they are immediately greeted by the minimalist, spacious design – a hallmark of Apple's brand aesthetic. This open layout, free from clutter and obstructions, invites customers to explore products freely. Sleek wooden tables at an accessible height are carefully arranged to display the latest iPhones, iPads, MacBooks and accessories, all fully powered and functional. Every item is out of its box and ready to be tested, touched and held, allowing customers to explore each product's design, usability and features without restrictions.

Apple's layout is intentional and methodical, with devices positioned at a comfortable height, encouraging customers to reach out and interact naturally. The absence of barriers like glass cases or locked display units creates an atmosphere that feels less like a traditional retail store and more like an experiential tech gallery. Customers are encouraged to linger, try out different devices and ask questions. By allowing them to touch and use devices as they would in real-life settings, Apple helps demystify its technology, making it approachable and intuitive.

This hands-on engagement has been shown to have a significant impact on customer satisfaction and purchasing confidence. Research indicates that tactile interaction with products can lead to more favourable evaluations and increased purchase intent, as customers feel more connected to the products they can touch and experience directly. By placing every device within reach and encouraging customers to explore, Apple builds a strong sense of ownership and satisfaction that makes customers more likely to complete their purchase in-store and less likely to return items due to unmet expectations.

The strategic use of touch in Apple Stores doesn't just enhance the shopping experience; it aligns closely with Apple's brand philosophy. The in-store experience mirrors Apple's design ethos of simplicity, accessibility and user-friendliness. From the interactive Genius Bar, where customers receive hands-on technical support, to Today at Apple sessions, where users can learn about their devices through practical workshops, every aspect of Apple's stores is designed to foster a tactile, interactive experience.

Apple's tactile-centric approach also reinforces its reputation for creating intuitive, easy-to-use products. By giving customers the chance to handle devices, experiment with features and engage with Apple staff, the company reinforces the perception of its products as accessible and user-friendly. This consistency between product design and the in-store experience has helped Apple build an intensely loyal customer base, with customers returning to Apple Stores not only to purchase but also to learn, explore and engage in the Apple ecosystem.

In addition to building customer loyalty, this model has proven financially effective. Apple's stores, with their unique design and focus on customer engagement, rank among the highest-performing retail spaces in the world. In 2021, Apple Stores were estimated to generate around $5,546 in sales per square foot, a testament to the success of its hands-on retail strategy.[11] This figure highlights the substantial impact that a well-designed, interactive store environment can have on sales performance and customer engagement.

This attention to touch in the store experience not only makes Apple Stores some of the most distinctive retail environments but also serves as a model for how sensory engagement can drive both customer satisfaction and financial success.

This chapter has explored the transformative power of retail theatre – where spaces are not merely designed to sell products but to engage consumers on a sensory and emotional level. Whether through sight, sound, smell, taste or touch, these elements create immersive experiences that resonate with customers and foster deeper brand connections. The idea is to go beyond transactions, crafting experiences that are memorable, emotive and capable of driving loyalty in a crowded retail landscape.

REAL-WORLD EXAMPLE
Roja Dove: The power of scent in retail theatre

Roja Dove is a world-renowned British perfumer and a leading authority on fragrance, celebrated for his work in the luxury perfume industry and for transforming retail fragrance experiences. Known for his opulent and carefully crafted scents, Dove has pioneered innovative fragrance retail concepts that blend the sensory with the theatrical, creating immersive experiences that capture the essence of luxury. His expertise has been acknowledged through multiple record-breaking fragrance launches, particularly in prestigious locations like Harrods, where his work has set new standards for luxury retail.

The following interview with Roja Dove explores the unique role of scent in retail theatre, particularly within the luxury space. Positioned at the intersection of sensory experience and brand identity, scent plays a powerful part in engaging customers on an emotional level, much like the tactile focus seen in Apple Stores. Dove's insights bring a deep understanding of how scent can transform a retail environment, making it memorable and enhancing the brand's allure.

Kate Hardcastle

(KH): Roja, you've been an essential figure in the world of fragrance and luxury retail. Today, I want to talk about how scent influences the retail theatre, particularly in the luxury environment, and touch on your record-breaking launches at Harrods. Let's start with this – how did you first discover the power of scent, particularly in retail?

Roja Dove

(RD): Thank you. Scent has an incredible, almost magical ability to transport and transform. It is the most emotionally evocative of all senses. My fascination began when I realized how a simple aroma could stir up forgotten memories or alter the mood in an instant.

In the retail world, scent is the invisible thread that weaves through a consumer's journey. It can elevate a space, making it feel luxurious, memorable and immersive. When a customer walks into a beautifully scented space, they aren't just walking into a store – they are stepping into a carefully curated experience. That's the power of scent – it's immersive, it's intimate, and it stays with you long after you've left the space.

KH: I completely agree. The world of retail has shifted dramatically, and creating an experience is now at the heart of successful brands. As someone who has partnered with Harrods, a quintessential symbol of luxury, can you speak to the importance of retail theatre and how scent plays a role in that?

RD: Retail theatre is exactly the right phrase. It's about creating a space where the consumer is the main actor in an unfolding story, something we should never forget. In a place like Harrods, it's essential to make every visitor feel like they are part of something extraordinary. Theatricality in retail, particularly luxury retail, is not just about what they see or touch; it's about engaging every sense. Scent is the invisible backdrop – it sets the stage without you even realizing it. It heightens every experience, whether you're trying on a gown, examining a timepiece, or simply browsing.

When we launched The Dove Haute Parfumerie in Harrods, we wanted to create something unlike anything else. Every detail was considered: the lighting, the product displays and of course, the scent that would welcome and envelop our clients. When people walked through the doors, they were hit with this beautiful wave of fragrance – distinct, elegant and unforgettable. That's the true essence of retail theatre – making sure that every element, seen and unseen, works in harmony to create something beyond the transactional.

KH: What I love about what you're saying is how scent is almost the silent architect of the experience. And you've created some of the most successful fragrance launches in Harrods history. Can you share more about how you crafted that success?

RD: With pleasure. For me, creating a successful fragrance launch is about more than just the scent – it's about the story, the emotion and the connection it forges with the customer. When we launched Roja Parfums at Harrods, we didn't want to simply put perfumes on display. It had to be a journey, an invitation into a world of luxury and sophistication.

One of our most successful launches involved the use of exclusive in-store events, where our most loyal clients were invited to an intimate setting. We created a narrative around the fragrance – a story about craftsmanship, artistry, and the heritage behind each bottle. This created a sense of exclusivity and personal connection.

KH: I think it's fascinating how you've managed to elevate fragrance beyond a mere product and turn it into a storytelling tool. How do you see the role of scent evolving in retail spaces going forward, especially with the growing influence of digital retail?

RD: Scent will always have a vital role in physical spaces, even as digital retail continues to grow. There's something irreplaceable about the way scent can enhance a physical experience. That said, I think the challenge for brands will be finding ways to translate that sensory experience into digital spaces. While scent can't be directly transmitted online, brands can create a narrative around their fragrances through digital storytelling – videos, virtual tours, immersive storytelling.

But physical stores will still be the heart of luxury retail. And as we move forward, I believe we'll see even more integration of scent into the overall brand identity. For instance, some hotels and luxury car brands are now creating signature scents that reflect their brand ethos and resonate with their clientele. I think retail will continue in that direction, with brands crafting more personalized, immersive experiences through scent.

KH: You've touched on something important – the idea of a signature scent for brands. It's something that can anchor an entire sensory experience, something people instantly associate with a brand. Can you share more about the future of scent in retail and how it may continue to develop?

RD: Certainly. As we've seen, there's a growing recognition of how scent can be a powerful branding tool. It's subtle yet highly impactful. I predict that in the future, more brands will move towards creating unique, signature scents that encapsulate their identity. This is already happening with luxury hotels, airlines and high-end retailers – each using scent to create a more immersive brand experience.

Furthermore, as technology advances, we might see even more sophisticated ways to incorporate scent into retail spaces. Imagine walking into a store where the scent changes based on the time of day or even the specific products you're browsing. Or an environment where the scent intensifies as you approach certain displays, subtly guiding you through the space. It's an exciting time, and I think we've only scratched the surface of what's possible.

KH: It's such a fascinating world you've built, Roja. Before we close, can you reflect on your journey and what stands out to you as the most rewarding part of bringing your creations to your customers?

RD: What stands out to me most is the emotional connection we've been able to create through scent – those moments when you see a client's eyes light up because a fragrance has transported them somewhere special, as you watch them walk away a centimetre taller without the need of a heel. That's the reward for me – knowing that what we do can evoke such powerful emotions and create lasting memories.

KH: Roja, thank you for sharing your insights today. The art of scent in retail is so essential, and your perspective is invaluable. I'm certain our readers will walk away with a new appreciation for how scent shapes their shopping experiences.

Key interview takeaways

1 **Scent as a subtle yet powerful retail tool:** Dove explains how scent can evoke strong emotions and memories, turning a retail space into an immersive experience that goes beyond the visual.

2 **Retail theatre as a layered experience:** Dove describes how scent complements other sensory elements, helping to create a cohesive and memorable experience that supports the brand's story.

3 **Signature scents as a brand differentiator:** Dove highlights the potential of brands adopting signature scents, a unique fragrance that customers associate with the brand's identity and values.

4 **Future of scent in personalized retail experiences:** Dove envisions advanced scent strategies, where brands adjust scents based on time, products or customer demographics, offering a highly personalized experience.

5 **Emotional connections build long-term loyalty:** According to Dove, customers form stronger attachments to brands that create meaningful emotional experiences. Scent can evoke powerful responses that deepen brand loyalty in a competitive retail space.

KEY TAKEAWAYS

1 **Retail theatre transforms shopping into an experience:** Modern consumers look for experiences that are immersive and memorable. Retail theatre turns shopping into a unique event, going beyond mere transactions to engage and captivate audiences.

2 **Sensory engagement drives emotional connections:** Engaging multiple senses – sight, sound, smell, taste and touch – allows brands to create deeper emotional connections with customers. These sensory interactions leave lasting impressions that enhance brand recall and loyalty.

3 **Strategic store design influences consumer behaviour:** Thoughtfully designed store layouts, like Apple's hands-on approach, encourage customers to engage with products, helping them feel more connected and confident in their purchases.

4 **Sensory elements can boost customer loyalty:** Incorporating sensory cues like inviting scents, interactive displays and ambient soundscapes creates a memorable experience that customers associate with positive feelings, making them more likely to return.

5 **The future of retail combines sensory and digital innovations:** As retail continues to evolve, stores will blend sensory experiences with data-driven personalization. Retail theatre's role will only grow, integrating emotional engagement with technology to meet the expectations of modern consumers.

References

1 Colateral (nd) Window displays: How to supercharge your visual merchandising, *Colateral*, www.colateral.io/en/blog/window-displays-supercharge-your-visual-merchandising (archived at https://perma.cc/28BP-BHMH)

2 Flonomics Staff (2016) The psychology of color in retail marketing, Flonomics

3 Allbranded (2023) Green color psychology: Unleashing the power of green in marketing, 26 July, www.allbranded.com/Blog/Green-Color-Psychology-in-Marketing (archived at https://perma.cc/GP54-225U)

4 Garlin, Francine V and Owen, Katherine (2006) Setting the tone with the tune: A meta-analytic review of the effects of background music in retail settings, *Journal of Business Research*, 59 (6), 755–64, https://doi.org/10.1016/j.jbusres.2006.01.013 (archived at https://perma.cc/C2AL-9MJ6)

5 Mattila, Anna S and Wirtz, Jochen (2001) Congruency of scent and music as a driver of in-store evaluations and behavior, *Journal of Retailing*, 77 (2), 273–89, https://doi.org/10.1016/S0022-4359(01)00042-2 (archived at https://perma.cc/Y67J-34KV)

6 Lush (2024) Lush Fresh Handmade Cosmetics Financial Report 2023, 8 May, https://weare.lush.com/lush-life/company-statements/lush-audited-accounts-year-ending-june-2023 (archived at https://perma.cc/5Y3S-G5E2)

7 Johnson, Bobby (2022) Infographic: Consumer sampling – how trying leads to buying, Inspira, 12 April, www.inspiramarketing.com/infographic-consumer-sampling-how-trying-leads-to-buying (archived at https://perma.cc/NKB5-GLB4)

8 Berlinger, Max (2021) How Erewhon became L.A.'s hottest hangout, *New York Times*, 17 February, www.nytimes.com/2021/02/17/style/erewhon-los-angeles-health-food.html (archived at https://perma.cc/DC4N-S6B6)

9 Peck, Joann and Shu, Suzanne B (2009) The effect of mere touch on perceived ownership, *Journal of Consumer Research*, 36 (3), 434–47, https://doi.org/10.1086/598614 (archived at https://perma.cc/R9UP-LQWN)

10 NRF (2021) $428 billion in merchandise returned in 2020, National Retail Federation, 11 January, www.nrf.com/media-center/press-releases/428-billion-merchandise-returned-2020 (archived at https://perma.cc/ZL4M-6DJR)

11 Thomas, Lauren (2017) Bucks from bricks: These retailers make the most money per square foot on their real estate, *CNBC*, 29 July, www.cnbc.com/2017/07/29/here-are-the-retailers-that-make-the-most-money-per-square-foot-on-their-real-estate.html (archived at https://perma.cc/HK8T-VUC9)

7

The art of shopping perception

The roles of influencers, celebrities and other customer advocates in brand perception

Brand endorsements have become an omnipresent force in today's consumer landscape, yet their influence stretches back far further than many of us realize. Over the years, I've developed the instincts of a sceptical shopper, able to see past the glamour of celebrity endorsements and influencer tie-ins. But as a parent, I'm reminded daily of the enduring impact these figures have on younger generations. Watching my own children (Gen Z and Gen Alpha) make purchasing decisions based on the latest product promoted by their favourite YouTubers or sports icons is a striking reminder: celebrity influence is deeply woven into our culture, shaping our habits, values and preferences.

This chapter explores the origins and evolution of brand endorsements, tracing the journey from early forms of association with royalty and the aristocracy to today's digital landscape, where influencers wield considerable power over consumer behaviour. It's a history that reveals just how long we have associated certain names and faces with trust, prestige and aspiration. In fact, studies indicate celebrity endorsements can significantly impact consumers' attitudes and behaviours towards advertised products or brands, underscoring the role that familiar, aspirational figures play in driving our purchasing decisions.[1]

In this chapter, we'll trace this fascinating journey, exploring the role of endorsements from monarchs to modern celebrities and examining how the psychology of influence remains much the same, despite changes in media and culture. We'll look at case studies that reveal both the power and pitfalls of endorsements and consider how consumers today – particularly younger generations – are influenced by social media figures in ways that parallel the historic appeal of celebrity influence. This chapter serves as a reminder that while the faces have changed, the human tendency to trust, admire and be influenced by those we look up to is as powerful as ever, reinforcing the timelessness of endorsements in shaping consumer behaviour.

The historical roots of brand endorsements

Brand endorsements by celebrities and influencers are often viewed as a phenomenon born in the digital age, yet their roots extend centuries back. The idea of associating products with admired public figures has been a powerful strategy for influencing consumer behaviour, shaping brand perceptions and driving purchases for generations. From royal endorsements to Hollywood icons, the evolution of brand endorsements reflects a consistent and enduring appeal: the trust and credibility a well-known figure can lend to a brand.

Early endorsements: Josiah Wedgwood and royal patronage

One of the earliest examples of celebrity endorsement can be traced back to the 18th century with English potter Josiah Wedgwood. Recognized for his craftsmanship, Wedgwood sought royal approval to elevate his pottery's status. In a strategic move, he secured Queen Charlotte, wife of King George III, as a patron of his work, branding his pottery line as 'Queen's Ware' This connection with the British monarchy allowed Wedgwood to position his pottery as luxury items suitable for royalty, a reputation that helped establish his brand's prestige across Europe and beyond. By associating his products with the royal family, Wedgwood laid the foundation for modern endorsement strategies, where a figure's authority or popularity lends added value to a product.

This instance reveals the lasting power of associating products with prestigious figures to enhance perceived quality and desirability. Wedgwood's Queen's Ware marked a foundational moment in influencer marketing, showing that the approval of a respected personality could elevate a product's appeal.[2]

The Royal Warrant system: A symbol of quality and prestige

The tradition of royal endorsements did not end with individual cases like Wedgwood's. The British Royal Warrant system, formalized in the

15th century and regulated in the 18th century, provides ongoing endorsement to brands that supply goods or services to royal households. This system remains one of the most recognizable forms of quality assurance today, with brands like Fortnum & Mason, Twinings and Heinz proudly displaying their Royal Warrants.[3]

The Royal Warrant serves as a mark of excellence and reliability, communicating to consumers that a brand meets the high standards required by the royal family. This form of endorsement transcends the typical notion of a celebrity endorsement, as it symbolizes trust and quality rather than mere popularity. Fortnum & Mason, a luxury department store known for fine foods, has held a Royal Warrant since 1863. This endorsement solidifies its status as a trusted purveyor, enhancing its brand image in the minds of consumers. Similarly, Heinz's Royal Warrant reinforces its association with quality and reliability, appealing to both domestic and international markets.

The Royal Warrant system highlights the effectiveness of trusted endorsements, as it assures consumers of a brand's integrity. Today, while platforms and methods have evolved, the core appeal of influencer marketing remains rooted in the credibility and authority the endorser can lend to the product.

Coca-Cola and the modern image of Santa Claus

In the 20th century, as advertising became more sophisticated, brands began to establish their own iconic characters to serve as ambassadors. A prime example is Coca-Cola's transformation of the image of Santa Claus.[4] Prior to the 1930s, depictions of Santa varied greatly across cultures, with his attire and demeanour changing from region to region. In 1931, Coca-Cola commissioned artist Haddon Sundblom to create holiday advertisements featuring a jolly Santa in a red suit – a look that complemented Coca-Cola's brand colours. This image resonated widely with consumers and ultimately cemented the modern image of Santa Claus in popular culture, an image that continues to connect Coca-Cola with the holiday season.

This strategic use of a fictional character demonstrated the potential of brand-created icons in building emotional connections with consumers. By associating itself with the cheerful, festive image of Santa Claus, Coca-Cola positioned itself as a beloved part of the holiday tradition. This case illustrates that brand endorsements need not always involve real-life celebrities; carefully crafted characters can become enduring ambassadors that build lasting consumer relationships.

Marilyn Monroe and Chanel No. 5: The allure of Hollywood glamour

As celebrity culture grew in the 20th century, brands began to capitalize on the influence of Hollywood icons to elevate their products. A quintessential example is Marilyn Monroe's association with Chanel No 5. Monroe's famous 1952 statement that she wore only Chanel No 5 to bed remains one of the most memorable endorsements in advertising history. This association cemented the fragrance's status as an emblem of sophistication and allure, aligning Chanel No 5 with Monroe's own image as a symbol of beauty and glamour.

Monroe's endorsement added an element of mystique and desirability to Chanel No 5, transforming it from a mere product to an icon of Hollywood glamour. This shift marked a new phase in the history of endorsements, where the aspirational appeal of celebrities became central. Consumers weren't just buying a product; they were buying into a lifestyle that epitomized elegance and allure.

The digital age: Trust and authenticity with social media influencers

Today, the endorsement landscape has expanded dramatically with the rise of digital platforms and social media. Modern-day influencers range from A-list celebrities to niche content creators, each wielding the power to shape consumer preferences and drive purchasing decisions. The unique strength of today's influencers lies in the personal connections they cultivate with followers, creating a level of relatability that traditional advertising cannot match.

According to a 2012 Nielsen study, 92 per cent of consumers trust recommendations from individuals, even if they don't know them personally, over brand-driven advertisements.[5] This trust factor underscores why influencer marketing has become such an effective tool, as followers often view influencers as friends or trusted sources, not just promotional figures. This shift marks a significant evolution in the way brands connect with audiences, where personal connection and authenticity have become paramount.

Modern influencer marketing draws on these historical precedents but is uniquely suited to today's landscape. Unlike earlier endorsements rooted solely in prestige or glamour, today's influencer marketing relies on building trust and emotional resonance with followers. Brands now can reach highly specific audiences, aligning with influencers who reflect the brand's values and appeal to targeted demographics.

The rise and rise of social media influencers

Social media platforms like Instagram, YouTube and TikTok have revolutionized the advertising landscape, leading to the rise of influencers who can reach vast audiences with a single post. Unlike traditional celebrities, social media influencers often cultivate niche followings, enabling brands to target specific demographics effectively. This modern-day marketing strategy has reshaped how consumers connect with brands, offering a more personal and relatable approach to product endorsements.

HUDA KATTAN: A BEAUTY MOGUL BUILT ON SOCIAL MEDIA

Huda Kattan, a beauty influencer and entrepreneur, exemplifies the success potential for social media influencers. With over 50 million Instagram followers, Kattan has leveraged her platform to build a multi-million-dollar business. Known for her make-up tutorials and product reviews, she established a brand, Huda Beauty, that has gained global recognition and loyal consumer support. Her make-up line, launched initially with false eyelashes, expanded rapidly, becoming a comprehensive beauty empire valued at over $1 billion.[6]

Kattan's success stems from her deep understanding of her audience's desires. By consistently sharing beauty tips, insights and authentic reviews, she has built a loyal following that trusts her recommendations. This trust has translated into a high level of consumer engagement and strong sales for Huda Beauty. As Kattan's influence grew, so did her brand's value, illustrating how an influencer's genuine connection with their audience can yield significant commercial success.

The psychology behind influencer marketing: The power of authenticity

The effectiveness of influencer marketing hinges on its ability to leverage psychological principles like social proof and authenticity. Social proof refers to the human tendency to look to others when making decisions, especially in uncertain situations. When influencers endorse a product, followers are more likely to trust and purchase it because they see someone they admire using it.

This sense of authenticity sets influencer marketing apart from traditional advertisements, which can feel impersonal and detached.

When discussing the impact of celebrity endorsements and the rise of celebrity-driven brands, one name inevitably comes to mind: Kim Kardashian. Kim's influence on product sales and brand perception is monumental, making her one of the most influential figures in modern retail.

THE KIM KARDASHIAN EFFECT

Kim Kardashian's transition from a reality television star to a business mogul represents the pinnacle of influencer-driven brand success. With over 300 million Instagram followers, Kardashian has a unique ability to drive consumer behaviour on a massive scale. Her shapewear brand, SKIMS, launched in 2019, reflects her understanding of social media dynamics and consumer preferences. Within three years, SKIMS grew into a business valued at over $3.2 billion, showcasing the powerful impact of Kardashian's influence.[7]

The success of SKIMS is rooted in Kardashian's direct engagement with her audience and careful attention to brand messaging. By positioning SKIMS as an inclusive brand with a wide range of sizes and tones, Kardashian tapped into the growing demand for body-positive, accessible fashion. Her regular updates and behind-the-scenes glimpses of product development give her followers a sense of involvement, reinforcing their loyalty to the brand. This approach to brand building, focused on authenticity and consumer connection, has set a new standard for celebrity-owned brands.

THE CHANGING FACE OF INFLUENCER MARKETING

Based on the latest data from the Influencer Marketing Hub's 2024 Benchmark Report, the influencer landscape has evolved to include a wide range of influencer types, each with distinct advantages for brand engagement. While celebrity influencers like Kim Kardashian and Huda Kattan reach broad audiences, 'micro-influencers' and 'nano-influencers' (those with fewer than 10,000 followers) are gaining traction for their highly engaged, niche audiences. According to the report, micro-influencers tend to have engagement rates up to 2 per cent higher than macro-influencers, offering brands a more personalized and authentic touchpoint with consumers, which has proven effective for targeting specific demographics.[8]

Nano-influencers are noted for their close-knit communities and genuine interactions, which translate into higher levels of trust. As consumers seek more relatable and credible sources of information, brands are increasingly valuing the unique advantage that smaller influencers bring by fostering meaningful and loyal relationships with their audiences.

Moreover, the rise of virtual influencers – computer-generated personas managed by brands or digital agencies – is reshaping the influencer market. These virtual influencers, often indistinguishable from real people, provide brands with a fully controllable influencer model that can align closely with brand values and messaging without the unpredictability of human influencers. As of 2025, virtual influencers are increasingly popular, particularly in fashion and luxury markets, where they often showcase products to large online audiences without the logistical constraints of traditional influencers. This trend is a testament to the dynamic nature of the influencer landscape, where brands continue to explore innovative ways to connect with audiences.

To sustain success, celebrity-driven brands must prioritize authenticity, quality and innovation. They need to continue engaging with their audience in meaningful ways and demonstrate a genuine commitment to their products and customers. This approach not only helps build lasting brand loyalty but also ensures that these brands can withstand the test of time. *Perceived authenticity is key.*

Everyday people as influencers and the shift in marketing

The retail marketing landscape has undergone a significant transformation, with influence now extending well beyond traditional celebrities and social media stars to include everyday consumers who wield considerable power through genuine connections and personal recommendations. Today, consumers seek authentic, relatable endorsements over brand-driven advertising, looking to voices they trust. This shift underscores the importance of peer-to-peer influence, where personal connections have become pivotal in shaping purchasing decisions. According to research, 89 per cent of consumers now prioritize recommendations from people they know and trust over traditional advertising channels, signalling a major change in how brand loyalty and consumer choices are built.[9]

The rise of consumer advocates and community-driven marketing

As influence becomes more democratized, brands increasingly understand the power of cultivating loyal communities who act as advocates. This shift has led to initiatives like LEGO's 'LEGO Ideas' platform, a community-driven project that invites fans to submit their own designs for potential production as official LEGO sets. The project highlights a new level of consumer engagement, allowing loyal customers to shape brand offerings directly. One standout example is the 'Women of NASA' set, submitted by science communicator Maia Weinstock. This set achieved widespread acclaim and became a bestseller, showing how passionate consumers can play a vital role in product innovation.[10]

The impact of community-driven marketing extends beyond sales; it fosters a sense of loyalty and ownership. Brands like Lego effectively harness the authentic enthusiasm of their customers, leveraging peer-to-peer recommendations as a powerful tool. Research reinforces this trend, showing that brands with strong consumer advocacy see over 50 per cent higher likelihood of influencing purchases compared to traditional advertisements.[11] By empowering consumers to become co-creators, brands build trust, increase engagement and create long-lasting relationships that go beyond the transactional.

In the realm of trusted advertising channels, recommendations from friends and family are clear front runners, surpassing other popular channels such as brand sponsorships, TV advertisements and influencer placements. This shift emphasizes that consumers today are not just looking for products; they seek genuine connections and experiences that resonate with their values and engage their community. This trend is underscored by the growing influence of testimonials and reviews, which have become a cornerstone of modern retail.

The importance of testimonials and reviews

Testimonials and reviews now serve as digital word-of-mouth endorsements, bridging the gap between traditional and peer-driven marketing. They act as social proof, offering insights that help consumers feel confident in their purchasing decisions. Amazon exemplifies the success of this approach, with its robust review system shaping consumer perceptions and guiding purchasing behaviour. Amazon's review system includes verified purchase badges and helpfulness ratings, creating a credible and transparent source of information. These features allow consumers to make informed decisions, with reviews often playing a decisive role in whether a product is purchased.

The impact of reviews on sales is significant. Research found that products with five or more reviews are 270 per cent more likely to be purchased than those with no reviews, highlighting the substantial influence that customer feedback has on sales.[12] This demonstrates how positive testimonials not only boost confidence but also contribute directly to higher conversion rates and increased revenue.

Navigating negative reviews and maintaining authenticity

While positive reviews can be powerful, negative reviews also play a crucial role. When managed appropriately, they provide valuable insights for brands to improve their offerings and foster transparency. Some retailers often address negative reviews with solutions such as refunds or replacements, demonstrating a commitment to customer satisfaction. This proactive approach helps mitigate dissatisfaction and shows that the brand values its customers, reinforcing a reputation of trust and reliability.

To maintain credibility, businesses must prioritize authenticity in their reviews. Consumers are often quick to spot inauthentic or overly promotional feedback, which can damage a brand's reputation. Encouraging genuine reviews is key, and brands achieve this by following up with customers after purchase, offering incentives for honest feedback, or simply delivering an outstanding customer experience that inspires positive responses.

The rise of video testimonials has added another layer of authenticity to the review landscape. Platforms like YouTube and Instagram provide a place for consumers to share their experiences in detail, making product reviews more personal and relatable. For instance, beauty brands often collaborate with content creators to showcase products through in-depth tutorials, giving potential customers a closer look at how products perform in real-life settings. This approach deepens engagement and builds trust, as consumers can visually assess a product's benefits.

COMBATING FAKE REVIEWS WITH TECHNOLOGY

The issue of fake reviews remains a challenge for many brands. Fraudulent feedback can mislead consumers and erode trust, making it essential for companies to implement measures to verify review authenticity. Amazon and other major platforms have turned to advanced technology, such as machine learning, to detect and address suspicious review patterns. Looking forward, emerging technologies like artificial intelligence and blockchain may further strengthen the reliability of reviews. AI can identify unusual review behaviour, while blockchain can provide a tamper-proof system to verify the source and authenticity of feedback, ensuring that consumers receive accurate information.

LOOKING FORWARD: THE FUTURE OF TESTIMONIALS AND REVIEWS

As retail evolves, the role of testimonials and reviews will continue to grow, becoming more sophisticated with the integration of new technologies. The rise of augmented reality (AR) and virtual reality (VR) in retail is expected to further enhance the testimonial experience. Imagine a virtual fitting room where consumers can try on clothing, and access reviews and ratings alongside the product. This integration of reviews with immersive technology would provide a richer, more engaging shopping experience, bridging the gap between online and in-store retail.

The importance of peer-driven influence in today's retail environment cannot be overstated. As consumers seek authenticity and connection, brands that prioritize customer advocacy, encourage genuine reviews and embrace emerging technology will be well-positioned to thrive. The emphasis on trust and community-driven recommendations reflects a fundamental change in how consumers relate to brands, shifting from passive observation to active participation.

The rise of social selling trends

The landscape of retail has been dramatically transformed by the rise of social media, giving birth to new and innovative trends designed to captivate audiences and drive sales. These trends, such as unboxing videos, mystery item reveals and 'Get Ready With Me' (GRWM) segments, have redefined how brands engage with consumers.

The rise of child influencers

The influence of young trendsetters is not limited to the beauty industry. Child influencers are also making waves in various other sectors, including toys, fashion and technology.

The phenomenon of child influencers highlights the growing trend of peer-to-peer marketing, where recommendations from trusted peers or relatable figures carry more weight than traditional advertisements. This trend is particularly pronounced among younger audiences, who are more likely to trust and follow the recommendations of influencers who they feel understand their interests and preferences.

However, the rise of child influencers also raises important ethical considerations. The line between authentic content and commercial promotion can become blurred, making it crucial for brands and influencers to maintain transparency and integrity. Ensuring that young influencers are not exploited and that their content adheres to ethical standards is essential for sustaining trust and credibility.

The evolving landscape of social media marketing has transformed how brands connect with consumers, leveraging the influence of both young trendsetters and beauty influencers. The integration of children into the social media ecosystem as influencers is reshaping marketing strategies, emphasizing authenticity and personal connection. As we move forward, it is crucial for brands to navigate this space responsibly, maintaining transparency and ethical standards to build lasting trust and loyalty among their audience. The power of personal recommendations, whether from young influencers or established beauty icons, continues to shape consumer behaviour, highlighting the enduring importance of genuine connections in the world of marketing.

Unboxing: The art of anticipation

Unboxing videos have become a significant trend, offering viewers a sense of excitement and anticipation as they watch products being unwrapped. These videos often feature influencers or regular consumers showcasing new purchases, from gadgets and beauty products to toys and fashion items. The appeal lies in the shared experience of discovery and the authenticity of seeing a product unveiled for the first time.

One notable example is Ryan's World, a YouTube channel run by Ryan Kaji. Ryan's World has amassed millions of subscribers and billions of views, making it one of the most popular channels on YouTube. The channel's success has even led to a line of Ryan's World branded toys, highlighting the significant commercial impact of unboxing videos.

In 2020 alone, Ryan Kaji earned $29.5 million, making him the highest-paid YouTuber. Ryan's World started as a simple unboxing channel where Ryan, a young child, would open and review toys. His genuine reactions and childlike excitement resonated with audiences, particularly young viewers and their parents. The channel quickly grew, leading to partnerships with major toy manufacturers and the creation of Ryan's World branded products sold in stores like Walmart and Target. The success of Ryan's World demonstrates the powerful influence that child influencers can have on both online and offline retail.[13]

Mystery item reveals, where consumers purchase products without knowing exactly what they will receive, have also surged in popularity. This trend taps into the excitement of surprise and the human desire for discovery. Products like mystery boxes, blind bags and subscription services offer consumers a chance to receive a curated selection of items, often themed or collectible.

REAL-WORLD EXAMPLE
Funko Pops: A cultural phenomenon

Funko Pops, the iconic vinyl figures produced by Funko Inc. have evolved from niche collectibles to a cultural mainstay, capturing the imagination of both avid collectors and casual fans. This case study delves into the rise of Funko Pops, their impact on retail and pop culture, and the strategic moves that have propelled them to global success.

The origins and growth of Funko Pops

Funko Inc. was founded in 1998 by Mike Becker as a modest venture aimed at creating retro-themed toys. Initially, Funko gained attention with bobbleheads, but it was the introduction of the Funko Pop line in 2010 that truly ignited the brand's popularity. The first Pop figures, featuring characters from DC Comics, struck a chord with consumers, leading Funko to expand its offerings across a vast array of franchises, from Marvel and Star Wars to Disney and Harry Potter. This early success laid the groundwork for Funko to capture a diverse consumer base spanning various fandoms.

Design and mass appeal

The unique design of Funko Pops, characterized by large heads and minimalistic facial features, has been instrumental in their appeal. The figures' simplicity and uniformity make them easily recognizable, yet versatile enough to adapt to any character. This accessible design has also allowed Funko to scale production efficiently, creating an extensive catalogue of figures that caters to a broad spectrum of interests. The approachable aesthetic of Funko Pops appeals to collectors and non-collectors alike, contributing to their mainstream popularity.

Funko's extensive licensing strategy has been another cornerstone of its success. By securing partnerships with leading franchises across entertainment, gaming and music, Funko can consistently release figures that resonate with fans of all ages. Funko holds licenses for major franchises, including Marvel, Star Wars, Harry Potter and popular television shows. This broad range of characters ensures an evergreen appeal, drawing in new customers with each release and keeping established collectors engaged.

Retail strategy and accessibility

Funko Pops are available across various retail channels, from major outlets like Walmart, Target and Amazon to speciality stores and online platforms. This wide distribution network makes Funko Pops accessible to an expansive audience, while limited editions and exclusive releases at conventions like Comic-Con add an element of scarcity that appeals to collectors. Convention-exclusive figures often become sought-after items, driving demand and fostering a dedicated collector community.

The accessibility of Funko Pops through both mass-market and niche retailers has been pivotal in maintaining brand visibility and accessibility. By tapping into multiple retail avenues, Funko ensures its products reach consumers wherever they shop, reinforcing the brand's presence and appeal.

The collector community and secondary market

The collector community has played a crucial role in Funko Pop's enduring success. Collectors are drawn to the thrill of hunting for exclusive, limited-edition and 'chase' variants, some of which are produced in highly limited quantities. These rare figures often fetch substantial prices on the secondary market, creating a sense of urgency and excitement around each release. The community-driven aspect of Funko collecting fosters a strong sense of belonging, as fans connect through social media groups, online forums and conventions dedicated to their shared passion.

Funko has actively nurtured this community by engaging with fans directly and hosting events that bring collectors together. The rise of social media platforms has only amplified the excitement, with collectors sharing their 'Funko hauls', discussing new releases and trading rare items online. This sense of community and exclusivity has turned Funko Pop collecting into a vibrant subculture.

Financial impact and market success

Since the introduction of Funko Pops, Funko Inc. has seen substantial financial growth. In 2019, Funko reported a revenue of $795 million, with a significant share attributed to the Pop line.[14] This impressive financial performance highlights the strong market demand for Funko products and reflects the brand's success in appealing to both mainstream and niche audiences. Funko's initial public offering (IPO) in 2017 further underscored its impact, positioning the company as a dominant player in the collectible toy market.

Funko's ability to maintain financial stability and growth amid changing consumer trends underscores the strength of its brand and business model. The company's focus on community engagement, licensing and consistent product innovation has helped it remain relevant in an increasingly competitive market.

The broader cultural impact of Funko Pops

Funko Pops have transcended their role as simple collectibles, embedding themselves into broader pop culture. The figures regularly appear in social media posts, YouTube unboxings and fan collections, further solidifying their cultural impact. Funko has also expanded its product lines, launching clothing, board games and other branded merchandise, reinforcing its presence beyond vinyl figures.

Funko's diversification into merchandise has strengthened its brand identity, enabling fans to engage with the brand across multiple platforms. This multifaceted approach has helped Funko extend its reach, appealing to both collectors and those drawn to Funko's unique aesthetic and broad product offering.

Criticisms and challenges

Despite its success, Funko has faced criticism, particularly regarding the environmental impact of producing plastic figures. The use of plastic raises sustainability concerns, with calls for the company to adopt more eco-friendly practices. Additionally, some critics argue that the proliferation of limited editions and exclusives has led to market saturation, which could risk diluting the brand's appeal among collectors.

Funko has accepted the need to address environmental concerns and is exploring ways to reduce its environmental footprint. The company's response to these challenges will be crucial in maintaining its brand integrity and continuing to resonate with a more environmentally conscious consumer base.

The future of Funko Pops

As Funko Inc. looks to the future, the brand shows no signs of slowing down. With an expanding list of franchises and properties, Funko is poised to release an endless array of new figures. The company's ability to adapt to market trends and consumer interests will be vital in sustaining its relevance. Funko's approach of tapping into consumer nostalgia while aligning with current pop culture phenomena suggests it will continue to capture the zeitgeist, at least in the short term.

The rise of Funko Pops offers a compelling example of how a simple yet effective product design, combined with strategic licensing and community engagement, can create a cultural movement. As a retail success story, Funko exemplifies how brands can leverage consumer passion, exclusivity and nostalgia to build lasting connections with their audience.

Marketing to children is not a new phenomenon, but the intensity and reach of these new social selling trends have raised ethical concerns. The addictive nature of unboxing videos and mystery item reveals, coupled with the fact that they are often targeted at young, impressionable audiences, can be troubling. Parents and regulators alike worry about the impact of such content on children's development and consumer habits.

Brands need to tread carefully, ensuring that their marketing methods are ethical and transparent. It is crucial for companies to consider the long-term effects of their strategies on young consumers. For instance, setting limits on the frequency of ads and ensuring that content is age-appropriate are steps in the right direction. Moreover, balancing entertainment with educational value can help mitigate some of the negative impacts of these trends.

In the evolving landscape of social media and digital marketing, the boundaries for marketing products to children have become increasingly fluid. The integration of children into the social media ecosystem as influencers and trendsetters is reshaping how products are marketed, not just to children but also through them to broader audiences.

Historically, advertising to children has been highly regulated to protect their impressionable minds. However, the rise of social media has blurred these boundaries, creating a new frontier where children themselves become the conduits for marketing messages. Social media platforms regularly feature content with young influencers who unbox toys, review products and even provide beauty tutorials, effectively turning them into miniature marketers. This shift is significant as it shows a transition from traditional, regulated advertising spaces to the more dynamic and less regulated realms of social media.

The rise and rise of influencers in beauty and fragrance

In recent years, beauty influencers have redefined what it means to connect with consumers in the digital era. Unlike traditional celebrity endorsements, these influencers cultivate followings through (mostly) genuine, relatable content and direct engagement with their audiences. Through personalized storytelling and the creation of digital communities, beauty influencers have emerged as powerful voices that shape consumer preferences, especially in the beauty industry, where authenticity and personal connection have become essential.

This transformation has allowed beauty influencers to rise as pivotal forces in modern marketing, bridging the gap between brands and consumers in ways that were once unimaginable. The power they hold is evident not only in their massive online followings but in their ability to drive product launches, influence buying behaviours and establish brands that resonate deeply with consumers.

The rise of influencer-led brands

As discussed earlier, a striking shift has emerged in the beauty industry with the rise of influencer-led brands. These brands are not merely the result of product endorsements; instead, they represent a new kind of business model, where influencers are not only recommending products but building entire lifestyle brands. This phenomenon illustrates how beauty influencers have transformed from content creators into entrepreneurs, leveraging their audiences and market insights to create products that cater directly to their followers' needs and aspirations.

Unlike traditional beauty brands that rely on polished, high-budget campaigns, influencer-led brands build their appeal on authenticity and relatability. Followers feel that they 'know' these influencers through their stories, struggles and successes. Influencers have become experts at crafting an aspirational yet accessible image, which allows their audiences to connect with them on a deeply personal level. This connection has proven invaluable, as followers are often more inclined to try products endorsed by someone they perceive as genuine, trustworthy and relatable.

AUTHENTICITY AS THE FOUNDATION OF INFLUENCE

One of the defining characteristics of beauty influencers is their ability to foster an authentic relationship with their followers. Unlike scripted advertisements, influencers share candid moments from their lives, reveal behind-the-scenes insights and speak openly about their experiences. This level of transparency and vulnerability builds trust, which is crucial in an era where consumers are increasingly sceptical of traditional advertising.

Followers appreciate influencers who are open about their personal journeys, including both successes and setbacks. This authenticity enables influencers to connect with audiences on an emotional level, encouraging a sense of loyalty that goes far beyond a typical brand–consumer relationship. For example, when an influencer endorses a product, it is often perceived as a recommendation from a friend rather than a sales pitch. This trust, built on years of genuine engagement, is a powerful driver in converting followers into loyal customers.

ENGAGING THROUGH COMMUNITY AND INTERACTIVE CONTENT

A significant part of an influencer's success lies in their ability to create a sense of community among their followers. Unlike traditional beauty brands, which primarily communicate through one-way advertising channels, beauty influencers engage with their audience through interactive content. From live make-up tutorials and Q&A sessions to behind-the-scenes glimpses into their daily routines, influencers create an exclusive and immersive experience that followers feel personally invested in.

Through these interactions, influencers foster a sense of community that is difficult for conventional brands to replicate. Followers feel they are part of a shared journey, and this connection goes beyond just product recommendations. Influencers who effectively create these digital communities become trusted figures, curating not only beauty products but also entire lifestyle choices that resonate with their audiences. This engagement is powerful, as followers see themselves as participants rather than mere consumers.

A new standard for inclusivity and representation

Beauty influencers have also set a new standard for inclusivity and representation in the industry. In an era where consumers demand diversity and inclusivity influencers have played a key role in pushing brands to address gaps in the market. Many influencers use their platforms to advocate for broader representation, encouraging brands to cater to a more diverse range of skin tones, body types and cultural backgrounds.

This push for inclusivity has led to tangible changes in the industry, with major brands expanding their product ranges to cater to previously under-served groups. Influencers are not only meeting a demand for diversity but are actively creating it, influencing brands to prioritize inclusivity as part of their core values. This shift is particularly powerful, as consumers increasingly support brands that reflect their own identities and values.

Moving beyond endorsements: Influencers as entrepreneurs

As the influence of beauty influencers grows, many have moved beyond traditional endorsements to establish their own brands, becoming entrepreneurs. Rather than simply partnering with brands, these influencers leverage their market insights and loyal followings to create products that directly meet their audiences' needs. This shift highlights the entrepreneurial potential of influencers, who now hold the ability to build their own companies based on years of understanding their followers' preferences.

Influencers who become brand founders bring an added layer of authenticity to their ventures. Unlike established beauty brands, which may be seen as corporate and distant, influencer-led brands feel personal and accessible. Followers often view these influencers as role models and visionaries, who create products with a deep understanding of their preferences. This entrepreneur-influencer model represents a new era of consumer-driven product development, where influencers hold significant sway over what products succeed in the market.

REAL-WORLD EXAMPLE
Jackie Aina: Driving diversity in a retail sector, powered by influence

In an industry where representation has historically been limited, Jackie Aina has emerged not only as a leading beauty influencer but as an advocate for inclusivity and diversity. A Nigerian-American influencer, Aina has used her platform to call out the lack of diverse products in the beauty sector and to champion more inclusive options, making a tangible impact on how the industry caters to various skin tones and backgrounds.

Jackie Aina's journey began in 2009 when she started her YouTube channel, sharing make-up tips and tutorials. Over time, her honest and engaging content resonated with millions, allowing her to build a substantial following. Today, Aina has over 3.6 million subscribers on YouTube and 1.8 million followers on Instagram, demonstrating the significant reach she has achieved.[15] Through collaborations with major beauty brands, Aina has played a pivotal role in bringing more inclusive products to market. Her partnership with a leading brand, for example, resulted in an extended foundation range, a landmark moment that highlighted the importance of inclusivity in beauty.

Reflecting on her advocacy, Aina has emphasized the need for brands to create products for everyone, arguing that inclusivity is not simply a trend but an essential element of modern beauty. Her influence has sparked critical conversations in the beauty sector, challenging brands to rethink their product lines and marketing strategies to become more inclusive.

Jackie Aina's impact extends beyond the beauty products themselves. She has been vocal on social issues, using her platform to support movements for social equality and to address systemic issues within the industry. Her willingness to engage with difficult topics has earned her respect and loyalty from her audience, showcasing the potential for influencers to drive positive change while simultaneously building a brand.

Building on her influence and expertise, Aina launched her own brand, Forvr Mood, in August 2020. Forvr Mood is a lifestyle brand that offers luxury candles, skincare and home goods, each product reflecting Aina's personal taste and commitment to quality. Her launch was met with overwhelming enthusiasm, with the brand's initial candle line selling out within hours. The success of Forvr Mood exemplifies how an influencer's connection with their audience can translate directly into successful retail ventures.[16]

Forvr Mood's offerings, from the sophisticated scents of its candles to the luxurious packaging, reflect Aina's commitment to quality and representation. Each product, from 'Cuffing Season' to 'Left On Read,' carries a sense of modern culture and relevance, appealing to a younger demographic that values authenticity and self-care. The brand's partnership with major retailers further highlights its market impact and Aina's ability to bridge her digital influence with mainstream retail success.

Aina's journey, from a beauty enthusiast to a powerful voice in the industry and a successful brand owner, underscores the shift in modern marketing. Her work illustrates how authenticity, representation and advocacy can be foundational elements in building an influential brand.

But Aina is not alone. As I discussed earlier, other influencers, such as Huda Kattan, founder of Huda Beauty, and Emily Weiss of Glossier, have similarly transitioned from influencers to influential brand creators. Each of these women has leveraged their understanding of consumer needs to build brands that resonate on a deeply personal level with their followers. Kattan's Huda Beauty and Weiss's Glossier have become global powerhouses, with Huda Beauty valued at approximately $1.2 billion in 2020, underscoring the profound impact that beauty influencers have had on the industry.

The future of beauty influencers in retail

The rise of influencer-led brands has given way to social selling trends such as unboxing videos, mystery item reveals and 'Get Ready With Me' (GRWM) segments, all of which have transformed the way brands connect with consumers. These trends demonstrate the importance of authenticity and personal connection, highlighting how influencers can shape consumer behaviour in ways that traditional advertising cannot. As the retail landscape continues to evolve, these influencer-led approaches will likely remain integral to successful marketing strategies, reinforcing the value of experiential and community-driven marketing.

The impact of beauty influencers has redefined not only beauty standards but also retail culture itself. Through their personal stories, engagement and genuine connections with followers, influencers are shaping a more inclusive, responsive beauty industry. By leveraging the unique power of their platforms, influencers have proven that individuals with a deep understanding of their audience can create dynamic, consumer-centred brands that challenge traditional business models and redefine success in the beauty sector. This shift towards authenticity and community engagement showcases the lasting potential of beauty influencers to impact the industry in meaningful and enduring ways.

Aina's impact goes beyond product lines. She has been a vocal advocate for social issues, using her platform to support movements for equality and inclusivity, addressing systemic challenges within the beauty industry. Her authenticity and willingness to speak openly about these issues have solidified her influence, creating a loyal and respectful following. Aina's advocacy reflects a broader trend among beauty influencers, who increasingly leverage their reach to promote change and make a difference in the industry.

Building authentic relationships and amplifying the message

A prime example of this strategy is the collaboration between Patagonia and environmental activists. Clothing brand Patagonia has built its brand around environmental sustainability and social responsibility, and its partnerships with activists and organizations have helped amplify its message and reach a broader audience. By aligning its brand with causes that resonate with its audience, Patagonia has created a strong and authentic brand identity that fosters loyalty and trust.

The role of micro-influencers in amplifying brand messages cannot be overlooked. Unlike traditional influencers with millions of followers, micro-influencers have smaller but highly engaged audiences. Their recommendations are often perceived as more genuine and trustworthy, making them powerful advocates for brands. According to research, micro-influencers have 22 times more conversations about purchasing recommendations than the average consumer. This highlights the potential of micro-influencers to drive engagement and influence purchasing decisions.[17]

As the landscape of influencer marketing continues to evolve, the future promises even more integration between brands and their advocates. With advancements in technology and data analytics, brands can now identify and engage with their most influential customers in more personalized and meaningful ways. This shift towards data-driven influencer marketing allows brands to create highly targeted campaigns that resonate with specific segments of their audience.

One of the key trends in the future of influencer marketing is the rise of virtual influencers. A study in the United States found that 58 per cent of respondents followed a virtual influencer. These computer-generated characters, like Lil Miquela and Shudu, have gained significant popularity on social media and have become powerful tools for brands to reach younger, tech-savvy audiences. Virtual influencers offer brands complete control over their image and messaging, ensuring consistency and authenticity in their campaigns.[18]

The future of influencer marketing lies with greater integration of e-commerce and social media platforms. Social commerce, where consumers can purchase products directly through social media, is becoming increasingly popular. Platforms like Instagram and TikTok have introduced shopping features that allow brands to showcase their products and drive sales within the app. This seamless integration of content and commerce creates a frictionless shopping experience for consumers and provides brands with valuable data on consumer behaviour and preferences.

The role of artificial intelligence (AI) in influencer marketing is also set to grow. AI-powered tools can analyse vast amounts of data to identify trends, predict consumer behaviour and optimize influencer campaigns. By leveraging AI, brands can create more effective and personalized marketing strategies that drive engagement and conversions.

Dynamic and ever-changing, the future of influencer marketing and retail is exciting to be part of. As technology continues to advance, brands must adapt and innovate to stay relevant and connect with their audience in meaningful ways. By embracing authenticity, leveraging data-driven insights and creating immersive experiences, brands can build strong relationships with their consumers and drive long-term loyalty.

The future of influence: Shaping tomorrow's retail

As we navigate the constantly shifting landscape of retail, a new kind of influencer is taking the reins. The influencers of tomorrow will be worlds apart from those we know today. We're witnessing a pivot from metrics like sheer follower numbers and commercial endorsements to a model where authenticity, values and community engagement are paramount. In this evolving paradigm, influence is no longer something you can buy – it's earned through genuine connection and expertise. As we move into this new era, we see traditional influencer models, often criticized for their transparency issues, facing competition from a new wave of purpose-driven voices and industry experts who prioritize long-term impact over quick commercial gains.

Introducing the 'impact influencer': The future of authenticity and values

Let's consider a new term – *impact influencer* – to define this next generation. These individuals are driven not by the pursuit of fame or quick wins but by purpose, depth and true engagement. Impact influencers are specialists who don't just work within their fields but live and breathe their craft. They connect with followers on a values-based level, moving beyond superficiality to build a legacy through their platforms. Unlike traditional influencers who may prioritize monetization, impact influencers are invested in creating meaningful change, crafting content that resonates deeply with those who share their values and passions.

The influence these individuals wield is not about reaching the broadest audience but about engaging a highly committed community. Their content often goes beyond product endorsements, aiming to inspire positive societal changes. Brands that partner with these voices will find that alignment on shared values is essential. Collaborations will feel less transactional and more like a shared mission, fostering consumer trust and loyalty in ways that are increasingly rare.

Supporting this shift, recent data reflects the public's increasing alignment with this new model. According to research, a significant 58 per cent of consumers express trust in brands that actively champion social causes aligned with their values. This metric signals a seismic shift: influence in retail is not just about consumer appeal – it's about impact.[19]

The rise of brand trips: From traditional influencers to customer advocacy

An increasingly popular strategy that reflects this shift towards deeper connection and authenticity is the evolution of the brand trip. Once the domain of Instagram influencers and social media personalities, brand trips have traditionally been an opportunity for brands to showcase new products or experiences to a curated group of popular influencers, expecting high-reach content in return. However, these trips are now evolving to feature actual customers rather than the regular Instagram influencers typically seen promoting products.

This shift towards inviting brand enthusiasts or loyal customers speaks volumes about the importance of genuine advocacy. When real customers become the face of brand experiences, the authenticity of their engagement shines through, reaching audiences in a far more relatable way. These brand advocates represent a direct connection to the consumer base, offering a sincere voice that resonates more strongly than that of a paid influencer.

By transforming brand trips into customer-led experiences, brands create ambassadors who are truly invested in the brand, not just the perks. It reflects an understanding that influence isn't solely about reach; it's about relevance, honesty and building trust. This trend represents a powerful way for brands to solidify loyalty and demonstrate that they value genuine consumer relationships. Moving forward, the evolution of brand trips may set a precedent for other marketing strategies where the voice of the customer is not only heard but celebrated.

The evolution of retail influence: From trusted retailers to niche digital curators

Once upon a time, trust in retail stemmed directly from the retailers themselves. Consumers sought guidance from their local stores or favourite department stores, places where staff could offer informed advice, genuine expertise and trustworthy product selections. This reliance built strong, lasting relationships where expertise was the bedrock of consumer trust.

However, with the advent of the internet and e-commerce, this model has been turned on its head. Retailers, once the gatekeepers of quality and information, are now part of an endless digital marketplace where influencers have become the new curators. Much like traditional retailers, influencers have served as a bridge between consumers and the countless products available online, testing, reviewing and ultimately shaping consumer opinions in an increasingly complex market.

As we stand on the brink of a new phase, we're beginning to see signs of an influencer model in transition. Technological advancements are paving the way for innovations that offer the same trusted recommendations influencers provide but with an added layer of personalization, made possible through AI and data-driven insights.

Moreover, as brands turn more frequently to direct-to-consumer (D2C) models, the need for intermediaries diminishes. Retailers and influencers alike may find themselves redefined as brands connect directly with consumers, drawing on customer insights and tailoring their offerings in ways previously unimaginable.

In this landscape, the role of influencers is becoming increasingly niche and specialized, resonating with smaller, more tightly knit communities. Today's consumers are holding brands and influencers accountable, demanding transparency, ethical business principles and authentic engagement – a trend that signals an era of recalibrated expectations.

Influencer fatigue and the quest for quality over quantity

The rapid proliferation of influencers and brand endorsements across social media platforms has led to what's now being termed 'influencer fatigue'. Audiences, once captivated by the glamour and exclusivity of influencer-driven content, are growing weary of repetitive posts, predictable formats and seemingly endless product promotions.

The path forward will likely see a consolidation of the influencer space, where only the most unique, entertaining and authentic voices hold sway. The parallels to retail are clear: just as consumers gravitate towards more curated, boutique shopping experiences, they are also seeking influencers who offer fresh insights, real expertise and meaningful relationships.

The role of data and technology in shaping the future of influence in retail

In today's digital world, data has evolved from a passive asset to a powerful driver of strategy. For brands navigating the shifting terrain of influencer marketing, data offers a way to dig beneath surface-level metrics and understand what truly resonates with consumers.

Brands are no longer just measuring influence through followers or likes; they're analysing deeper metrics such as engagement, demographics and content performance to ensure that marketing budgets are used effectively. The integration of AI and machine learning now enables brands to process and analyse this data at a scale previously unimaginable.

As we see the constant evolvement in this arena, the skill of data interpretation – knowing how to translate insights into impactful marketing strategies – will become invaluable. Brands that can connect the dots between data and consumer behaviour will stand out, creating more personalized and effective campaigns. For instance, by honing in on what truly matters to their audiences, brands can elevate their reach beyond what's possible with traditional influencer models alone.

Retailers who understand the unique insights hidden within their data are poised to excel in the years ahead. By marrying data-driven strategy with human insights, brands can position themselves as leaders in the new age of retail influence.

The continued rise of TikTok Shopping: Redefining retail influence

TikTok has become a major force reshaping the retail landscape, merging entertainment with commerce through TikTok Shopping. The app's 'What's Next Shopping Trend Report' reveals the platform's rapid growth as a shopping hub, highlighting how users are more likely to discover, engage with and purchase products directly through the app's unique shopping format. With 62 per cent of TikTok users stating they feel more connected to brands that interact with them, TikTok has positioned itself as an authentic space where brand–consumer relationships flourish.[20]

Yet, this should be seen not as the final evolution of digital retail influence, but as one part of a larger journey. While TikTok Shopping's format is currently revolutionizing consumer engagement and purchase behaviour, future technologies will undoubtedly emerge, offering new ways to deepen customer connections. For brands, staying nimble and ready to adapt to the unknown remains key, even as they embrace the opportunities that platforms like TikTok present.

Balancing tech and human connection in the age of AI-powered influence

With advancements like AI-powered chatbots and virtual influencers, brands face new opportunities – and challenges – in shaping retail influence. While these tools offer streamlined, data-driven insights, they raise questions about authenticity. As these technologies gain traction, the role of human connection in influencer marketing becomes increasingly complex. The key to future success will lie in finding the optimal balance where technology enhances but doesn't replace the invaluable human touch.

The path ahead for retail influence: Embracing a new era of community and values-based marketing

Looking to the future, the potential of influencer marketing as a tool for retail remains significant, but the rules of engagement are changing. Retailers that wish to stay relevant must embrace a values-based approach that fosters community, transparency and authenticity. Brands that succeed in this new era will be those that choose their partnerships carefully, aligning with impact influencers who share their core values and are willing to champion causes that resonate with their audiences.

The impact influencer heralds a shift in what it means to be influential. In this new era, success is no longer defined by the size of the follower count but by the quality of engagement and the positive impact on society. As consumers grow more discerning, the influence wielded by these new, purpose-driven voices will only become stronger.

As we close this chapter, it becomes evident that influencer and celebrity endorsements are deeply woven into consumer habits and brand perception. The journey from historical endorsements by royalty to today's digital influencers shows a lasting appeal for figures who represent trust, prestige and aspiration. This chapter traced how the psychology of influence has endured through media and cultural shifts, with modern social media influencers and niche advocates now commanding the type of trust once reserved for royalty or Hollywood icons.

Today's consumers, especially younger generations, navigate a landscape where personal recommendations, peer testimonials and relatability carry as much weight as fame. The brands that succeed are those that balance authenticity with innovation, fostering loyalty through both established and emerging influence channels.

As Emmanuel Eribo, co-founder of LØCI, reflects on the journey of building a brand in the heart of this changing retail landscape, he provides a unique lens on the role of influence today. Emphasizing the importance of authenticity and values, Eribo speaks to the delicate balance of establishing credibility while remaining true to brand ethos. At LØCI, influence isn't just about reaching consumers but about inspiring a conscious and connected community that supports both the brand and its mission.

REAL-WORLD EXAMPLE
Emmanuel Eribo, Co-founder and CEO of LØCI

Kate Hardcastle

(KH): Emmanuel, LØCI is an exciting brand that has made waves in both the sustainability space and the sneaker world, especially with your high-profile partnerships. But what strikes me most is how well you seem to understand the science of shopping itself. Can you talk to us about how LØCI taps into the consumer psyche so effectively?

Emmanuel Eribo

(EE): Thanks Kate. It's been quite the journey! When we started LØCI, we knew we wanted to be more than just a sneaker brand. From day one, we focused on understanding why people shop the way they do. This isn't just about buying a product – it's about making a statement, about identity. For us, it was crucial to tap into the emotions behind purchasing decisions, especially with a growing audience who are not just conscious about fashion but also deeply concerned about the environment.

The science of shopping is fascinating because it's not just rational – it's emotional. When people buy LØCI sneakers, they're not just thinking about comfort or style. They're making a choice that reflects their values, especially when it comes to sustainability. That's why we've been so intentional about how we communicate what LØCI stands for. We've combined the science of decision making with our commitment to sustainability, and I think that's what has resonated with people.

KH: You've hit the nail on the head there. Many brands fail to grasp the deeper emotional and psychological triggers behind a purchase. What specific strategies have you employed to ensure LØCI strikes that balance between function, fashion and sustainability?

EE: One of the first things we focused on was transparency. We know from research that today's consumers – especially millennials and Gen Z – are hyper-aware of greenwashing. They don't just want to hear that a brand is sustainable; they want to see the data, the proof. So, we laid everything bare – our materials, our processes and even where we could improve. That honesty has built trust with our customers. They know we're not perfect, but we're striving every day to be better.

We also understand that consumers are driven by experiences. LØCI isn't just about sneakers – it's about the lifestyle around it. The brand has enjoyed celebrity A-list support too, from actor and environmental campaigner Leonardo DiCaprio and musician and entrepreneur Nicki Minaj both taking an interest in the business. We're curating an experience that our customers want to be part of. These collaborations aren't just endorsements – they're about creating a community, a shared mission.

KH: You've touched on partnerships, which leads me to one of LØCI's defining moments – your collaboration with Leonardo DiCaprio. It wasn't just another celebrity partnership. It was rooted in shared values around sustainability. How do you decide which partnerships to pursue, and how do you ensure they align with LØCI's mission?

EE: That's a great question. We've always been very selective about who we work with. For us, it's not about slapping a celebrity's name on our product – it's about creating meaningful partnerships that elevate our mission. When we partnered with Leonardo, it wasn't about getting a big name for publicity. It was about the fact that he's been advocating for environmental causes for decades. His values were already in line with what we stand for.

Before we work with anyone, we ask ourselves a few key questions: Do they care about sustainability? Do they share our vision for ethical fashion? Are they invested in the long term, or are they just looking for a quick deal? That's how we ensure every partnership is rooted in authenticity. It's why people trust us when we say we're committed to sustainability – they know we mean it.

KH: And it's clearly working! You've gained quite a loyal following. What's interesting is that your products are premium, yet you manage to attract customers who care about both luxury and sustainability. How do you strike that balance between exclusivity and accessibility?

EE: That's one of the biggest challenges, to be honest. Sustainability is often seen as a luxury – something that comes with a higher price tag. But we've worked hard to ensure that we're accessible while still maintaining the quality and craftsmanship that people expect from a premium brand.

We do this in a few ways. First, we've streamlined our operations to cut unnecessary costs. Second, we offer a direct-to-consumer model, which allows us to keep our prices more competitive while maintaining the luxury aspect of the product. And third, we're transparent about where every dollar is going. When consumers know they're paying for sustainably sourced materials and ethical manufacturing, they're more willing to invest in something that aligns with their values.

KH: Transparency really does seem to be a central theme for LØCI. But beyond materials and production, you also seem to have a strong grasp of behavioural economics – the idea that people don't always make decisions based on logic, but rather emotion and identity. How has that shaped LØCI's brand identity?

EE: Behavioural economics is a huge part of our strategy. People buy things for emotional reasons first and justify them with logic afterwards. When someone buys a pair of LØCI sneakers, they're not just buying footwear. They're buying into a movement – a set of beliefs. It's about belonging to a community of people who care about the planet, who want to make a positive impact. That's why the storytelling around our brand is so important.

Our customers want to know that they're contributing to something bigger than themselves. So, we make sure that every touchpoint – whether it's our social media, our packaging or our partnerships – communicates that shared mission. It's not just about selling shoes; it's about building a brand that people feel proud to be associated with.

KH: That emotional connection is so powerful, especially in today's market. I also noticed how quickly LØCI caught on to the concept of fluidity in shopping behaviour. You've blended both online and offline experiences effortlessly, from your website to pop-ups. How have you mastered that fluidity?

EE: The key is understanding that consumers don't see online and offline as separate any more. To them, it's all part of one continuous experience. We realized early on that the future of retail was hybrid. That's why we've invested in making our website as immersive as possible, while still maintaining the personal touch in our physical experiences, whether it's through pop-ups or collaborations with local stores.

KH: I love that you mention excitement. Consumers today, particularly younger generations, crave novelty and excitement. How do you ensure that LØCI continues to capture that excitement, while staying true to your sustainability mission?

EE: It's a fine balance. We want to be exciting, but we don't want to follow trends for the sake of it. Instead, we focus on innovation – whether that's in design, materials or the partnerships we form. We're constantly experimenting with new ways to integrate sustainability into our products.

For instance, we recently started using algae-based materials in some of our sneakers. This is not just a gimmick – it's a genuine solution to the problem of unsustainable materials in fashion. When we tell our customers that they're wearing sneakers made from ocean waste, it adds a layer of engagement because they feel like they're part of a solution, not just another trend.

KH: That's an incredible example of how innovation and sustainability can go hand in hand. But with so many brands jumping on the eco-friendly bandwagon, how do you differentiate LØCI and ensure you stay ahead of the curve?

EE: For us, it always comes back to authenticity. Sustainability must be more than a marketing buzzword. We're not just looking to tick boxes; we want to push the boundaries of what's possible. That means being transparent about where we're doing well, and where we still need to improve. We engage with our customers honestly, and we're not afraid to admit when we don't have all the answers.

Beyond that, we focus on staying innovative. We're constantly researching new materials, new manufacturing processes and new ways to reduce our footprint. At the same time, we're staying true to our design ethos – creating shoes that people want to wear, not just because they're sustainable, but because they're stylish and comfortable, too.

KH: Emmanuel, thank you for your insights. It's inspiring to hear how LØCI has managed to blend sustainability with innovation and emotional engagement so seamlessly. I can't wait to see what's next for the brand.

Key interview takeaways

1 **Emotional and identity-driven purchases:** Eribo highlighted that consumers choose LØCI sneakers as an expression of their values, connecting purchases to identity rather than pure utility – emphasizing the need for brands to tap into emotional motivators.

2 **Transparency as a trust-building strategy:** LØCI's commitment to transparency about materials and processes builds consumer trust, acknowledging that today's consumers, especially Gen Z, are wary of greenwashing and seek authenticity.

3   **Meaningful celebrity partnerships:** Eribo shared that LØCI's collaboration with celebrities is not just about publicity but shared values, demonstrating how partnerships with aligned figures can deepen consumer trust and brand mission.

4   **Sustainability meets luxury:** LØCI bridges sustainability with premium quality by refining operational efficiencies and educating consumers on where their spending goes, making eco-friendly products appealing without compromising on quality or accessibility.

5   **Balancing innovation with consistency:** LØCI stays ahead by experimenting with sustainable materials like algae-based fabrics, reinforcing its commitment to environmental solutions while delivering stylish, comfortable products that reflect the brand's core ethos.

KEY TAKEAWAYS

1   **Enduring influence of celebrity endorsements:** From Josiah Wedgwood's royal endorsement in the 18th century to Kim Kardashian's multi-billion-dollar SKIMS brand, celebrity influence has long shaped consumer perceptions, with each era adapting the psychology of trust to its cultural context.

2   **Rise of social media influencers and authenticity:** The shift from traditional celebrities to social media influencers has added layers of relatability and authenticity. Followers today are more likely to trust influencers who feel like peers, creating a unique bond that traditional advertisements struggle to achieve.

3   **Influence of micro- and nano-influencers:** With highly engaged and niche audiences, smaller influencers often wield more trust and relevancy, allowing brands to connect with specific demographics effectively and build community-driven loyalty.

4   **Community and peer-to-peer marketing:** The rise of platforms like LEGO's 'LEGO Ideas' and Amazon's robust review systems highlights the shift towards community advocacy, where loyal customers act as brand advocates, enhancing trust and engagement.

5   **Impact of technological advances:** As influencer marketing evolves, the integration of AI, blockchain and immersive experiences (like AR/VR) are shaping new ways for brands to foster trust and engagement, redefining the future of influencer-driven retail.

References

1 Newman Staff (2024) Celebrity endorsements: The influence and challenges of famous faces in marketing, Birmingham Newman University, 5 July, www.newman.ac.uk/news/celebrity-endorsements-the-influence-and-challenges-of-famous-faces-in-marketing (archived at https://perma.cc/WRG6-JBCD)

2 Wedgewood (nd) The Wedgewood Story, www.wedgwood.com/en-gb/welcometowedgwood/the-wedgewood-story (archived at https://perma.cc/4ZJG-B3QZ)

3 Royal Warrant Holders Association (nd) History, www.royalwarrant.org/#history (archived at https://perma.cc/8TAF-ZASY)

4 The Coca-Cola Company (nd) Did CocaCola invent santa? www.coca-colacompany.com/about-us/faq/did-coca-cola-invent-santa (archived at https://perma.cc/A35M-ZGQF)

5 Nielsen (2012) Consumer trust in online, social and mobile advertising grows, April, www.nielsen.com/insights/2012/consumer-trust-in-online-social-and-mobile-advertising-grows (archived at https://perma.cc/X92Y-3YKG)

6 Forbes (nd) Huda Kattan, www.forbes.com/profile/huda-kattan (archived at https://perma.cc/HJH2-G5RV)

7 Forbes (nd) Kim Kardashian,www.forbes.com/profile/kim-kardashian (archived at https://perma.cc/23DS-25U6)

8 Influencer Marketing Hub (2024) The State of Influencer Marketing 2024, https://influencermarketinghub.com/influencer-marketing-benchmark-report-2024 (archived at https://perma.cc/V3M7-TTUZ)

9 Briggs, Fiona (2024) 89 per cent of consumers trust recommendations above all other advertising channels, *Retail Times*, www.retailtimes.co.uk/89-of-consumers-trust-recommendations-above-all-other-advertising-channels (archived at https://perma.cc/NJ4W-HRZA)

10 BBC (2017) Toy company Lego to produce Women of NASA set, *BBC News*, 1 March, www.bbc.com/news/world-europe-39129674 (archived at https://perma.cc/DE32-Y2Z9)

11 Edelman (2019) In Brands We Trust? 2019 Edelman Trust Barometer special report, www.edelman.com/sites/g/files/aatuss191/files/2019-07/2019_edelman_trust_barometer_special_report_in_brands_we_trust_executive_summary.pdf (archived at https://perma.cc/QYW5-J7ZG)

12 Northwestern University (nd) How online reviews influence sales, Medill Spiegel Research Center, https://spiegel.medill.northwestern.edu/how-online-reviews-influence-sales (archived at https://perma.cc/DUA6-HXJF)

13 Neate, Rupert (2020) Ryan Kaji, 9, earns $29.5m as this year's highest-paid YouTuber, *Guardian*, 18 December, www.theguardian.com/technology/2020/dec/18/ryan-kaji-9-earns-30m-as-this-years-highest-paid-youtuber (archived at https://perma.cc/A2KT-UA42)

14 Funko (2020) Funko reports fourth quarter and fiscal 2019 financial results, press release, 5 March, https://investor.funko.com/news-and-events/press-releases/Press-Releases/2020/Funko-Reports-Fourth-Quarter-and-Fiscal-2019-Financial-Results/default.aspx (archived at https://perma.cc/7SRR-5U8L)

15 Farr, Adrienne (2023) Jackie Aina doesn't think talent is enough when it comes to finding success, *InStyle*, 9 August

16 Blanco, Lydia T (2024) Jackie Aina's FORVR Mood is a charge to live and do business by Design, *Forbes*, 5 April, www.forbes.com/sites/lydiatblanco/2024/04/05/jackie-ainas-forvr-mood-is-a-charge-to-live-and-do-business-by-design (archived at https://perma.cc/3ARH-YTY9)

17 Kirkpatrick, David (2016) Micro-influencers have major impact on buying behavior: Study, *Marketing Dive*, 31 March, www.marketingdive.com/news/micro-influencers-have-major-impact-on-buying-behavior-study/416579 (archived at https://perma.cc/R245-G8AY)

18 Kuzminov, M (2023) Consumer trust and virtual influencers, *Forbes*, 29 March, www.forbes.com/councils/forbesagencycouncil/2023/03/29/consumer-trust-and-virtual-influencers (archived at https://perma.cc/V7EF-7ABC)

19 Edelman (2023) 2023 Edelman Trust Barometer Special Report: The collapse of the purchase funnel, Edelman Trust institute, www.edelman.com/trust/2023/trust-barometer/special-report-brand-trust (archived at https://perma.cc/PKY6-Y64Q)

20 Savage, Olivia (nd) TikTok and commerce: 4 reasons why brands succeed with 'shoptainment', impact.com, https://impact.com/influencer/tiktok-and-commerce-4-reasons-why-brands-succeed-with-shoptainment (archived at https://perma.cc/CVR5-FF5A)

8

Goldilocks and the pricing strategy

Finding a price point that's just right

The psychology of pricing: A personal perspective

Pricing. It's the first thing that catches our eye when we walk into a store, scan a website or pick up a product. Yet, most of us don't stop to think about the intricacies that go into setting that number. As consumers, we believe we're making rational decisions, weighing cost against value. But in truth, every price tag is a carefully calculated tool designed to engage our senses, appeal to our emotions and, yes, guide our wallets. The difference between a price that feels 'just right' and one that feels too high or too low isn't random – it's often the result of sophisticated psychology.

Here's a confession. As someone who's been around the retail block more than a few times, I'll admit to being wise to the allure of strategic pricing. Years of hard experience in the retail industry have taught me that price isn't just about numbers; it is about perception, emotion, and ultimately, the permission we give ourselves to spend. Yet, even now, as a parent, I'm continually surprised by how easily pricing strategies can still influence buying decisions – my children's included.

The art of pricing is as much about human psychology as it is about economics. It is about how we feel when we see a price tag, how we rationalize our decisions and how retailers skilfully nudge us towards that all-important 'just right' price point. In this chapter, we'll explore the deep psychological underpinnings of pricing, and why even the savviest consumers can be swayed by a well-placed price tag.

As we journey through the science and art of pricing, you'll see how these numbers shape our experiences and influence our choices. The retail world is filled with subtle tricks and clever tactics, all meant to bring you to that

'Goldilocks' moment where the price feels perfect. And while these strategies may seem complex, they're often anchored in simple principles.

To help you navigate the path, here's a light-hearted glossary to get familiar with some key terms. Think of it as your 'insider's guide' to the strategies
retailers use to create an engaging, even enjoyable, pricing experience.

GLOSSARY OF KEY PRICING TERMS

Charm pricing: The subtle tactic where £9.99 feels worlds apart from £10.00.
This psychological trick leverages the tiny difference of one penny to make
a product feel more affordable than it is.

Dynamic pricing: Pricing that fluctuates in real time, based on demand,
competition or even external factors like the weather. It's a staple in digital
and e-commerce, with prices rising or dropping depending on market
conditions.

Goldilocks pricing: The pursuit of the 'just right' price that feels balanced –
not too high, not too low. This sweet spot is where consumers feel
comfortable making a purchase, convinced they're getting value without
overpaying.

Loss leader: A heavily discounted item designed to get you into the store or
onto the site. Once there, the retailer hopes you'll pick up additional
full-price items along the way.

Price anchoring: The display of a high-priced item next to a lower-priced one
to make the latter seem like a great deal. Imagine a £3,000 designer bag
next to a £300 option – the second bag suddenly seems much more
reasonable.

Now that you're armed with these essentials, let's dive into the intricacies of
pricing strategy and explore how retailers shape our shopping experiences,
guiding us to make purchases that feel 'just right'.

When we think about pricing, we often overlook the emotional journey
it involves. Pricing strategies are designed to tap into our emotions, creating
a sense of urgency, excitement, or even comfort. Consider the widespread
use of pricing that ends in .99. It is a tactic so ubiquitous that it is easy to
dismiss as insignificant. But research has shown that this tiny detail can
make a significant difference in how consumers perceive value. A price of
£9.99 feels psychologically lower than £10.00, even though the difference is

just one penny. It is a phenomenon known as 'left-digit bias,' where the left-most digit disproportionately impacts our perception of price.

This psychological manipulation is key in understanding why certain pricing tactics, such as this method – known as 'charm pricing', are so effective. Charm pricing is the simple tactic of a retailer pricing a product just below a round number, such as £19.99 instead of £20.00. This seemingly small difference plays a significant role in consumer decision-making. According to behavioural economist Richard Thaler, people tend to 'round down' prices subconsciously when the price is just below a round number, making the purchase decision feel more comfortable.[1]

However, psychological pricing isn't just about the small change. Retailers also use strategies like 'good, better, best' pricing to guide consumer choices. This tactic, often referred to as the 'Goldilocks effect', involves offering three tiers of products at different price points. Consumers generally gravitate towards the middle option because it feels like the best value – neither too cheap nor too expensive – it's 'just right', hence 'the Goldilocks effect'. It is a classic strategy seen across various industries, ranging as vastly from groceries through to higher-priced technology goods, where companies like Apple use it masterfully to steer customers towards mid-range products, which are often the most profitable.[2]

But pricing strategies go beyond just manipulating perceptions – they also tap into our deep-seated desire for a good deal. Retailers understand that consumers derive a sense of satisfaction and even delight from finding bargains. This is why sales and discounts are so effective. When we see a product with a slashed price, it triggers a response in our brains that tells us we're getting something valuable for less. It is not just about saving money; it is about the thrill of the hunt, the joy of winning a small victory in our everyday shopping.

As we move forward in this chapter, we'll delve deeper into how pricing has evolved over time, from the early days of the cash economy to the sophisticated strategies employed in today's retail environment. We'll also examine how pricing impacts consumer behaviour, and why it remains a crucial element in the retail experience.

The history of price-oriented retail strategies

To understand where we are today in the world of pricing, we need to take a step back and look at how price-oriented retail strategies have evolved over time. The concept of pricing is as old as trade itself, but the mainstream strategic use of pricing to influence consumer behaviour is a more modern phenomenon. The origins of price-oriented retail strategies can be traced back to the early 20th century when mass production and the rise of consumer culture began to reshape the retail landscape.

One of the earliest and most influential examples of price-oriented retailing is the 'five-and-dime' stores that emerged in the United States in the late 19th and early 20th centuries. These stores, like Woolworth's in the UK, offered a wide range of goods at fixed prices, with a limit of sixpence. The concept was revolutionary at the time because it made shopping predictable and affordable for the average consumer. These stores were the precursors to the modern-day pound shops and discount retailers that dominate the low-price segment of the market today.[3]

The idea of pricing goods at .99 or .95 rather than rounding up to the nearest pound also has its roots in this era. This tactic became widespread in the early 20th century to prevent theft by ensuring that cashiers had to open the register to give change, thus recording the sale. But it quickly became clear that this pricing strategy also had a psychological impact on consumers, making prices seem lower and more attractive. This method has persisted for decades and is still widely used in retail today.

As retail evolved, so too did the strategies around pricing. The mid-20th century saw the rise of big-box retailers and supermarkets, which introduced the concept of loss leaders – products sold at or below cost to draw customers into the store, like milk and bread. The idea was that once customers were in the store, they would make additional purchases at regular prices, offsetting the loss on the discounted items. This strategy is still used today, particularly in grocery stores where staple items like bread or milk are often priced low to attract shoppers.[4]

In the luxury market, pricing strategies can work a little differently. High-end retailers understood that price could be a symbol of status and exclusivity. This led to the development of premium pricing strategies, where high prices are used to create an aura of luxury and exclusivity around a product. This strategy is based on the idea that consumers associate higher prices with higher quality and are willing to pay more for products that convey status and prestige. Brands like Rolex, Hermès and Louis Vuitton have built their entire business models around this concept, creating products that are as much about the price tag as they are about the product itself.

Another significant development in retail pricing was the introduction of tiered pricing strategies. This concept involves offering different versions of a product at different price points, catering to a range of consumers with varying budgets. The automotive industry is a prime example of this strategy in action. When you see an advertisement for a car, the price quoted is often the base model, stripped of any luxury features. However, the car in the advertisement is usually a top-of-the-line model with all the bells and whistles. This creates a perception of affordability while simultaneously encouraging consumers to 'upgrade' to a more expensive version. This tiered pricing approach is used across various industries today, from technology to fashion.

As we explore the art of pricing in this chapter, it is important to recognize that while these strategies may result in maximizing profit, they are also geared to shaping consumer perception and behaviour. Whether it is the low prices of discount retailers or the high prices of luxury brands, the goal is the same: to create a sense of value that resonates with the consumer. As we move forward, we'll look at how these historical strategies have laid the foundation for the sophisticated pricing tactics used in retail today.

The psychological manipulation of pricing

A powerful psychological tool is the use of price anchoring. This involves placing a high-priced item next to a more reasonably priced one, making the latter seem like a better deal. Price anchoring works by creating a reference point in the consumer's mind. For instance. In a department store if we browsed to find a £3000 designer handbag next to a similar £300 version, the latter suddenly seems much more affordable, even if it is still expensive by most standards. This technique is particularly effective in environments where consumers are unsure of what constitutes a fair price but may well be seduced by luxurious surroundings and ambience. By anchoring consumer expectations to a higher price point, retailers make regular prices appear more attractive.

Now we understand the theories of charm pricing and price anchoring, let's talk about the strategy of price bundling. Bundling involves offering several products or services together at a single price point, often at a discount compared to purchasing each item separately. This tactic plays on the perception of value, making customers feel they are getting more for their money. Bundled pricing is common in the telecommunications industry, where companies bundle internet, phone and TV services together. The appeal of bundled pricing lies in its ability to make the overall package seem like a better deal, even if the consumer only needs one of the items included.

However, the psychological manipulation of pricing isn't just about what's on the price tag – it is also about how prices are presented. For instance, many online retailers now use dynamic pricing, where prices fluctuate based on demand, time of day and other factors. This technique creates a sense of urgency, encouraging consumers to make a purchase before the price goes up. It is a strategy commonly used in industries like travel, where flight and hotel prices can change multiple times a day. Dynamic pricing takes advantage of the fear of missing out (FOMO), pushing consumers to act quickly before they miss a perceived good deal. This strategy is particularly prevalent in the travel sector and, of course, concert and event ticket sales.

The 'decoy effect' is another psychological tactic, and in that case retailers introduce a third, less attractive option to nudge consumers towards choosing the more expensive of the two other options. This is particularly effective in settings where consumers might be torn between two choices. By introducing a decoy – a product that is priced close to the higher option but offers far less value – retailers can guide consumers to see the higher-priced item as the better deal. This technique is often used in subscription services, where companies offer multiple tiers of service, with the middle option being the most popular, thanks to the presence of a deliberately unattractive 'decoy' tier. This can be seen in play as part of the Goldilocks effect to bolster chances of the middle or higher option being selected.

One of the more controversial aspects of psychological pricing is its impact on consumer trust. While these strategies can be effective in driving sales, they can also lead to consumer scepticism if overused. For example, constant markdowns and sales can create a perception that the regular prices are inflated, leading consumers to doubt the value of the product. This has been particularly problematic in the fashion industry, where frequent sales events have trained consumers to wait for discounts rather than pay full price. As a result, brands must strike a delicate balance between using psychological pricing to boost sales and maintaining the integrity of their pricing strategies to build and sustain consumer trust.

As we delve further into the nuances of pricing, it becomes clear that while these tactics can significantly influence consumer behaviour, they also require a thoughtful and balanced approach to maintain long-term success and consumer loyalty. Retailers must be mindful of the potential downsides of these strategies, ensuring that they do not undermine the trust and loyalty they seek to build with their customers.

REAL-WORLD EXAMPLE

Death by Blue Cross: The perils of perpetual discounting

The story of Debenhams, once a giant of British retail, serves as a prime example of the dangers inherent in the overuse of discounting and sales. The department store, which had been a fixture on the UK high street for over two centuries, became increasingly reliant on its infamous 'Blue Cross Sales' in its later years. These events, characterized by their deep discounts and heavy promotional campaigns, were initially successful in driving footfall. However, over time the constant sales began to erode the perceived value of the brand. What was once an occasional treat for bargain hunters became a constant expectation, ultimately leading to a devastating cycle that contributed to the store's downfall.

The erosion of value through perpetual discounting

Debenhams's reliance on frequent sales events like the Blue Cross Sales created a culture where consumers became conditioned to wait for discounts rather than purchasing items at full price. This expectation of constant sales led to a devaluation of the products themselves. Consumers began to perceive the regular prices as inflated, and the once prestigious brand became synonymous with discount shopping. The regularity of these sales undermined the brand's pricing strategy, resulting in reduced margins and an inability to invest in other areas of the business, such as store refurbishments and staff training.

This phenomenon wasn't unique to Debenhams. The concept of perpetual discounting has plagued many retailers that overuse sales as a primary driver of traffic. The overemphasis on discounts can create a short-term boost in sales but at the cost of long-term brand equity. Shoppers begin to associate the brand with cheapness rather than quality, and paying full price becomes almost unthinkable. This strategy is a far cry from the carefully managed sales periods that once characterized the retail calendar, where discounts were a way to clear end-of-season stock, rather than a constant fixture.

REAL-WORLD EXAMPLE
Sears: A parallel story across the Atlantic

Sears, once the largest retailer in the United States, faced a similar fate. Like Debenhams, Sears became overly reliant on constant sales and markdowns to drive footfall. The frequent sales events created a sense of desperation, with stores often cluttered with clearance items that no one seemed to want. The perpetual discounting contributed to a decline in consumer trust and an overall devaluation of the brand, leading to a loss of market share and, ultimately, the company's downfall.

Sears's downfall, much like Debenhams, highlights the risks associated with overusing discounts as a primary retail strategy. When a brand becomes too dependent on sales, it risks alienating consumers who no longer see value in the regular prices. This can lead to a vicious cycle where sales become necessary to move inventory, but each sale further erodes the brand's value, leading to a slow but steady decline.

So how does this work for some?

REAL WORLD EXAMPLE
TK Maxx (TJ Maxx, US)

Interestingly, while Debenhams suffered from this discounting strategy, other brands like TK Maxx have thrived using a similar model. The difference lies in the perception and the business model. TK Maxx is built on the concept of offering brand-name goods at lower prices, creating a treasure hunt experience for its customers. Shoppers enter TK Maxx expecting to find deals, and the store delivers by offering a constantly changing assortment of products at reduced prices. This is a core part of TK Maxx's identity, and consumers don't see the discounts as devaluing the brand because the brand's value is based on the idea of finding great deals. Indeed, in one UK advertisement for TK Maxx, the concept of 'TK Maxxing' and how to do it right (and wrong) has been promoted, creating a verb around the action of discount shopping. The brand to this day promotes range categories such as 'Treasures', the idea of a valuable find.

The key difference is that for the TK/TJ Maxx model, discounting is not a sales event; it is the entire business model. The store buys surplus stock from manufacturers and passes the savings on to consumers. In contrast, for a store like Debenhams, the discounts were an attempt to clear excess stock that had been overpriced to begin with. The constant sales diluted the brand, whereas for TK Maxx, it is a business strategy that creates customer loyalty and consistent foot traffic.

The shift to online clearance and outlet stores

As department stores grapple with the challenges posed by perpetual discounting, many have shifted their clearance activities online or to purpose-built outlet stores. This allows them to maintain the integrity of their primary brand while still offering deep discounts. For example, brands like Ralph Lauren and Coach operate outlet stores where they can sell last season's items or surplus stock at reduced prices without affecting the pricing structure or aesthetics of their mainline stores. This strategy allows them to cater to discount shoppers without diluting the value of their flagship brand.

REAL-WORLD EXAMPLE

Value retail and the success of Bicester Village

The shift to premium outlets with an experience-driven model

In the rapidly evolving retail landscape, Value Retail's Bicester Village has emerged as a trailblazer in outlet shopping. Unlike traditional outlets that focus solely on offering discounts, Bicester Village has redefined the concept by combining luxury brands with an immersive shopping experience. This unique approach has transformed it into a global destination, attracting millions of visitors annually from more than 120 countries.

Bicester Village, in Oxfordshire, UK is home to more than 160 high-end brands, including Gucci, Prada, Burberry and Dior. However, the focus isn't just on clearing surplus inventory; instead, the outlet carefully curates its merchandise to reflect the prestige of its participating brands. By doing so, Bicester ensures that discounts are appealing without compromising the sense of exclusivity and value that these brands embody. This careful curation is critical to the outlet's success, as it allows luxury retailers to participate confidently without fearing damage to their core brand.

The experience at Bicester Village goes far beyond the products on offer. The outlet is designed to resemble a charming British countryside village, with picturesque architecture, beautifully landscaped pathways and a focus on ambience. This attention to detail creates an inviting environment that feels far removed from the utilitarian style of conventional outlet malls. Shopping at Bicester is not just a transaction – it is an event, encouraging visitors to linger, explore and indulge.

Another factor that sets Bicester Village apart is its global appeal. Through strategic marketing, Value Retail has positioned it as a must-visit destination for international tourists. Features like multilingual staff, tax-free shopping services and exclusive VIP perks cater to the needs of affluent travellers, particularly those from China, the Middle East and the United States. These tailored services, combined with partnerships with travel companies and luxury hospitality providers, have helped cement Bicester Village's reputation as a leader in retail tourism.

One of Bicester's most significant achievements is its ability to preserve the integrity of the brands it hosts. By managing the perception of discounts as rare opportunities in a premium setting, the outlet reassures luxury brands that their equity will remain intact. In fact, many brands see their participation at Bicester as complementary to their flagship stores and online operations. The outlet serves as an entry point for new customers who may later purchase full-price items, creating a cycle of brand engagement that benefits all parties involved.

The success of Bicester Village also stems from its customer-centric approach. From valet parking and personal shopping services to gourmet dining options, every element is designed to enhance the visitor experience. This commitment to excellence encourages loyalty, making Bicester Village a favourite destination for both value-conscious shoppers and those seeking a taste of luxury.

The Bicester Village model offers valuable lessons for the retail industry. By elevating the outlet experience and creating a seamless blend of affordability and aspiration, Value Retail has demonstrated that discounts need not come at the expense of brand equity. Retailers can learn from this approach, particularly the importance of creating an environment that complements their brand values and attracts a diverse audience.

The move to online clearance sales also offers significant advantages. By moving discounts online, retailers can segment their customer base more effectively, offering deals to price-sensitive shoppers without eroding the value perception among their core customers. Online clearance sections can be more discreet, and the segmentation of these customers allows the main brand to continue positioning itself as premium in physical stores. Furthermore, online platforms can offer retailers greater flexibility in managing inventory and pricing strategies, adjusting prices in real time based on demand and stock levels.

Discounting: It is all in the delicate balance

The experiences of Debenhams and Sears serve as stark reminders that while discounting can be an effective short-term strategy, it must be managed carefully to avoid long-term damage to the brand. Retailers must strike a delicate balance between offering value to customers and maintaining the integrity of their pricing strategies. Brands like TK Maxx demonstrate that discounting can be a successful business model when it is part of the brand's identity. However, for traditional department stores, the shift towards online clearance and outlet stores represents a necessary evolution to protect the main brand from the pitfalls of perpetual discounting.

> **The lesson here is clear:** discounting should be used strategically, not as a crutch. When done correctly, it can drive traffic and boost sales without compromising the brand's overall value. But when overused, it can lead to a slow erosion of trust and, eventually, the demise of the business.

The evolution of dynamic and real-time pricing

In recent years, the advent of digital technologies has revolutionized the way retailers approach pricing, giving rise to dynamic and real-time pricing strategies that allow prices to fluctuate based on a variety of factors. Dynamic pricing, often referred to as surge pricing, is a strategy where prices are adjusted in real time in response to changes in supply and demand, competitor pricing and other external factors. This strategy, though not entirely new, has been significantly enhanced by advancements in data analytics and artificial intelligence (AI).

Dynamic pricing is most famously used by companies like Amazon and Uber, where prices can change within minutes depending on demand and market conditions. For example, during peak shopping times, such as Black Friday or Cyber Monday, Amazon's algorithms may raise prices on high-demand items to maximize profits, while lowering prices on less popular items to clear inventory. This pricing model is not static; it is a fluid system that responds to market behaviour in real time, making it incredibly effective in maximizing revenue.[5]

One of the significant advantages of dynamic pricing is its ability to optimize pricing for different customer segments. For instance, airlines have long used dynamic pricing to offer different prices for the same seat on a flight depending on when and how the ticket is purchased, and through which platform. Early bookers may get lower prices, while last-minute buyers might pay a premium. This pricing strategy leverages the urgency and willingness to pay of different consumer groups, thus maximizing revenue. However, this approach can sometimes backfire, leading to customer dissatisfaction if consumers perceive the pricing as unfair or manipulative.

Real-time pricing is an extension of dynamic pricing, where prices are adjusted instantly based on data inputs such as inventory levels, competitor prices and consumer behaviour. This strategy is particularly effective in online retail, where retailers can monitor competitors' prices and adjust their own prices accordingly to remain competitive. Retail giants like Walmart and Best Buy have adopted real-time pricing to stay ahead in the highly competitive retail market, using sophisticated algorithms to ensure that their prices are always competitive.[6]

The concept of dynamic and real-time pricing is a powerful tool that leverages consumer behaviour, market conditions and technological advancements to adjust prices in response to demand and supply fluctuations. This approach is increasingly driven by AI and machine learning, allowing retailers to predict consumer behaviour with remarkable accuracy and adjust prices dynamically to optimize both sales and customer satisfaction. However, the implications of such strategies are multifaceted, particularly when considering the fine balance required to maintain consumer trust.

But surely you wouldn't pay more for the exact same item willingly, would you? It is interesting how many of us do just that.

Weather as a pricing influence

One significant and often underappreciated factor in dynamic pricing is the impact of weather on consumer demand. For instance, during my time working on a BBC news programme, we explored how something as constant and seemingly innocuous as the weather can drastically influence retail trends and interviewed businesses whose sole purpose is the analysis and trend prediction of weather for retailers.[7]

On a sunny day, demand for certain products, such as ice cream, cold beverages and barbecue supplies, can skyrocket. Retailers that can respond quickly to these shifts by adjusting prices can capitalize on this sudden surge in demand. Conversely, on cold or rainy days, products like hot drinks, soups and cozy indoor items might see an uptick in sales. This responsiveness to environmental factors is key to the future of dynamic pricing and of course the product's placement in store, online and on social media – allowing retailers to be more agile and customer focused. Similarly, extreme weather conditions like a snowstorm can boost sales of certain items like snow shovels, winter coats and canned goods, as people prepare to hunker down, but it can also deter shoppers from visiting stores altogether, impacting foot traffic and in-store sales.

Retailers that have learnt to harness this information effectively can tailor their marketing and inventory strategies accordingly. For example, a retailer might ramp up promotions on barbecue grills and picnic supplies in anticipation of a warm weekend forecast, or discount winter coats earlier in the season if a mild winter is predicted.

More sophisticated retailers are now using real-time weather data as part of their dynamic pricing strategies. By integrating weather forecasts with inventory management systems, retailers can adjust prices on the fly to match expected demand. For instance, an outdoor gear retailer might lower prices on rain jackets ahead of a predicted storm to move inventory quickly, while a sporting goods store could increase prices on summer sports equipment during an unexpected heatwave.

REAL-WORLD EXAMPLE

Bravissimo and weather-based marketing in action

Bravissimo, a leading lingerie and swimwear retailer in the UK, provides an excellent example of how weather-based marketing can significantly impact sales. By dynamically adjusting its marketing messages based on local weather conditions, Bravissimo achieved a significant increase in both online engagement and sales.

When the weather was warm, Bravissimo would emphasize its swimwear and lighter lingerie collections, with tailored messaging that resonated with customers enjoying the sunshine. Conversely, during colder periods, the focus would shift to more insulated and comfort-oriented products, ensuring that the brand remained relevant regardless of the weather outside.

This targeted approach yielded impressive results. According to a case study by WeatherAds, Bravissimo saw a 600 per cent increase in pay-per-click-driven sales revenue, and a conversion rate of browsers to buyers increasing by 103 per cent when utilizing weather-based marketing tactics. This demonstrates how aligning marketing strategies with real-time environmental factors can not only enhance customer relevance but also drive substantial financial returns.[8]

The key takeaway from Bravissimo's experience is that weather-based marketing is not just a trendy gimmick; it is a powerful tool that can significantly enhance the effectiveness of marketing campaigns. By understanding and anticipating the impact of weather on consumer behaviour, retailers can craft more relevant, timely and engaging marketing messages that resonate with their target audience and drive sales.

Retailers should consider investing in weather-based marketing tools and strategies, especially if they operate in sectors where consumer demand fluctuates with the weather.

Looking ahead, the integration of AI and machine learning with weather data will likely make these strategies even more affordable, precise and effective. Imagine a future where your favourite retailer sends you a personalized offer for sunscreen and beachwear, with guaranteed speedy delivery, the day before a predicted heatwave, or a discount on hot chocolate and blankets just before the cold front moves in. This kind of hyper-relevant marketing, powered by real-time data, is where the future of retail is headed.

However, the widespread use of dynamic and real-time pricing raises ethical concerns, particularly around transparency and consumer trust. Critics argue that these pricing strategies can lead to price discrimination, where different consumers are charged different prices for the same product based on their browsing history, location or even device type. This has sparked debates around the fairness of dynamic pricing, with some advocating for greater transparency in how prices are set and adjusted in real time.

As retailers embrace these sophisticated strategies, I believe they must also ensure that they maintain a greater level of transparency and fairness in their pricing. Dynamic pricing should enhance the shopping experience, not lead to a perception of constant opportunism. As with any powerful tool, the key is to use it judiciously, always with the consumer's best interest in mind.

Click to subscribe: Lessons in subscription pricing

One of the key psychological pricing strategies that has gained traction in the digital age is the use of subscription models. Services like Netflix, Spotify and Amazon Prime have popularized the subscription model, where consumers pay a recurring fee to access a product or service. The psychological appeal of subscription pricing lies in its perceived value and convenience.

Consumers are more likely to perceive a monthly fee of £9.99 as affordable, compared to a one-time payment of £120, even though the annual cost is the same. This strategy taps into the concept of mental accounting, where consumers mentally categorize and evaluate their spending in ways that make recurring payments feel less burdensome

The rise and rise of subscription models in modern retail pricing

Subscription models have also transformed the landscape of consumer goods retail, offering a unique pricing strategy that not only locks in customers but also creates a sense of exclusivity and value. By providing products and services through subscriptions, companies can establish a recurring revenue stream while delivering convenience and personalized experiences to their customers. This approach has become especially popular in sectors like coffee, meal prep and beauty, where perceived value often exceeds the actual cost of the products.

REAL-WORLD EXAMPLE

Grind Coffee London: Revolutionizing coffee consumption

Grind Coffee London, a major disruptor in the coffee industry, exemplifies the effectiveness of the subscription model. Founded in 2011, Grind started as a single café in Shoreditch and quickly expanded into a chain known for its high-quality coffee and vibrant atmosphere. Recognizing the growing trend towards at-home coffee consumption, particularly post the Covid-19 pandemic, Grind launched a subscription service for its compostable coffee pods.

The subscription model allows customers to receive a regular supply of coffee pods delivered directly to their doors, creating a convenient alternative to purchasing pods from the store. Customers can choose the frequency of deliveries, ensuring they never run out of their favourite coffee. Additionally, the subscription comes with a discount, compared to one-time purchases, making it feel like a special deal. This approach not only locks in customers for the long term but also cultivates a sense of belonging to the Grind community.

One of the most significant factors contributing to the success of Grind's subscription service is the emphasis on sustainability. Grind's pods are fully compostable, appealing to environmentally conscious consumers who want to reduce their carbon footprint. The combination of convenience, sustainability and perceived value has helped Grind's subscription model thrive, demonstrating the power of aligning pricing strategies with consumer values.

Meal prep subscriptions: Convenience over cost

The meal prep industry has seen a significant surge in popularity, with companies like HelloFresh, Blue Apron and Gousto leading the charge. These services offer weekly subscriptions that deliver pre-portioned ingredients and recipes directly to customers' homes, simplifying the cooking process and saving time.

While meal prep subscriptions are often more expensive than buying the same ingredients from a supermarket, their appeal lies in the convenience they offer. Consumers are not just paying for the food itself but for the time saved in meal planning, shopping and preparation. This shift in value perception has allowed meal prep companies to charge premium prices for what is essentially a curated grocery service.

Moreover, meal prep subscriptions tap into the growing trend of health-conscious eating. Many services offer options for specific dietary needs, such as vegan, gluten-free or low-carb diets. This level of customization adds to the perceived value, as consumers are willing to pay more for meals that align with their dietary goals.

Financially, meal prep companies have seen substantial growth. The rapidly expanding market of online meal kit delivery services has seen significant growth since its debut in 2012. Global meal kit market size was valued at US$20.54 billion in 2022, and expected to grow at a compound annual growth rate of 15.3 per cent from 2023 to 2030.[9]

REAL-WORLD EXAMPLE

Beauty Pie: Reinventing the beauty subscription model

In 2016, Marcia Kilgore, the beauty industry maven behind successful brands like Bliss and Soap & Glory, took the subscription model to new heights with the launch of Beauty Pie. The concept behind the brand is simple yet revolutionary: offer luxury beauty products directly to consumers at factory prices, cutting out the middleman and retail markup.

Beauty Pie operates on a membership basis, where subscribers pay a monthly fee to access the high-end quality of beauty products at significantly reduced prices. This model disrupts the traditional beauty retail space, where luxury products are often sold at high premiums due to branding, marketing and retail costs. By offering transparency in pricing and allowing members to purchase products at cost, Beauty Pie as an own brand has attracted a dedicated following of consumers who value both quality and affordability.

Kilgore's vision for Beauty Pie is not just about affordability; it is about democratizing luxury and making high-quality beauty products accessible to a broader audience. The success of Beauty Pie underscores the power of the subscription model in transforming consumer perceptions of value. By leveraging the direct-to-consumer approach, Beauty Pie eliminates the layers of markup typically associated with luxury beauty, offering a compelling value proposition that resonates with cost-conscious yet quality-driven consumers.

REAL-WORLD EXAMPLE
FabFitFun: The allure of bundled beauty boxes

The beauty industry has also embraced bundling through the subscription model, with companies like FabFitFun capitalizing on the appeal of product trends and also self-gifting. FabFitFun offers a quarterly subscription box filled with a mix of full-sized beauty, wellness, interiors, fashion and fitness products. Each box is curated based on seasonal themes, and subscribers often receive products that are collectively worth significantly more than the subscription cost.

The appeal of FabFitFun lies in the element of surprise and the perceived value of receiving a box of products that exceed the cost of the subscription. This model also allows brands to offload surplus inventory or introduce new products to a targeted audience. By bundling these items together, FabFitFun creates a sense of exclusivity and value, encouraging subscribers to maintain their memberships.

FabFitFun has demonstrated strong financial success, with a reported peak revenue of $300 million in 2023. The company employs 590 people, resulting in a revenue-per-employee ratio of $508,475.[10]

The company's ability to maintain a high level of customer engagement through social media and influencer partnerships has further solidified its position in the market.

Subscription models and consumer perception of value

What makes these subscription models particularly effective is the way they alter consumer perceptions of value. In each case – whether it is coffee pods, meal prep kits or beauty boxes – the actual cost of the products might be lower than what consumers would pay if they purchased them individually. However, the convenience, personalization and perceived exclusivity of these subscriptions justify the higher price points.

Let's be honest – for many, the thrill of receiving a package in the mail, the anticipation of unboxing and the joy of 'self-gifting' create an experience that some consumers liken to 'Christmas every day'.

Furthermore, these models often create a sense of 'membership' or belonging to a community, which can be a powerful motivator for continued engagement. Consumers who subscribe to these services often feel like they are part of an exclusive club, enjoying benefits and products that nonsubscribers don't have access to.

The future of subscription pricing

As subscription models continue to evolve, we can expect to see even more innovation in pricing strategies. Dynamic pricing, where the cost of a subscription can change based on demand, time of year or customer behaviour, is one potential development. Additionally, we may see more hybrid models that combine traditional purchasing options with subscription benefits, allowing consumers to choose how they engage with a brand.

Ultimately, the success of subscription models in retail pricing underscores the importance of understanding consumer psychology. By offering convenience, customization and a sense of exclusivity, brands can command higher prices and foster deeper customer loyalty. As the retail landscape continues to change, subscription models will likely remain a key strategy for brands looking to build long-term relationships with their customers.

Pay £0 today...

Another effective psychological pricing tactic in the digital age is the use of free trials and 'freemium' models. Companies like Dropbox, LinkedIn and Zoom offer basic services for free, with the option to upgrade to premium features for a fee. This strategy is designed to lower the barrier to entry, allowing consumers to experience the product without financial commitment.

The psychological principle at play here is the 'endowment effect', where consumers place higher value on something they already own or use. Once consumers have invested time and effort into a free service, they are more likely to upgrade to a paid version, perceiving the cost as justified.[11]

In addition to subscription and freemium models, the digital age has also seen the rise of personalized pricing. With the advent of big data and AI, retailers can now offer personalized prices based on individual consumer profiles. This strategy leverages consumer data, such as browsing history, past purchases and demographic information, to tailor prices that are most likely to convert into sales. For example, an online retailer might offer a discount to a customer who has abandoned their shopping cart, to incentivize them to complete the purchase.

While personalized pricing can be highly effective, it also raises ethical concerns around privacy and fairness. Consumers may feel uncomfortable knowing that their personal data is being used to determine the prices they see, leading to potential backlash against such behaviours.

The science and strategy behind premium pricing

Premium pricing, often referred to as prestige or luxury pricing, is a strategy where businesses set prices higher than their competitors to create the perception of exclusivity, quality and value. This approach is particularly effective in industries where brand reputation and consumer perception play a critical role in purchasing decisions, such as luxury goods, high-end fashion and technology.

At the heart of premium pricing is the concept of perceived value. Consumers are willing to pay more for products that they believe offer superior quality, craftsmanship or status. This perception is often carefully cultivated through branding, marketing and the overall customer experience. For example, brands like Apple, Rolex and Tesla have mastered the art of premium pricing by creating products that are not only high in quality but also carry a strong brand identity that resonates with their target audience. Consumers who purchase these products are not just buying a phone, a watch or a car – they are buying into a lifestyle, a sense of belonging and a statement of their personal values.

A critical element of successful premium pricing is the ability to maintain price integrity. This means that the brand must consistently deliver on its promise of quality and exclusivity, without resorting to frequent discounts or promotions that could undermine its premium positioning. For example, luxury fashion brands like Chanel and Louis Vuitton rarely, if ever, offer discounts on their products. This approach reinforces the perception of exclusivity and maintains the brand's status as a premium offering. Consumers who purchase these products do so with the understanding that they are paying a premium for something that is rare, valuable and not easily accessible.[12]

In addition to perceived value and price integrity, scarcity is another key factor that drives premium pricing. Limited edition-products, exclusive collections and restricted availability all contribute to the allure of premium-priced items. The luxury car market is a prime example of how scarcity can be used to justify high prices. Luxury car brands produce a limited number of vehicles each year, creating a sense of urgency and exclusivity among potential buyers. This scarcity, combined with the brand's reputation for quality and performance, allows these companies to command premium prices that far exceed those of mass-market vehicles.

However, premium pricing is not without its challenges. In a world where consumers have access to more information than ever before, brands must be careful to ensure that their premium prices are justified by the quality and value of their products. If consumers perceive that a brand is charging more for a product without offering any tangible benefits, they may become sceptical and seek alternatives. This perception can lead to a loss of brand loyalty, and in some cases, the decline of the brand itself. To avoid this, companies employing premium pricing strategies must continuously innovate and maintain the quality that justifies their higher prices. They must ensure that every aspect of the customer experience – from the product itself, to the purchasing process, to after-sales service – reflects the brand's premium status.

Furthermore, the rise of social media and digital platforms has introduced new challenges and opportunities for premium brands. On one hand, these platforms allow brands to showcase their products to a global audience, reinforcing their exclusivity and desirability. On the other hand, they also make it easier for consumers to compare prices and find alternative options. In this context, maintaining the integrity of a premium pricing strategy requires careful management of online and offline brand messaging.

Luxury items out of reach for some may be afforded by the success of recommerce – reselling previously owned goods, fuelled by tech advancements. Once just down to the luck of finding these items in charity shops, and at flea markets and car (trunk) boot sales, this has now become a burgeoning market, birthing new retailers, particularly in the luxury recommerce sector. For example, high-end brands like Hermès and Louis Vuitton have seen certain models of their handbags and accessories resell for prices that exceed their original retail value. This phenomenon is driven by the same principles of scarcity and brand prestige. Limited production runs, high demand and a robust market for second-hand luxury goods contribute to this dynamic. The secondary market for luxury items is thriving, with platforms like The RealReal, Vestiaire Collective and StockX allowing consumers to buy and sell pre-owned luxury goods at premium prices.

The growing trend of recommerce reflects a shift in consumer behaviour, where the value of an item is not solely determined at the point of purchase but can appreciate over time due to its enduring desirability and limited availability.

One example of how a brand has successfully navigated these challenges is Tesla. Tesla's pricing strategy is rooted in its commitment to innovation and sustainability. By consistently delivering high-quality electric vehicles that push the boundaries of technology, Tesla has been able to command premium prices. However, unlike traditional luxury car brands, Tesla also leverages digital platforms to engage with its customers directly, bypassing traditional dealerships. This direct-to-consumer approach not only reinforces Tesla's premium positioning but also allows the company to maintain tighter control over its pricing and customer experience.[13]

Premium pricing can be a complex strategy that requires a delicate balance between perceived value, price integrity and scarcity. When executed correctly, it can elevate a brand to iconic status, allowing it to command prices far above those of its competitors. However, in a world where consumers are more informed and connected than ever before, maintaining a premium pricing strategy requires constant vigilance, innovation and a deep understanding of consumer psychology. As we look to the future, the brands that succeed with premium pricing will be those that can adapt to changing consumer expectations while staying true to their core values of quality, exclusivity and excellence.

The future of pricing strategies in a changing retail landscape

As we move further into the 21st century, the future of pricing strategies is likely to be shaped by several key trends and technological advancements. The increasing digitization of retail, coupled with changing consumer expectations, is pushing retailers to rethink how they approach pricing.

The future of pricing could also be influenced by the growing importance of sustainability in consumer decision-making. As more consumers prioritize environmentally friendly products, we may see the emergence of 'green pricing' strategies, where products that are sustainably sourced or have a lower environmental impact are priced at a premium. This approach not only appeals to eco-conscious consumers but also allows brands to differentiate themselves in a crowded market. However, the success of green pricing will depend on consumers' willingness to pay more for sustainable products and the transparency of the brand's sustainability claims.

The future of pricing strategies will be shaped by the continued evolution of technology. Innovations like blockchain could revolutionize pricing by providing unprecedented transparency into the supply chain, allowing consumers to see exactly where their products come from and how they are priced. This could lead to more informed purchasing decisions and greater trust in brands that embrace transparency. Additionally, the rise of the metaverse and virtual reality could create entirely new pricing models, where consumers pay for digital goods and experiences in a virtual reality.

While the future looks dynamic, I want to take the theory of pricing back to something a little simpler – a pin badge. And how something as simple as a motif on a pin can still create a fascinating case study in pricing.

REAL-WORLD EXAMPLE
Pricing and Disney Pin Trading: A case study in scarcity and pricing dynamics

For some, Disney Pin Trading is more than just a hobby; it is a subculture that illustrates the power of scarcity in driving demand and influencing pricing. Since its inception at Walt Disney World in 1999, pin trading has exploded into a global phenomenon, with Disney enthusiasts actively seeking out limited-edition pins, rare designs and exclusive releases to add to their collections.

One of the most compelling aspects of Disney Pin Trading is how the scarcity of certain pins dramatically increases their value, sometimes far beyond their original retail prices. Disney capitalizes on this by releasing pins in limited quantities, creating a sense of urgency among collectors. Special events, such as the annual Epcot International Food & Wine Festival, the D23 fan convention or more recently, Disney's 100th anniversary celebrations, often feature exclusive pins that are only available for a short period or in very limited numbers. This limited availability drives collectors to pay premium prices, both in the parks and on the secondary market.

The secondary market for Disney pins is a prime example of how scarcity can inflate prices. A pin that originally retailed for $10 to $15 can sell for several times that amount once it becomes hard to find. For instance, a limited-edition pin featuring a beloved character or a unique design might be resold for 10 times or more the original selling price, depending on its rarity and demand among collectors. This resale value is fuelled by the emotional attachment that collectors have to the pins, as well as the community that has grown around the hobby. Enthusiasts are often willing to pay a premium to complete their collections or to own a piece of Disney history.

Disney's strategy with pin trading aligns perfectly with broader themes of scarcity and premium pricing. The pins themselves become artefacts of Disney's extensive brand narrative, serving as tangible connections to experiences, events and memories. For collectors, owning these pins is not just about possessing a physical item but about owning a piece of the magic that Disney represents. This emotional connection further drives the perceived value of the pins, making them highly sought after.

The robust secondary market for Disney pins is facilitated by auction platforms like eBay and specialized collector sites, where pins are bought, sold and traded among fans. Some collectors even engage in in-person trades at Disney parks, where the community aspect of pin trading is most evident.

The Disney Pin Trading community is alive and well, with enthusiasts sharing stories of their most treasured pins, rare finds and the lengths they've gone to acquire certain pieces.

The power of scarcity in premium pricing

As discussed previously, scarcity is another key factor that drives premium pricing. Factors including limited-edition products, exclusive collections and restricted availability all contribute to the allure of premium-priced items.

The scarcity of these items, whether real or perceived, fuels demand and allows brands to maintain or even increase their prices over time. In the case of Disney pins, as well as these high-end products, scarcity is not just a marketing tactic; it is a fundamental part of the product's value proposition.

Recommerce and the premium pricing of pre-owned goods

The rise of recommerce – the buying and selling of pre-owned goods – further underscores the power of scarcity and perceived value in premium pricing. In the luxury market, certain items, such as vintage Hermès bags or rare Disney pins, often appreciate over time. This trend is evident on platforms like The RealReal and StockX, where consumers are willing to pay significant premiums for items that are no longer available in stores.

For instance, a limited-edition Disney pin or a rare Louis Vuitton handbag might be purchased at a premium on the secondary market due to its rarity and the emotional connection it holds for the buyer. In some cases, these items may even sell for more than their original retail price, highlighting the enduring appeal of products that are both scarce and desirable.

Recommerce has also gained traction in the tech industry, where pre-owned smartphones, laptops and other electronics are resold at competitive prices. The perceived value of these items is often linked to their scarcity, as well as their condition and brand reputation. For consumers, buying a pre-owned item can be a way to access high-quality products at a lower price point, while still enjoying the benefits of brand prestige.

REAL-WORLD EXAMPLE
Vinted: Supercharging recommerce and enabling 'home sellers'

In the evolving landscape of retail, recommerce – the buying and selling of pre-owned goods – has emerged as a significant force, reflecting a shift towards sustainability and conscious consumption. This movement is not merely a resurgence of thrift shopping but a comprehensive transition towards a circular economy, where consumers reassess the concepts of ownership and value. Within this context, Vinted has positioned itself as a pivotal player, transforming the second-hand fashion market and redefining consumer engagement.

How Vinted was born

Founded in 2008 in Vilnius, Lithuania, by Milda Mitkutė and Justas Janauskas, Vinted began as a solution to a personal challenge: Mitkutė's need to declutter her wardrobe before moving house. This simple idea evolved into an online platform enabling users to buy, sell and exchange pre-owned clothing and accessories. Over the years, Vinted has expanded its reach, operating in multiple countries and amassing a substantial user base.

Vinted's growth trajectory has been marked by strategic decisions and timely adaptations. In 2016, the company appointed Thomas Plantenga as CEO, who steered Vinted through a critical restructuring phase. Under his leadership, Vinted eliminated seller fees, enhancing the platform's appeal and fostering a more user-friendly environment. This move was instrumental in increasing user engagement and expanding the platform's community.

The company's commitment to continuous improvement is evident in its technological advancements. Vinted has invested in developing a robust mobile application and an intuitive user interface, ensuring a seamless experience for both buyers and sellers. These enhancements have been pivotal in attracting a diverse demographic, including tech-savvy younger consumers and those seeking sustainable fashion alternatives.

A community for resellers

At the heart of Vinted's success lies its emphasis on community and consumer engagement. The platform has cultivated a vibrant community where users can interact, share fashion insights and build trust. Features such as user profiles, follow options and feedback mechanisms have transformed Vinted into more than just a marketplace; it has become a social platform for fashion enthusiasts.

Vinted's approach to consumer engagement is multifaceted. The platform offers detailed product listings with high-quality images and comprehensive descriptions, enabling buyers to make informed decisions. Additionally, Vinted provides a secure payment system and buyer protection policies, further building trust and encouraging transactions.

Navigating challenges

As Vinted has scaled, it has encountered challenges typical of rapid growth, particularly in maintaining customer service quality. The platform has faced scrutiny regarding its ability to handle the increasing volume of transactions and user interactions. To address these concerns, Vinted has invested in expanding its customer support teams and implementing advanced AI-driven solutions to manage queries efficiently.

Ensuring the authenticity and quality of items is another critical aspect of Vinted's operations. The platform has introduced verification processes for high-value items and established clear guidelines for sellers to maintain standards. These measures are designed to uphold the platform's integrity and provide a reliable marketplace for users.

Financial milestones and market position

Vinted's financial performance reflects its robust market position. In 2023, the company reported its first annual profit, with net earnings of €18 million and a 61 per cent increase in sales, reaching €596 million. This achievement underscores Vinted's effective business model and its ability to scale sustainably.[14]

Vinted's success is closely tied to its responsiveness to market trends and consumer preferences. The platform has capitalized on the growing demand for sustainable fashion and the increasing acceptance of second-hand goods. By offering a user-friendly platform with a vast selection of items, Vinted has made second-hand shopping accessible and appealing to a broad audience.

The role of sustainability in Vinted's mission

Sustainability is a core component of Vinted's mission. The platform promotes the reuse of clothing, thereby reducing waste and the environmental impact associated with fast fashion. By facilitating the exchange of pre-owned items, Vinted encourages consumers to adopt more sustainable consumption habits.

Vinted's commitment to sustainability resonates with a growing segment of consumers who prioritize environmental considerations in their purchasing decisions. This alignment with consumer values has been instrumental in building brand loyalty and expanding Vinted's user base.

Looking ahead

Despite its successes, Vinted faces challenges inherent in the recommerce sector. Ensuring the authenticity of items, managing quality control and maintaining customer satisfaction are ongoing concerns. Additionally, as the market becomes more competitive, Vinted must continue to innovate and differentiate itself to retain its leading position.

The company has said it plans to expand into new markets and categories, invest in technology to improve platform functionality, and strengthen its logistics and customer support systems. By staying attuned to consumer needs and market dynamics, Vinted aims to continue its trajectory as a leader in the recommerce space.

Vinted's journey from a local Lithuanian start-up to a leading international recommerce platform exemplifies the transformative power of aligning business models with evolving consumer values. Through strategic growth, community engagement and a steadfast commitment to sustainability, Vinted has redefined the second-hand fashion market and set a benchmark for others in the industry. As the recommerce sector continues to expand, Vinted's story offers valuable insights into the potential of combining technology, sustainability and consumer-centric strategies to drive success.

Vinted's success is a testament to how modern pricing strategies can align with evolving consumer values. By creating a community-oriented platform that prioritizes affordability, transparency and sustainability, Vinted has redefined how consumers perceive second-hand fashion. Its ability to deliver value through a combination of emotional engagement, ease of use and ethical positioning provides a powerful lesson for retailers everywhere.

This shift towards consumer-centric pricing, as seen with Vinted, underscores a critical truth: the future of pricing lies in more than just clever tactics – it requires building trust, fostering loyalty and meeting the deeper needs of today's shopper. As brands increasingly embrace concepts like recommerce and sustainable pricing, the challenge will be to balance profitability with purpose, ensuring that pricing strategies resonate not only financially but ethically.

Pricing isn't merely a numbers game – it's a powerful dialogue between the retailer and the consumer. This chapter has uncovered the intricate mechanics of that dialogue, where psychology, perception and strategy intersect. The art of pricing isn't about arbitrary figures; it's about story-telling – shaping how we think, feel and act when confronted with those digits on a price tag.

From the persuasive charm of £9.99 to the thrill of exclusivity in premium pricing, we've explored the hidden levers that guide our buying decisions. Pricing strategies aren't static; they evolve with cultural shifts, technological advancements and changing consumer expectations. They tap into our emotions, influence our decisions and, at their best, foster loyalty and trust.

As we close this chapter, the question isn't whether pricing will evolve, but how we, as consumers, can remain aware of its impact. Because in the world of retail, every price tells a story – and understanding that story is the key to becoming a smarter, more empowered consumer.

This chapter reminds us that pricing is not a static number but a living, dynamic force – capable of influencing industries, shaping consumer percep-tions and redefining how we find value in the things we buy. By understanding these strategies, we arm ourselves with the knowledge to navigate the retail world with confidence and clarity.

KEY TAKEAWAYS

1 **The power of emotional pricing:** Pricing strategies are not only about financial equations but emotional resonance. Techniques like charm pricing and decoy pricing target our subconscious biases, making decisions feel intuitive even when they're influenced.

2 **Scarcity can create both value and loyalty:** Limited editions, premium products and even the psychology of 'last chance' sales leverage scarcity to drive urgency. But they also build loyalty – consumers are drawn to brands that make their offerings feel exclusive and special.

3 **Dynamic pricing reflects consumer and market realities:** Advanced technologies, like AI and real-time data analysis, allow retailers to adjust prices dynamically, creating tailored experiences. But this comes with the need for greater transparency to maintain consumer trust.

4 **Perpetual discounts: a double-edged sword:** Overusing sales erodes brand value, as seen in the demise of retailers like Debenhams. Effective pricing strategies balance short-term sales with long-term consumer confidence in the product's inherent value.

5 **The future of pricing is ethical, technological and transparent:** As pricing evolves, sustainability, equity and consumer data protection will shape its direction. The most successful brands will be those that combine innovation with fairness, using pricing as a tool to enhance – not exploit – the consumer relationship.

References

1 Thaler, Richard H (2016) *Misbehaving: The making of behavioral economics*, W.W. Norton & Company, New York, NY

2 Mohammed, R (2018) The good-better-best approach to pricing, *Harvard Business Review*, September-October.

3 The Woolworths Museum (nd) Farewell 3d and 6d, hello rationing, www.woolworthsmuseum.co.uk/1940s-byebye6d.htm (archived at https://perma.cc/EYA9-YQQF)

4 Banton, C (2021) Loss leader strategy: Definition and how it works in retail, *Investopedia*, 27 May, www.investopedia.com/terms/l/lossleader.asp. (archived at https://perma.cc/W997-TDFX)

5 Boardfy (nd) A guide to Amazon's pricing strategy, www.boardfy.com/a-guide-to-amazons-pricing-strategy (archived at https://perma.cc/E4PM-F3Y7)

6 Cramer, A (2024) Walmart's everyday low price strategy, Pricefy, 29 August, www.pricefy.io/articles/walmarts-everyday-low-price-strategy (archived at https://perma.cc/X3TZ-6YV6)

7 Kate Hardcastle (nd) Latest media clips: TV, radio & documentaries, www.katehardcastle.com/media-clips (archived at https://perma.cc/J3R9-4GXK)

8 WeatherAds (nd) How effective is weather-based marketing? 4 Case studies with ROI stats, www.weatherads.io/blog/how-effective-is-weather-based-marketing-4-case-studies-with-roi-stats (archived at https://perma.cc/WA7B-A3YL)

9   Grand View Research (nd) Meal kit delivery services market size, share & trends analysis report, 2023–2030, www.grandviewresearch.com/industry-analysis/meal-kit-delivery-services-market (archived at https://perma.cc/AEK6-LSVG)

10 Zippia (nd) FabFitFun revenue, www.zippia.com/fabfitfun-careers-1405260/revenue (archived at https://perma.cc/Y33W-5YDL)

11 Ganti, A (2023) Endowment effect: Definition, what causes it, and example, Investopedia, 17 February, www.investopedia.com/terms/e/endowment-effect.asp (archived at https://perma.cc/92XB-NMP6)

12 Lastre, D (2018) Luxury brand pricing strategy: Consistency is key to brand success, Wealth-X, 20 February, www.wealthx.com/articles/luxury-brand-pricing-strategy-consistency-key-brand-success (archived at https://perma.cc/M568-NKP3)

13 Tesla (2011) Tesla reinvents the car buying experience, press release, 13 April, https://ir.tesla.com/press-release/tesla-reinvents-car-buying-experience (archived at https://perma.cc/9CGV-JHY8)

14 Vinted (2024) Vinted delivers strong year of growth and reaches profitability, while investing for the future, 29 April, https://company.vinted.com/newsroom/vinted-reaches-profitability (archived at https://perma.cc/DV7D-RKSG)

9

Mastering promotional strategies to boost sales

The psychology of discounts and promotions

The human heart beats over 35 million times a year. Sometimes, it flutters – with love, excitement and yes, even for a great deal. There's a unique thrill that comes with snagging a discount, a rush that many of us know all too well. But what is it about promotions that captures our hearts and makes them race? The answer lies in the psychology behind discounts and promotions.

Promotions are far more than just a tactic to lower prices; they are a tool to influence consumer behaviour, create a sense of urgency and drive sales. At the heart of every successful promotion is a deep understanding of consumer psychology. Even those of us seasoned in the retail industry can't help but be drawn in by a well-crafted deal. This behaviour isn't purely rational; it is driven by a complex mix of emotions and perceptions that marketers have long since learnt to tap into. So following on from the discussion of different price strategies in Chapter 8, how can retailers maximize the impact by considering the consumer psychology around it?

Perceived value: Why percentages pack a punch

One of the most powerful concepts in promotional psychology is *perceived value*. The notion that something is 'worth it' isn't always tied to its actual price, but to the value consumers believe they're getting. Consider this: why does a 20 per cent discount often seem more attractive than a flat £10 reduction, even when the latter offers more savings? It is all about perception.

Percentages feel more impactful. The idea of saving 20 per cent plays into our emotions more effectively than a straightforward pound amount, especially when percentages are tied to higher-priced items.

Retailers are acutely aware of this and frequently use percentage discounts to entice consumers. The strategy is simple: by framing a deal in terms of percentage savings, they appeal to a consumer's sense of value. It is not just about the money saved; it is about the psychological satisfaction of securing a 'better' deal. This satisfaction is heightened when the percentage discount is paired with a reference price, a tactic known as anchoring.

Anchoring: Setting the psychological reference point

Anchoring is a psychological concept where the original price of a product is presented alongside the discounted price, creating a reference point in the consumer's mind. This reference, or 'anchor', makes the discount appear more significant. For instance, a product originally priced at £100 marked down to £70 feels like a better deal than a product simply priced at £70. The higher original price serves as a benchmark, making the discount seem more substantial and therefore more appealing.

Take Kohl's, the US department store, as a case study. The retailer is well-known for its aggressive promotional tactics, particularly with Kohl's Cash. Customers earn $10 for every $50 spent, which they can then use on a future purchase. The psychology behind this promotion is fascinating. Customers feel like they're getting something extra, even though they must spend more to redeem their Kohl's Cash. This strategy not only encourages repeat visits but also increases the average transaction value. However, there's a downside. When consumers start viewing Kohl's Cash as a necessity rather than a bonus, it creates a cycle where the brand must continually offer promotions to maintain sales. This can erode profit margins over time, turning what was once a clever marketing tactic into a crutch.

Discount saturation: The dangers of overdoing it

While discounts can be incredibly effective, they are not without their risks. One significant danger is discount saturation, where consumers become desensitized to deals, or worse, where discounts start to erode the perceived value of a brand. This is particularly true for brands not built around discounting, such as luxury goods. Excessive discounting can lead to a situation where customers purchase only when a discount is offered, which damages long-term profitability and brand equity.

For brands like Louis Vuitton, which rarely offer discounts, the strategy is to maintain brand prestige. Offering discounts can diminish a brand's exclusivity and allure. For most brands, especially those in the mid-tier, it is essential to strike the right balance. Promotions should entice, not cheapen. The right strategy can create a sense of urgency and drive sales, but if over-used, it can backfire, leading consumers to question the true value of the product.

The psychology behind promotions is a delicate balance between creating excitement and maintaining value. By understanding these psychological triggers, retailers can craft compelling deals that resonate with consumers while reinforcing the brand's value proposition.

Couponing: From clipping to digital

Couponing has long been a staple in the world of retail promotions. What began as a simple tactic to drive product trials has evolved into a sophisticated, multichannel strategy that spans both traditional and digital platforms. The history of couponing is as rich as it is fascinating, reflecting broader shifts in consumer behaviour, technology and retail marketing.

The golden age of clipping

In the early days, coupons were physical tokens clipped from newspapers or magazines, offering pennies-off on everyday items. These early coupons were an effective way for brands to introduce new products to the market and encourage consumers to try something new. The appeal was straightforward: save money on products you already buy or take a chance on something new with minimal financial risk. For many consumers, couponing became a way of life. Shoppers meticulously clipped and organized their coupons, carefully planning shopping trips to maximize savings.

One of the most iconic examples of traditional couponing's success is the FMCG (fast-moving consumer goods) industry. Brands like Kellogg's used couponing to drive massive product trials, often introducing new cereals with attractive savings offers. These coupons weren't just about reducing the price; they were about driving traffic to stores, encouraging customers to try something new, and ultimately building brand loyalty.

The digital revolution in couponing

Fast-forward to today, and couponing has undergone a digital transformation. What was once a labour-intensive process of clipping and organizing paper coupons has evolved into a seamless digital experience. Digital couponing offers a level of convenience and personalization that physical coupons never could. With the rise of smartphones and data analytics, retailers can now track consumer behaviour and offer targeted coupons based on past purchases. This shift has made couponing more efficient for both consumers and retailers. Shoppers can now load digital coupons directly onto their loyalty cards or apps, which are automatically applied at checkout, ensuring that they never miss out on savings.

The rise of digital couponing has also further grown the trend of extreme couponing. This phenomenon, often popularized by television shows and social media, involves savvy shoppers using multiple coupons, often stacked with store sales, to purchase large quantities of products at minimal cost. Extreme couponing generates buzz and drives short-term sales, but it also presents challenges for retailers. If not managed carefully, it can lead to stock shortages, lower profit margins and even instances of fraud.

REAL-WORLD EXAMPLE

JC Penney's couponing crisis

The importance of couponing in consumer expectations was dramatically highlighted by JC Penney's failed experiment with eliminating coupons under CEO Ron Johnson. To simplify pricing and eliminate the confusion surrounding discounts and coupons, JC Penney switched to an 'everyday low price' strategy, removing all coupons and promotions. The result was disastrous. Customers, who had come to expect and rely on JC Penney's coupons, felt betrayed and left the brand in droves. Sales plummeted, and Johnson was eventually ousted. The company reinstated its couponing strategy, but the damage was done, and JC Penney has struggled to regain its former market position.[1]

This case underscores the deep psychological attachment consumers have to coupons. Coupons create a sense of empowerment, allowing consumers to feel like they are getting a deal, even if the actual savings are minimal. They also foster brand loyalty, as customers return to the stores where they can redeem their coupons. In the digital age, where price comparison is just a click away, coupons continue to be a powerful tool for driving traffic, encouraging repeat purchases and building long-term customer relationships.

Loyalty cards as a promotional technique

In the ever-evolving world of retail, loyalty cards have stood the test of time as one of the most effective promotional techniques. What started as simple, physical cards tucked away in wallets has transformed into a digital power-house, capable of driving customer engagement, fostering loyalty and providing retailers with invaluable data. The shift from physical to digital loyalty programmes has not only changed how consumers interact with brands but has also revolutionized the way retailers approach customer relationships.

The evolution of loyalty cards: From physical to digital

Loyalty cards began as straightforward tools – physical cards that custom-ers could present at the checkout to accumulate points or rewards. These cards were often seen as a convenient way for consumers to get a little some-thing extra for their regular shopping. Early programmes, like the original rubber-stamped cards in coffee shops or the simple plastic cards used by grocery stores, were all about building a tangible connection between the consumer and the brand.

The physical nature of these cards played a significant role in their effec-tiveness. Having a loyalty card in your wallet was a constant reminder of the perks associated with frequent shopping at a particular store. However, as technology advanced, the limitations of physical cards became apparent. Lost cards, forgotten points and the hassle of carrying multiple cards from different stores started to diminish the appeal.

Enter the digital age. The rise of smartphones and data analytics trans-formed loyalty programmes into sophisticated, data-driven strategies. Today, most loyalty programmes have moved online, integrated into mobile apps that offer far more than just points accumulation. These digital platforms provide a seamless experience, allowing customers to access their rewards, view personalized offers and even track their spending habits all in one place. For retailers, the shift to digital has unlocked a treasure trove of data, enabling more targeted marketing and customer experiences.

The impact of data: From simple rewards to personalized experiences

One of the most significant advantages of digital loyalty programmes is the ability to collect and analyse vast amounts of customer data. Every time a customer interacts with a loyalty programme – whether by making a purchase, redeeming points or simply browsing products – valuable data is generated. This data provides insights into customer behaviour, preferences and shopping patterns, allowing retailers to tailor their marketing efforts more effectively.

For example, digital loyalty programmes can track what products a customer frequently purchases and then offer personalized discounts on those items. They can also send targeted promotions for complementary products, enhancing the overall shopping experience. This level of personalization was unimaginable with physical loyalty cards but is now a standard expectation in the digital era.

Statistics underscore the power of personalization in loyalty programmes. A study by Accenture found that 91 per cent of consumers are more likely to shop with brands that provide personalized offers and recommendations. Additionally, 77 per cent of consumers have chosen, recommended or paid more for a brand that provides a personalized service or experience.[2] These figures highlight the critical role that data-driven personalization plays in modern retail and the effectiveness of digital loyalty programmes in driving sales.

REAL-WORLD EXAMPLE
The success of the Boots Advantage Card

The Boots Advantage Card is a prime example of how a well-designed loyalty programme can drive customer engagement, retention and brand loyalty. Launched in 1997, the Boots Advantage Card has become one of the most successful and beloved loyalty schemes in the UK, with over 14.7 million active members by 2023. This loyalty card has not only boosted customer satisfaction but also solidified Boots's position as a leading health and beauty retailer.

When the Boots Advantage Card was introduced, the retail landscape was vastly different from today. Loyalty programmes were not as ubiquitous, and the concept of earning points that could be redeemed for future purchases was still relatively novel. Boots's decision to launch the Advantage Card was strategic, aimed at differentiating itself in a competitive market.

The programme was simple yet effective: customers earned four points for every pound spent, with each point equivalent to one penny. These points could be accumulated and redeemed on future purchases. This structure incentivized repeat visits, as customers saw tangible benefits from their spending. From the outset, the Advantage Card was designed to be more than just a rewards programme – it was a tool to build long-term relationships with customers and, of course, provide the retailer with essential data.[3]

The power of data: Personalization and targeted offers

One of the key reasons behind the success of the Boots Advantage Card is its effective use of customer data. From the beginning, Boots recognized the importance of understanding customer behaviour and preferences. The data collected from Advantage Card transactions allowed Boots to tailor its marketing efforts, delivering personalized offers that resonated with individual customers.

For example, if a customer frequently purchased skincare products, they might receive special offers or additional points for buying those products. This level of personalization made customers feel valued and understood, strengthening their loyalty to the Boots brand. As technology advanced, Boots continued to refine its data analytics capabilities, integrating these insights into its digital platforms.

In recent years, Boots has taken this to new heights by integrating the Advantage Card with its online and mobile platforms. Customers can now access their points balance, view personalized offers and even shop online with their loyalty points. This seamless integration of the physical and digital shopping experience has made the Advantage Card even more appealing to tech-savvy consumers.

Adapting to change: The digital transformation of the Advantage Card

The retail industry has undergone significant changes since the launch of the Boots Advantage Card, particularly with the rise of digital shopping. Boots has successfully adapted the Advantage Card to these changes, ensuring that it remains relevant and valuable to its customers.

In the digital age, convenience is key. Boots recognized this and invested in digital solutions to enhance the Advantage Card experience. Customers can now load digital offers directly onto their cards via the Boots app, which are automatically applied at checkout. This not only saves time but also ensures that customers never miss out on savings.

Moreover, Boots has leveraged digital channels to communicate with its Advantage Card members more effectively. Through personalized emails, push notifications and in-app messages, Boots keeps its customers informed about exclusive offers, new product launches and seasonal promotions. This constant engagement helps to maintain customer interest and loyalty.

The impact on sales and customer retention

The financial impact of the Boots Advantage Card on the company's sales and customer retention cannot be overstated. In 2023, Boots reported that its loyalty scheme delivered £50 million in savings for customers, a clear indicator of the programme's value. But beyond the immediate savings, the Advantage Card has played a crucial role in driving customer retention and increasing the average transaction value.[4]

Customers with an Advantage Card tend to spend more per visit and shop more frequently at Boots compared to non-members. This is a direct result of the points-based system, which encourages customers to accumulate and redeem points, thus increasing their purchase frequency. Additionally, the personalized offers delivered through the Advantage Card have proven effective in encouraging customers to try new products and services, further boosting sales.

Challenges and criticisms

While the Boots Advantage Card is widely regarded as a success, it has not been without its challenges. One criticism of the programme is that the points earned can sometimes feel insignificant, especially when compared to the total amount spent. For example, earning four points per pound means that a customer would need to spend £100 to earn £4 in rewards. For some customers, this return may not seem particularly compelling.

Moreover, as with any loyalty programme, there is the risk of over-reliance. Customers may become so accustomed to earning points and receiving discounts that they only shop at Boots when they can take advantage of a promotion. This could potentially erode profit margins if not managed carefully.

However, Boots has addressed these challenges by continually enhancing the value proposition of the Advantage Card. The introduction of 'Bonus Points' events, where customers can earn extra points on specific products or during shopping periods, has helped to keep the programme exciting and rewarding. Additionally, Boots has introduced tiered membership levels, offering even more perks to its most loyal customers, thereby increasing the perceived value of the programme.

The Boots Advantage Card is a prime example of how a well-executed loyalty programme can drive business success. By focusing on personalization, seamless integration between physical and digital platforms, and continually evolving the programme to meet changing customer needs, Boots has created a loyalty scheme that not only attracts new customers but also retains them for the long term.

The Advantage Card's success lies in its ability to make customers feel valued and rewarded for their loyalty. It is not just about the points; it is about the relationship that Boots has built with its customers over the years. As other retailers look to develop or enhance their loyalty programmes, the Boots Advantage Card serves as a powerful model of how to do it right.

The combination of thoughtful design, effective use of data and a relentless focus on customer experience has ensured that the Boots Advantage Card remains one of the most successful loyalty schemes in the UK, driving both customer satisfaction and business growth.

The evolution of competitions and sweepstakes

Competitions and sweepstakes have long been a cornerstone of promotional strategies, offering brands a powerful tool to engage consumers and drive sales. Over the years, these tactics have evolved from simple in-store raffles and mail-in forms to sophisticated digital campaigns that leverage the latest in technology and consumer behaviour insights.

In the early days of retail, competitions were often straightforward. Consumers might find a sweepstakes entry form in a cereal box or receive one through the post. These promotions tapped into the thrill of winning, creating an emotional connection that encouraged brand loyalty. Brands like Kellogg's and General Mills were pioneers in this space, using sweepstakes to boost sales and foster a sense of fun around their products.

Digital transformation

The advent of digital technology has revolutionized competitions and sweepstakes, making them more accessible, engaging and data driven. Today, entry forms are often a click away, integrated seamlessly into websites, apps and social media platforms. Brands are no longer limited to paper and post; they can now reach consumers instantly through their smartphones.

Digital platforms have also introduced new ways to engage with competitions. Social media platforms, for instance, allow for shareable content, turning every participant into a potential brand ambassador. Companies can now run sweepstakes that require participants to follow, share or comment on social posts, exponentially increasing their reach.

Furthermore, the shift to digital has provided brands with a treasure trove of consumer data. Every entry gives insights into consumer preferences, behaviours and demographics, allowing for more personalized and targeted future promotions. However, with this increase in data collection comes the responsibility to handle consumer information ethically and securely, a topic that has gained importance in recent years.

REAL-WORLD EXAMPLE
McDonald's Monopoly and BrewDog's gold can campaigns

One of the most successful examples of a competition evolving with the times is the McDonald's Monopoly campaign. Launched in 1987, the promotion has become a staple of McDonald's marketing strategy. The game allows customers to collect Monopoly property stickers attached to various menu items, with the chance to win everything from free food to cash prizes.

Over the years, McDonald's has adapted the game to keep it relevant. In recent iterations, digital components have been added, allowing consumers to scan game pieces with an app for additional chances to win. This digital integration has helped McDonald's maintain consumer interest in a campaign that could have otherwise grown stale.

However, the success of the Monopoly campaign also highlights potential risks. There have been instances of fraud and controversy, underscoring the need for brands to maintain transparency and fairness in their promotional strategies.

BrewDog's gold can sweepstakes

Not all sweepstakes end successfully. A cautionary tale comes from BrewDog, a popular craft beer brand known for its edgy marketing tactics. In 2021, BrewDog launched a promotion offering customers the chance to find a 'solid gold' can hidden in cases of their beer. Winners were told the cans were worth £15,000, adding an element of luxury and exclusivity to the campaign.[5]

However, the promotion quickly unravelled when it was revealed that the cans were not solid gold, but merely gold-plated. The actual value of the cans was significantly lower than advertised, leading to consumer backlash and accusations of misleading advertising. The Advertising Standards Authority (ASA) in the UK investigated the incident, and BrewDog was forced to apologize and clarify the true value of the prizes.

This incident highlights the importance of transparency and accuracy in promotional campaigns. Misleading consumers, even unintentionally, can lead to significant reputational damage and legal repercussions. Brands must ensure that all claims made in promotions are truthful and clearly communicated to avoid such pitfalls.

Benefits, challenges and considerations of sweepstakes

While competitions and sweepstakes are effective promotional tools, they are not without challenges. The rise of digital technology has brought about new legal considerations, particularly around the collection and use of consumer data. Brands must navigate these challenges carefully to avoid legal repercussions and maintain consumer trust.

Additionally, there is a risk of consumer fatigue. If promotions are not innovative or engaging, they can become just another form of marketing noise. To avoid this, brands need to continuously evolve their strategies, incorporating new technologies and consumer insights to keep their campaigns fresh and exciting.

Giveaways have the power to do more than just boost immediate sales – they can create lasting brand loyalty. When executed thoughtfully, a giveaway can turn a one-time customer into a lifelong brand advocate, deepening the emotional connection between the consumer and the brand.

At the heart of any successful giveaway is the emotional engagement it fosters. Consumers love the feeling of getting something for free – it triggers a psychological response that enhances the perceived value of the brand. When a brand offers a giveaway, it is not just about the physical item; it is about the gesture, the sense of being valued as a customer.

This emotional connection is what transforms a simple transaction into a relationship. The consumer feels a sense of reciprocity, where the brand's generosity fosters goodwill and loyalty. This is particularly effective when the giveaway is tied to a larger brand narrative or campaign that resonates with the consumer's values and lifestyle.

Branded giveaways: Boosting brand awareness

One of the most powerful ways to turn a giveaway into brand loyalty is through exclusivity. When consumers believe they are receiving something unique or limited, the value of the giveaway increases significantly. This is why limited-edition products or experiences are so effective – they create a sense of belonging and exclusivity among consumers.

Brands can leverage this by offering giveaways that are not just free, but also exclusive. For example, a limited-edition product that is only available to giveaway participants can drive significant consumer interest and engagement. This strategy not only boosts short-term sales but also strengthens long-term loyalty by making consumers feel like they are part of an exclusive community.

Pepsi Stuff campaign

Pepsi's 'Pepsi Stuff' campaign in the 1990s is a classic example of a giveaway that built lasting brand loyalty. The campaign allowed consumers to collect points from Pepsi purchases, which they could then redeem for branded merchandise. The more Pepsi products they bought, the more points they earned, creating a cycle of continuous engagement with the brand.

What made Pepsi Stuff so successful was its appeal to consumers' desire for exclusivity and reward. The merchandise was branded, making it a tangible symbol of loyalty to Pepsi. Consumers felt they were getting something extra for their purchases, which reinforced their connection to the brand.

The campaign was so successful that it was revived in 2005, and it continues to be a case study in how to use giveaways to build brand loyalty. However, the key takeaway is that the success of such campaigns hinges on offering rewards that are both desirable and aligned with the brand's identity.[6]

The balance of value and cost

While giveaways are a powerful tool for building loyalty, they must be carefully balanced in terms of cost. Offering high-value items may attract consumers, but it can also erode profit margins if not managed properly. Brands need to ensure that the cost of the giveaway is offset by the long-term value of the loyalty it generates.

Moreover, the effectiveness of a giveaway is not just in its monetary value, but in how well it resonates with the target audience. A well-chosen giveaway that aligns with the brand's image and the consumers' desires will always have a greater impact than a generic high-value item.

The power of scarcity

Scarcity is one of the most effective motivators in consumer behaviour. When people perceive that a product is in limited supply, their desire to obtain it increases. Timed promotions capitalize on this by creating a sense of urgency – if the consumer doesn't act now, they might miss out on a great deal.

This tactic is particularly effective in today's fast-paced retail environment, where consumers are bombarded with choices. A limited-time offer cuts through the noise by presenting a clear and compelling reason to buy now. Retailers can enhance this effect by highlighting the limited availability of the product, whether through stock counters, countdown timers or phrases like 'while supplies last'.

FOMO in marketing

The fear of missing out (FOMO) is a powerful driver of consumer behaviour, and it is a central element of many successful timed promotions. FOMO plays on the anxiety that others might be getting something valuable that the consumer is not, prompting them to take action to avoid being left out.

Flash sales, pop-up shops and exclusive product drops are all examples of promotions that use FOMO to drive sales. These tactics create a buzz around the product, encouraging consumers to act quickly to secure their purchase. In many cases, the anticipation of the sale is just as important as the sale itself, as it builds excitement and increases the perceived value of the promotion.

REAL-WORLD EXAMPLE
Amazon Prime Day

Amazon Prime Day is a prime example of how timed promotions can drive massive consumer engagement and sales. Launched in 2015, Prime Day has become one of the biggest shopping events of the year, rivalling even Black Friday in terms of sales and consumer participation.

What makes Prime Day so successful is its combination of limited-time deals and the exclusivity of being available only to Amazon Prime members. This creates a perfect storm of scarcity and FOMO, as consumers scramble to take advantage of the deals before they disappear.

Amazon also uses a rolling release of deals throughout the event, keeping consumers engaged and encouraging them to check back frequently for new offers. This strategy not only drives sales but also reinforces the value of the Amazon Prime membership, making it a key part of Amazon's overall customer retention strategy.

Strategic execution

While timed promotions can be incredibly effective, they require careful planning and execution. The key is to strike the right balance between urgency and accessibility. If a promotion feels too exclusive or difficult to access, it can alienate consumers rather than engage them. On the other hand, if it is too easy to obtain, it may lose its impact.

Brands should also consider the timing of their promotions carefully. Aligning a flash sale with a significant event or season can amplify its effectiveness. For example, launching a timed promotion around the holidays can tap into the increased consumer spending that occurs during this period, maximizing the promotion's impact.

The power of promotions

Promotions are a staple of retail, but their true power lies in their ability to evoke emotions, shape perceptions and influence behaviour. A great offer isn't just about offering a discount – it's about crafting an experience that resonates with the consumer. There's a unique thrill to securing a deal, a feeling of achievement that taps into human psychology. Retailers that understand and leverage this can transform a simple sale into a tool for building loyalty and driving engagement.

One of the most critical aspects of promotions is the concept of perceived value. Consumers often respond to how a deal makes them feel rather than the actual savings. For example, a 20 per cent discount can feel more rewarding than a £10 reduction, even when the latter provides greater savings. The psychology of anchoring – the practice of presenting the original price alongside the discounted price – reinforces this sense of value. By showing what could have been spent, retailers make the deal appear more significant, satisfying the consumer's desire to 'win' at shopping.

Scarcity and urgency are other powerful tools in the promotional arsenal. Limited-time offers, exclusive collections and countdown timers create a fear of missing out (FOMO) that compels consumers to act quickly. These strategies don't just drive immediate purchases – they create a sense of exclusivity that builds brand loyalty. However, overusing promotions can lead to discount saturation, where consumers only buy during sales, eroding long-term profitability and brand value.

The evolution of promotions is also evident in the rise of digital tools. From personalized coupons delivered through apps to loyalty programmes that use data to offer tailored rewards, technology has transformed how promotions are designed and delivered. Competitions and sweepstakes, too, have shifted from in-store raffles to sophisticated online campaigns that integrate seamlessly with social media and mobile platforms. These innovations provide retailers with powerful insights into consumer behaviour, enabling them to craft increasingly effective and engaging strategies.

But while promotions can be a powerful driver of sales, they must be used thoughtfully. Retailers must balance the excitement of discounts with the need to maintain their brand's perceived value and trust. When done well, promotions can create lasting emotional connections, turning one-time shoppers into loyal advocates.

Turning transactions into connections

Promotions are more than tools for boosting sales – they're opportunities to build trust, spark joy and create meaningful relationships. The most effective strategies combine emotional resonance with ethical transparency, ensuring consumers feel valued while reinforcing the brand's reputation.

In a competitive marketplace, retailers that understand the art and science of promotions can stand out, fostering loyalty and driving growth. By creating experiences that resonate on a human level, promotions become more than a marketing tactic – they become a bridge to lasting consumer connections.

KEY TAKEAWAYS

1 **Promotions are emotional, not just rational:** Effective promotions tap into the psychological thrill of securing a deal, leveraging tools like anchoring and percentage-based discounts to amplify perceived value.

2 **Balance is key to sustaining value:** Overuse of discounts can erode brand equity and profitability. Strategic use of promotions ensures excitement without creating dependency on sales.

3 **Loyalty programmes drive long-term engagement:** Digital loyalty programmes offer personalization and convenience, using data to create tailored rewards that strengthen customer relationships.

4 **Competitions and giveaways foster emotional connections:** Campaigns like McDonald's Monopoly or exclusive branded giveaways use the allure of rewards to deepen consumer trust and drive repeat engagement.

5 **Scarcity and urgency amplify impact:** Limited-time promotions and exclusive product launches create urgency and FOMO, driving immediate action while enhancing brand appeal.

References

1   Aisner, Jim and Lal, Rajiv (2013) What went wrong at JC Penney? Harvard Business School, 20 August, www.hbs.edu/news/articles/Pages/rajiv-lal-on-jcpenney. aspx (archived at https://perma.cc/CTH9-XZ52)

2   Robinson, John (nd) The future of customer experience – adapting to evolving customer preferences, Ant Marketing, www.antmarketing.com/the-future-of-customer-experience-adapting-to-evolving-customer-preferences (archived at https://perma.cc/5U4J-9DH4)

3   Lewis, Georgia (2022) Turning loyalty into an advantage at Boots, *CX Network*, 11 August, www.cxnetwork.com/cx-retail/articles/turning-loyalty-into-an-advantage-at-boots (archived at https://perma.cc/8G37-CHZK)

4   Bhoora, Ritika (2023) Boots says rewards scheme delivers £50m savings for customers, *Retail Week*, 19 July, www.retail-week.com/health-and-beauty/boots-says-rewards-scheme-delivers-50m-savings-for-customers/7044195.article (archived at https://perma.cc/5PKA-SNHY)

5   Smart, Andrew (2023) Brewdog pays almost £500,000 after 'solid-gold' beer can claim, *Halstead Gazette*, 9 January, www.halsteadgazette.co.uk/news/national/uk-today/23238422.brewdog-pays-almost-500-000-solid-gold-beer-can-claim (archived at https://perma.cc/AZ7X-8PDX)

6   MRi (nd) Case study: Pepsi Stuff Program, Marketing Resources Incorporated, www.marketingresources.com/case-study/pepsi-pepsi-stuff (archived at https://perma.cc/GA66-EAWD)

10

It's time for you to check out...

Retail, at its core, reflects human behaviour, social patterns and economic structures, but what makes it particularly fascinating to me is how the process of shopping also reveals our deeper, more personal needs. Throughout this book, we've explored the evolution of retail, unpacked the psychological underpinnings of consumer behaviour and discussed the major forces shaping the industry today.

I've long been fascinated by the intersection of storytelling and retail. Storytelling is part of our DNA – a skill passed on from generation to generation – and the stories that captivate will always work.

Why? Because, at the end of the day, it is human to tell and listen to stories. We use the skill to make sense of the world, and retail is no different. Shopping is about more than acquiring products – it's about how those products fit into the larger narrative of our lives.

Think of brands like Apple, Patagonia or Disney. What sets them apart isn't just their product offering – it's their ability to tell stories that resonate with their customers on a deeper level. Apple doesn't just sell iPhones; it sells a vision of innovation and creativity. Patagonia doesn't just sell outdoor gear; it sells an ethos of sustainability and environmental stewardship. These brands understand that their products are part of a larger brand narrative – and that's what makes them powerful.

This idea ties into narrative transportation theory, which suggests that people can become so deeply immersed in a story that it alters their beliefs and behaviours. When applied to retail, it helps us understand why compelling brand stories are so effective in driving consumer loyalty. A well-crafted story not only sells a product but also creates an identity for the consumer, allowing them to align themselves with the values and aspirations of the brand.

However, the critical element in modern storytelling is authenticity. Consumers are savvier than ever – they can spot inauthenticity from a mile away. The rise of transparent branding appeals to the modern consumer but also enhances the perceived value of the product.

Retailers should focus on developing authentic narratives that resonate with their audiences' values and aspirations. It's not enough to tell a story – brands must live that story, ensuring that every touchpoint reflects their core message and ethos.

Now, as we remind ourselves of these ideas, I want to remind you of two of the frameworks that I've developed over the years: the *Buyerarchy of Needs* and the *Equation of Value*. Both have been instrumental in shaping my approach to understanding the ever-changing world of retail and consumerism. Let's recap the chapter highlights.

Chapter 1: The evolution of retail: From high-street store to online marketplace

Retail is much more than a mechanism for transactions – it is a mirror of our lives, shaped by the societal shifts that influence how we live, think and connect. From the bustling markets of ancient times to the rise of department stores, and now the dominance of online shopping giants, the journey of retail has been one of continuous adaptation. At its core, retail is about people: their needs, their desires and their stories.

But shopping is not merely functional; it is deeply personal. It's a way to express individuality, to connect with trends and even to define identity. Whether buying out of necessity or indulgence, the act of shopping reveals the interplay between practicality and aspiration. While macro changes like technological advancements and globalization have transformed the industry, the heart of retail remains unchanged – the ability to create meaningful connections with consumers.

A new framework for understanding consumer behaviour

In navigating this complex relationship, the *Buyerarchy of Needs* emerges as a critical tool. Inspired by Maslow's hierarchy but adapted for the retail world, it recognizes that consumer behaviour is fluid, not fixed. While Maslow's pyramid suggests a progression from basic to higher-order needs, the *Buyerarchy* reflects the realities of modern retail: consumers frequently move between levels, driven by emotions, peer influence or changing circumstances.

Take, for instance, the meteoric rise of fast fashion. On the surface, it addresses a practical need – affordable clothing. Yet brands like Zara and H&M have mastered the art of triggering emotional responses. They play on the desire for novelty, the influence of social media and the fear of missing out, encouraging consumers to prioritize wants over needs. This dynamic interplay between necessity and desire lies at the heart of retail's evolution.

Similarly, ethical considerations have begun to factor into consumer choices. Shoppers are increasingly balancing their aspirations for affordability and trendiness with the desire to support sustainable and socially responsible brands. These shifting priorities illustrate the layered complexity of modern consumer behaviour, where financial means, emotional desires and social values constantly interact.

KEY TAKEAWAYS

1 Emotional triggers drive behaviour

While practical needs often form the foundation of shopping behaviour, it is emotional triggers that frequently dictate purchasing decisions. Retailers must understand this fluidity and address both functional and aspirational needs to stay relevant.

2 Desire is as important as need

Successful brands don't just meet needs – they create desire. By appealing to higher levels of the *Buyerarchy*, they can transform their offerings into objects of aspiration. Value creation lies in building emotional connections that resonate with consumers on a deeper level.

3 Retail mirrors society

The evolution of retail reflects broader societal changes, from the rise of convenience and speed championed by Amazon to the growing consumer demand for sustainability. Retailers must remain agile, recognizing these shifts to remain aligned with consumer expectations.

4 A constant interplay of factors

Financial constraints, social influence and emotional drivers operate in tandem to shape consumer choices. Retailers that can navigate these layers effectively will be better positioned to anticipate and fulfil their customers' evolving needs.

As we continue to explore the future of retail, it's important to remember that retail is not static – it evolves with society, technology and consumer expectations. Yet its essence remains rooted in human connection. Brands that thrive in this ever-changing landscape are those that understand their customers not just as buyers, but as people with emotions, aspirations and stories.

The evolution of retail reflects how far we've come – and where we're going. By focusing on personalization, building emotional resonance and tapping into the fluid nature of the *Buyerarchy of Needs*, retailers can position themselves to meet the demands of today's consumers while paving the way for tomorrow. The journey is not just about selling products; it's about shaping experiences that matter.

Chapter 2: The psychology of shopping

Shopping is far more complex than a simple exchange of money for goods or services. At its core, it is a deeply human act shaped by emotions, perceptions and desires. It is about meeting needs – not just practical ones, but emotional and psychological needs too. Understanding the motivations behind why people shop is essential for any retailer that wants to connect meaningfully with its customers.

In today's consumer-driven world, rational decision-making is often only part of the story. While price and practicality play a role, they are frequently overshadowed by emotional triggers – desires, fears and aspirations. To thrive in this environment, retailers need to go beyond functional benefits and focus on creating emotional value for their customers.

The Equation of Value

Central to this is the Equation of Value:

$$\text{Product/Service} + \text{Perceived Value} = \text{Price Paid}$$

This simple yet profound formula highlights that value is not a fixed concept; it is shaped by perception. A product is not just judged on its price tag but on how it makes the consumer feel. Does it evoke a sense of pride, security or joy? Is the emotional pay-off worth the monetary cost?

Luxury brands like Louis Vuitton or Chanel illustrate this perfectly. Their appeal goes far beyond the product itself. A handbag or a pair of shoes from these brands carries the weight of cultural significance, status and emotional resonance. For their customers, the perceived value – what the product represents – far exceeds its physical worth, justifying the premium price.

Emotional drivers in consumer behaviour

Consumers are often motivated more by the desire to avoid loss than by the prospect of gain. This is why strategies such as limited-time offers or scarcity models are so effective. These approaches heighten the perception of value by playing on the fear of missing out (FOMO), triggering emotional responses that lead to action.

At the same time, modern consumers seek reassurance in their purchases – what can be called *emotional insurance*. They want to feel that their choices are smart, responsible and rewarding. Brands like Apple and Patagonia excel in providing this emotional safety net. Apple's ecosystem of products creates a sense of reliability and innovation, while Patagonia's sustainability narrative offers consumers the satisfaction of aligning their purchases with their values.

KEY TAKEAWAYS

1 Emotional security is a priority
Consumers today are as driven by the emotional aspects of shopping as they are by practical needs. Retailers must understand that their customers seek more than products – they seek emotional reassurance and connection.

2 Perceived value drives purchasing decisions
The *Equation of Value* reminds us that value is largely about perception. Retailers must craft compelling narratives around their products, enhancing the consumer's emotional investment and justifying their price.

3 The power of scarcity and urgency
Urgency-driven models like limited-time offers or exclusive collections work because they heighten the emotional stakes. Retailers can use these tools to amplify the perceived value of their products.

4 Emotional narratives build loyalty
Narratives that focus on emotional storytelling – whether through sustainability, innovation or community – create connections that are harder to replicate, and help foster loyalty in a competitive market.

THE EMOTIONAL HEART OF RETAIL

At its essence, shopping is a deeply personal act. It is a way for consumers to express their identity, fulfil their desires and find emotional satisfaction. The most successful retailers are those that recognize the human side of shopping, crafting experiences that resonate on an emotional level.

As the industry evolves, the importance of connection will only grow. Retailers that embrace this understanding will not only sell products but create lasting relationships with their customers. By focusing on the emotional drivers behind consumer behaviour and crafting value-driven narratives, they can ensure their relevance in an ever-changing landscape.

The psychology of shopping reminds us that the act of buying is rarely just about the product – it is about the feelings, stories and aspirations tied to it. Retailers that understand and embrace this will not only meet consumer needs but become an integral part of their lives.

Chapter 3: Mastering the digital landscape of e-commerce

In today's retail landscape, e-commerce isn't just a channel; it's a mindset. The digital transformation of shopping has redefined consumer expectations, making it essential for businesses to evolve. Success now hinges on mastering a seamless blend of technology, convenience and personalization.

The modern consumer is no longer confined to a single shopping format – they expect a unified experience that moves effortlessly between physical stores, online platforms and mobile devices. This is where the concept of *shape-shifting retail* becomes crucial: businesses must be agile, adaptive and ready to meet customers wherever they are.

The pillars of digital mastery

1 **Seamless integration**

   Consumers don't think in silos, and neither should retailers. Whether browsing a store's website, engaging on a mobile app, or stepping into a bricks-and-mortar location, they expect the same experience and service. Achieving this requires consistency across all touchpoints, from branding to customer interactions, ensuring that each channel feels like part of a cohesive whole.

2 **Personalization through data**

Data analytics is no longer optional; it's the foundation of effective engagement. By leveraging customer data, retailers can create highly tailored experiences that resonate with individual preferences. Whether through specialized product recommendations or customized promotions, the ability to make customers feel seen and valued fosters deeper loyalty.

3 **Flexible fulfilment options**

Convenience is king in e-commerce, and flexible fulfilment is its crown jewel. Offering options like kerbside pickup, same-day delivery, or buy online, pick up in-store (BOPIS) meets diverse customer needs while reinforcing trust in a brand's ability to deliver – literally.

4 **Robust technology infrastructure**

Behind every seamless shopping experience lies a powerful technological backbone. Scalable, secure platforms are essential to real-time inventory management, efficient order processing and responsive customer service. Retailers must view technology as a core investment, not a secondary tool.

5 **Sustainability as strategy**

Today's consumers are increasingly choosing brands that align with their values. Incorporating eco-friendly practices throughout the supply chain – whether through reduced packaging, sustainable sourcing or carbon-neutral operations – is not only an ethical imperative but a competitive advantage.

The future is adaptive

Shape-shifting is the ultimate key to thriving in the digital era. As technology and consumer behaviours continue to evolve, retailers must remain flexible, anticipating and responding to changes with agility. It's not just about keeping pace – it's about staying one step ahead.

KEY TAKEAWAYS

1 **A seamless, omnichannel approach is vital**
   It ensures that customers experience consistency and ease, no matter how they choose to shop.

2 **Personalization, backed by data insights enables growth**
   It builds stronger customer relationships and drives loyalty.

3 **Flexible fulfilment options enhance convenience and trust**
   These make it easier for consumers to choose your brand.

4 **Investing in robust technology infrastructure is key**
   It supports operational excellence and prepares retailers for future growth.

5 **Embracing sustainability is no longer optional**
   It's now a necessary component of long-term success.

6 **Mastering the digital landscape isn't just about technology**
   It's also about creating a customer journey that feels effortless, personal and
   meaningful at every step.

Chapter 4: Redefining retail in the age of technology

The power of physical retail spaces lies in their ability to create an emotional connection that extends beyond the product. Despite the rise of e-commerce, consumers continue to crave tactile, immersive experiences that online shopping alone cannot fulfil. Physical stores remain a vital part of the retail ecosystem, offering opportunities for discovery, interaction and connection.

However, the role of these spaces has shifted. It's no longer enough to simply present products; retailers must now craft environments that invite consumers to stay, explore and engage. Today's shoppers are seeking more than transactions – they want meaningful experiences that align with their values and needs. This evolution is a testament to the enduring importance of bricks-and-mortar stores, not as stand-alone entities but as critical anchors in an omnichannel strategy.

The new rules of physical retail

1 Interactive, experience-rich spaces
   Modern stores are no longer places to simply browse and buy; they are destinations. Retailers are redesigning spaces to offer workshops, product demonstrations and sensory experiences that make shopping memorable. By creating environments that encourage exploration and interaction, brands can build emotional connections that drive long-term loyalty.

2 Omnichannel integration as a competitive edge
   Leading retailers like Walmart have demonstrated the value of using physical stores as part of a larger omnichannel strategy. Services such as

BOPIS seamlessly blend digital convenience with physical interaction, meeting consumer demands for flexibility and immediacy. This approach also brings customers into stores, creating opportunities for additional purchases and deeper engagement.

3 **Personalization through data insights**
Incorporating digital tools like point-of-sale systems and customer data platforms allows retailers to tailor in-store experiences to individual preferences. By understanding consumer habits and needs, brands can provide personalized product suggestions, customized promotions and unique in-store events. These personalized touches transform the store visit into a curated experience that feels relevant and rewarding to the shopper.

4 **Interactive POP displays**
Point-of-purchase (POP) displays are becoming increasingly dynamic, integrating digital screens, augmented reality (AR) and interactive features that capture attention and spark curiosity. These displays allow consumers to engage with products in ways that mimic the convenience of online shopping while delivering the sensory satisfaction of in-person exploration.

5 **Physical stores as omnichannel anchors**
In a digitally dominated world, physical stores play a pivotal role in providing tangible brand experiences. They serve as the heart of omnichannel strategies, offering spaces where customers can see, feel and connect with products and services in real time. By integrating traditional layouts with innovative technology, retailers can create environments that feel both familiar and forward-thinking, ensuring that physical spaces remain indispensable.

The future of physical retail

Physical stores are not relics of the past but opportunities for innovation. By reimagining these spaces as hubs for connection, discovery and engagement, retailers can deliver something e-commerce cannot fully replicate – an emotional, sensory experience that resonates with the consumer.

As retail continues to evolve, the most successful brands will be those that understand the consumer's desire for balance: the convenience of digital with the richness of physical. Stores that embrace this duality will not only remain relevant but will thrive, providing the kinds of experiences that turn shoppers into loyal advocates.

KEY TAKEAWAYS

1 **Physical retail spaces are evolving into interactive, experience-rich environments**
These should look to cater to the emotional and sensory needs of consumers.

2 **Omnichannel strategies are only becoming more important**
Strategies like BOPIS and seamless integration are vital for ensuring that stores remain competitive and consumer-focused in a digital-first world.

3 **Personalization through data insights enhances the in-store journey**
These help to make shopping more relevant and rewarding for individuals.

4 **Interactive POP displays combine the convenience of digital engagement with the sensory satisfaction of in-person shopping**
These create a dynamic experience for customers.

5 **Physical stores are not just transactional spaces**
They are also essential touchpoints that anchor omnichannel strategies and foster lasting brand relationships.

The transformation of physical retail spaces represents an exciting moment for the industry – a chance to deliver what consumers truly want: memorable, meaningful experiences. By embracing innovation while staying true to the human side of shopping, retailers can ensure their stores remain vibrant, valuable and central to the future of retail.

Chapter 5: Retail spaces, evolving places

The retail environment is no longer confined to the traditional purpose of facilitating transactions. It has evolved into a dynamic space where brands engage with consumers in meaningful ways, blending commerce with experience, culture and innovation. Retail spaces are now designed to inspire and connect, transforming shopping into an activity that resonates emotionally and socially.

This shift has been driven by changing consumer expectations and technological advancements, forcing retailers to reimagine their physical spaces. As we look to the future, stores will need to do more than house products –

they must offer experiences that are immersive, personalized and reflective of the values consumers hold dear.

The future of retail environments

1   **From transactions to experiences**

    Retail spaces are becoming destinations, offering far more than products on shelves. By incorporating dining, entertainment, wellness services and cultural activities, retailers are creating spaces that encourage longer visits and foster deeper engagement. For example, flagship stores such as those of Nike and Lululemon have integrated fitness studios and event spaces, creating communities around their brands. The future of retail lies in this shift from functional spaces to experience-driven environments.

2   **Technology-driven personalization**

    Advanced technologies like augmented reality (AR), virtual reality (VR) and artificial intelligence (AI) are redefining how consumers interact with brands in-store. These tools allow for tailored experiences – think virtual try-ons, personalized recommendations, or smart mirrors that adjust lighting and style suggestions. Beyond enhancing customer satisfaction, these technologies provide valuable insights into consumer preferences, helping retailers refine their offerings and optimize their strategies.

3   **A greater commitment to sustainability**

    As consumer demand for eco-conscious practices grows, retail spaces must integrate sustainability into their design and operations. From sourcing eco-friendly materials for store interiors to minimizing energy consumption and waste, sustainability is no longer optional – it's a necessity. Brands that align with these values not only appeal to ethically minded consumers but also contribute to long-term business resilience.

4   **Non-traditional retail spaces**

    The rise of pop-up shops, hotel boutiques and hybrid spaces demonstrates how brands are breaking away from traditional retail formats. These innovative spaces often combine shopping with social, cultural or lifestyle experiences, such as art galleries or cafés. For example, Glossier's pop-up shops serve as community hubs, blending retail with brand storytelling and interactive installations. These flexible formats offer retailers opportunities to test markets, experiment with concepts and engage consumers in new ways.

5 The role of sensory marketing

Retail's power lies in its ability to engage all five senses. Sensory elements – like inviting scents, curated playlists, tactile displays or even sampling stations – help consumers form emotional connections with brands. For example, Abercrombie & Fitch is known for its signature scent, which creates a distinctive and recognizable atmosphere. By appealing to the senses, retailers can create memorable experiences that foster loyalty and enhance the shopping journey.

A template for the future

The evolution of retail spaces is a response to changing consumer needs, technological innovations and societal shifts. Physical stores are no longer merely places to shop – they are platforms for storytelling, interaction and discovery. Successful retailers are those that understand that the future of retail lies in creating environments that resonate emotionally and reflect consumer values.

KEY TAKEAWAYS

1 **Retail spaces must be destinations**
They now need to offer experiences that blend shopping with dining, entertainment and wellness to foster deeper engagement.

2 **Technology is central to personalization**
AR, VR and AI now enable tailored, interactive experiences that satisfy consumers while providing retailers with valuable insights.

3 **Sustainability is a priority**
Eco-friendly practices and materials are increasingly important to today's ethically minded shoppers.

4 **Non-traditional spaces, such as pop-ups and hybrid formats, are gaining traction**
These offer innovative ways to connect with consumers.

5 **Sensory marketing remains a powerful tool**
Retailers should think about engaging sight, sound, smell, taste and touch to create memorable, emotionally resonant shopping experiences.

THE ENDURING ROLE OF RETAIL SPACES

As the retail environment continues to evolve, one thing remains constant: the need to connect with consumers in meaningful ways. By embracing innovation, prioritizing sustainability, and creating spaces that engage the senses and inspire, retailers can redefine the purpose of physical stores.

These evolving places are not just where transactions happen – they are where brands come to life, where stories are told and where consumers find experiences that matter. The future of retail lies in spaces that are as dynamic and multifaceted as the people they serve.

Chapter 6: Roll up, roll up! This is retail theatre

Retail theatre is the transformative force that turns ordinary shopping trips into extraordinary experiences. In a world brimming with choices, the ability to surprise and delight has become a key differentiator. By blending storytelling, design and interactivity, retail theatre brings brands to life in ways that engage all the senses, connect emotionally and leave lasting impressions.

It's no longer enough for stores to display products on shelves – today's consumers seek immersive environments that excite and inspire. Retail theatre transforms shopping into an event, with customers as active participants in the brand story. From carefully orchestrated lighting to the integration of cutting-edge technology, every element is designed to captivate and engage, creating moments that linger long after the visit ends.

The role of retail theatre in modern shopping

Retail theatre taps into the psychology of human connection. By turning stores into stages and shoppers into co-creators of the experience, it delivers something intangible yet powerful: a sense of magic. Whether through flagship stores that evoke wonder, pop-ups that create a buzz, or sensory displays that make a lasting impression, retail theatre elevates shopping from a transactional act to a memorable journey.

For example, a visit to the flagship store of a luxury brand might feel like stepping into another world, where every detail – from the ambient scent to the curated soundtrack – is designed to convey the essence of the brand.

Similarly, a pop-up shop for an emerging brand might harness creativity and spectacle to make a bold statement, leaving visitors with a lasting emotional connection.

Retailers that embrace these theatrical elements aren't just selling products; they're offering an experience that becomes part of the consumer's story.

Techniques that bring retail theatre to life

1 **Sensory engagement**

Retail theatre excels at engaging the senses. Brands use sight, sound, smell, touch and even taste to create environments that feel vibrant and alive. For example, Abercrombie & Fitch's signature scent or Starbucks' curated playlists build sensory experiences that customers associate with the brand. These elements make the experience richer, more memorable and emotionally resonant.

2 **Immersive technologies**

Augmented reality AR, VR and interactive displays are adding new layers to retail experiences. From trying on virtual outfits to exploring product features in an interactive way, these technologies invite customers to actively engage with the brand, making shopping both entertaining and informative.

3 **Thoughtful store design**

Store layouts influence how customers explore and interact with products. Apple's minimalist design, with its open spaces and hands-on displays, encourages customers to experiment with technology, making them feel confident and connected. These design choices create an intuitive and enjoyable experience that fosters loyalty.

4 **Theatrical pop-ups and experiential flagships**

Temporary spaces like pop-ups and experiential flagship stores are a playground for retail theatre. Brands use these spaces to tell stories, launch new products or celebrate cultural moments. By making these experiences immersive and interactive, they capture attention, generate buzz and create an emotional bond with visitors.

5 **Emotional storytelling**

The heart of retail theatre lies in storytelling. Brands craft narratives that invite consumers into their world, creating experiences that align with their aspirations and emotions. Whether it's a sustainability story embedded in the design of a store, or a campaign brought to life through interactive displays, these narratives make shopping meaningful and memorable.

KEY TAKEAWAYS

1 Retail theatre transforms shopping into an experience

Consumers today crave immersive, memorable shopping experiences. Retail theatre engages audiences by turning stores into destinations that delight and inspire, going beyond transactions to create meaningful connections.

2 Sensory engagement drives emotional connections

Engaging multiple senses – sight, sound, smell, taste and touch – helps retailers create deep emotional bonds with their customers. Sensory-rich experiences leave lasting impressions, fostering brand recall and loyalty.

3 Strategic store design influences consumer behaviour

Thoughtful layouts and design elements, like those found in Apple stores, encourage customers to interact with products in meaningful ways. This not only enhances the shopping experience but also builds trust and confidence in the brand.

4 Sensory elements build loyalty

From ambient scents to interactive displays, sensory cues create an environment that customers associate with positive feelings. These memorable experiences are key to ensuring repeat visits and fostering loyalty.

5 The future of retail combines sensory and digital innovations

As retail evolves, the integration of sensory experiences with digital technology will become increasingly important. Retail theatre will blend emotional engagement with data-driven personalization, offering consumers the perfect balance of inspiration and convenience.

THE MAGIC OF RETAIL THEATRE

Retail theatre is more than a trend – it is a vital response to the modern consumer's desire for meaningful, emotional engagement. It takes shopping beyond the transactional, creating moments of joy, wonder and connection. By integrating sensory elements, storytelling and technology, retailers can transform their spaces into stages where unforgettable experiences unfold.

The future of retail lies in its ability to merge the digital and the physical, the practical and the magical. Retail theatre ensures that stores remain vibrant, dynamic places where brands can connect with their audiences in ways that go far beyond the product. In a competitive market, it's this artistry – the ability to craft experiences that resonate deeply – that sets brands apart and keeps consumers coming back for more.

Chapter 7: The art of shopping perception

Shopping has always been about more than the products we buy – it's about what those products represent and the trust we place in the people or brands that endorse them. From the royal seal of approval in centuries past to the rise of digital influencers today, perception plays a critical role in shaping consumer behaviour. At its heart, this chapter explores the power of influence: how individuals – celebrities, social media personalities and even everyday customers – shape brand narratives and drive consumer decisions.

As retail evolves, so does the psychology of influence. In the digital age, the lines between celebrities, influencers and advocates blur, creating new opportunities for brands to connect with audiences in ways that feel authentic and engaging. The future of retail is not just about the products – it's about who stands behind them and the stories they tell.

The evolving role of influencers in shaping brand perception

1 **The enduring power of celebrity endorsements**
   Celebrity endorsements have been a cornerstone of retail for centuries. Josiah Wedgwood famously leveraged a royal endorsement in the 18th century to position his ceramics as the pinnacle of quality and sophistication. Today, figures like Kim Kardashian elevate brands such as SKIMS into cultural phenomena, merging personal brand power with commercial success. These endorsements are rooted in trust, status and aspiration, evolving with each era's cultural priorities.

2 **Social media influencers and the appeal of authenticity**
   The rise of social media has shifted the focus from traditional celebrities to influencers who feel relatable and accessible. Influencers bridge the gap between aspirational and attainable, creating trust through perceived

authenticity. Followers see influencers as peers, valuing their opinions on products and experiences in ways that traditional advertising struggles to replicate.

3   The power of micro- and nano-influencers
While mega-influencers dominate headlines, micro- and nano-influencers are quietly reshaping the marketing landscape. With smaller, more engaged audiences, these influencers excel at connecting with niche demographics. For example, a food blogger with 10,000 followers may have a stronger impact on a local café's success than a celebrity with millions of followers, thanks to their community's trust and loyalty.

4   The rise of community-driven advocacy
In an age of peer-to-peer marketing, customers themselves are becoming powerful advocates. Platforms like Lego's Lego Ideas and Amazon's review system empower communities to champion brands, fostering trust and engagement. These grass-roots endorsements can be as influential as a high-profile campaign, proving that trust built from the ground up is invaluable in shaping brand perception.

5   Technological advances and the future of influence
Emerging technologies are revolutionizing how brands leverage influence. AI-driven algorithms identify trends and connect brands with the right advocates. Blockchain ensures transparency in influencer partnerships, enhancing credibility. AR and VR bring immersive experiences to life, enabling consumers to interact with products through the lens of their favourite influencers. These tools are redefining the boundaries of what's possible in influencer marketing.

KEY TAKEAWAYS

1   **Celebrity endorsements stand the test of time**
From historical royal endorsements to modern-day celebrity-led brands, the psychology of trust and status continues to underpin the success of high-profile partnerships.

2   **Authenticity drives trust in influencers**
Social media influencers have redefined brand advocacy, blending relatability with reach. Their perceived authenticity fosters trust, making them a cornerstone of modern marketing strategies.

3 **Niche influencers build community loyalty**
Micro- and nano-influencers excel at fostering genuine connections within specific communities, offering brands a powerful way to engage with targeted audiences.

4 **Community advocacy strengthens brand perception**
Platforms that encourage customer advocacy and peer-to-peer recommendations, like Amazon and Lego, showcase the growing influence of grass-roots marketing.

5 **Technology is shaping the future of influence**
AI, blockchain, AR and VR are redefining the influencer landscape, providing brands with innovative tools to enhance trust, engagement and consumer connection.

A NEW ERA OF INFLUENCE

As we move forward, the art of shopping perception will continue to evolve, shaped by the interplay of human connection and technological innovation. The most successful brands will be those that understand the shifting dynamics of influence – leveraging celebrity power, embracing authenticity and empowering communities to champion their stories.

In the end, influence is about trust. Whether it comes from a celebrity, a social media influencer or a fellow customer, the endorsement carries weight because it feels genuine. By harnessing the power of perception, brands can not only reach their audiences but create lasting relationships that transcend the transactional. The future of retail lies in this delicate balance between aspiration and authenticity, storytelling and connection.

Chapter 8: Goldilocks and the pricing strategy: Finding a price point that's just right

Pricing is far more than a mathematical equation; it is a strategic narrative that shapes consumer behaviour, builds loyalty and defines brand identity. At its best, pricing is a dialogue between retailers and consumers – a blend of perception, psychology and storytelling. From the allure of £9.99 to the exclusivity of luxury price points, pricing has the power to evoke emotions, influence decisions and foster long-term trust.

In today's rapidly evolving retail landscape, pricing strategies have become increasingly sophisticated. They are not static; they respond to cultural shifts, technological advancements and consumer expectations. Every price tells a story – one that appeals to our instincts, aspirations and subconscious biases. Understanding these narratives enables both retailers and consumers to engage in more meaningful transactions.

The art and science of pricing

1 **The emotional impact of pricing**
Pricing is not just about logic; it appeals to our emotions and instincts. Techniques like charm pricing (£9.99 instead of £10) and decoy pricing (introducing a slightly inferior option to make a more expensive one seem reasonable) leverage cognitive biases to make choices feel intuitive. These strategies highlight how pricing can guide decisions without overt persuasion.

2 **Scarcity as a driver of value and loyalty**
Limited editions, exclusive collections and 'last chance' sales thrive on the psychology of scarcity. By creating urgency, these tactics encourage immediate action. More importantly, they foster loyalty by making consumers feel like part of an exclusive group – a key factor in premium branding.

3 **Dynamic pricing in the digital age**
With advancements in AI and real-time data analytics, retailers can now adjust prices dynamically to reflect market trends, consumer behaviour and inventory levels. While this creates personalized experiences, it also raises the need for transparency. Trust is essential; consumers need to feel that dynamic pricing serves their interests, not just the retailer's bottom line.

4 **The risks of perpetual discounts**
Endless sales and markdowns can undermine a brand's value, as seen in the struggles of legacy retailers like Debenhams. Effective pricing strategies strike a balance between short-term gains and long-term confidence in a product's worth. Consumers are more likely to stay loyal to brands that maintain consistent value rather than relying on constant discounts.

5 **The future of pricing: Ethical, transparent and innovative**
As pricing continues to evolve, sustainability and fairness will play a growing role. Consumers increasingly demand transparency in pricing, as

well as practices that reflect social and environmental responsibility. Brands that prioritize these values – while leveraging technology to innovate – will lead the way in building stronger, trust-based consumer relationships.

KEY TAKEAWAYS

1 Pricing is emotional

Retailers use psychological techniques, like charm and decoy pricing, to influence subconscious decision-making, making prices feel more appealing and choices more natural.

2 Scarcity builds value and trust

Scarcity-driven strategies, such as limited editions and exclusivity, create urgency while also fostering brand loyalty by making consumers feel special.

3 Dynamic pricing reflects modern realities

AI-driven pricing offers tailored consumer experiences but must be paired with transparency to maintain trust.

4 Perpetual discounts undermine brand value

Overuse of sales and discounts can erode consumer confidence in a brand's products, while balanced pricing strategies reinforce long-term value.

5 Ethics and technology shape the future

The next phase of pricing innovation will prioritize fairness, sustainability and transparency, ensuring that pricing enhances rather than exploits the consumer relationship.

PRICING AS A LIVING DIALOGUE

Pricing is not static; it is a living, evolving tool that reflects the intersection of consumer psychology, market dynamics and cultural values. As we move forward, the most successful brands will be those that understand pricing as an emotional and ethical dialogue – one that fosters trust, loyalty and value.

For consumers, understanding the psychology behind pricing is empowering. It allows us to see beyond the numbers, recognizing the strategies at play and making more informed decisions. In the world of retail, every price tells a story, and by decoding that story, we gain the clarity and confidence to navigate an increasingly complex marketplace.

Chapter 9: Mastering promotional strategies to boost sales

Promotions are far more than simple tools for driving sales – they are an opportunity to build trust, deepen relationships and create emotional connections with consumers. This chapter has explored the multifaceted world of promotional strategies, from limited-time discounts to loyalty programmes and compelling giveaways. At their core, promotions are about more than financial incentives; they are about tapping into human psychology and fostering a sense of value, urgency and delight.

In the modern retail landscape, successful promotions go beyond short-term gains. They are crafted to amplify brand equity, align with consumer values and provide memorable experiences. Whether it's the thrill of an exclusive launch, the comfort of a personalized reward, or the excitement of a gamified campaign, promotions are a critical avenue for turning transactions into lasting connections.

However, the power of promotions must be wielded carefully. Overuse can lead to diminished trust and perceived value, while thoughtful execution can elevate a brand's standing and earn consumer loyalty. As retailers navigate the future, the emphasis will shift towards holistic promotional ecosystems that integrate sustainability, personalization and transparency, ensuring consumers feel not only rewarded but respected.

KEY TAKEAWAYS

1 Promotions spark emotion and loyalty

The best promotions tap into emotional triggers, offering consumers more than financial savings. They create experiences – whether through the thrill of securing a deal, winning a prize or feeling personally valued.

2 Balance short-term gains with long-term trust

Over-reliance on discounts and flash sales can erode brand value and train consumers to wait for deals. Strategic promotions should build trust, maintain equity and drive sustainable growth.

3 Gamification and rewards deepen engagement

Campaigns like McDonald's Monopoly or loyalty point systems engage consumers through play, fostering a sense of excitement and achievement. These strategies drive repeat visits while strengthening emotional connections.

4 Scarcity and urgency are key drivers

Limited-time offers, exclusive product launches and 'only while supplies last' messaging leverage FOMO to drive immediate action, while also enhancing brand desirability.

5 Sustainability and ethics enhance appeal

Promotions tied to sustainability or ethical causes resonate deeply with modern consumers, who seek alignment with their values. Brands that use promotions to support social or environmental initiatives create goodwill and long-term loyalty.

6 Technology enables personalization and precision

AI and data analytics allow retailers to tailor promotions to individual consumers, offering rewards, discounts and messaging that feel personal and relevant. This strengthens the bond between consumer and brand while maximizing promotional impact.

TURNING TRANSACTIONS INTO CONNECTIONS

Promotions are no longer just about driving traffic or boosting sales figures – they are a bridge between brand and consumer, an invitation to build trust, spark joy and create shared value. The most impactful promotions combine human emotion with ethical transparency, ensuring consumers feel respected, rewarded and connected.

As the competitive retail landscape continues to evolve, retailers must embrace promotions as a strategic tool to foster loyalty, reinforce brand reputation and create meaningful connections. By aligning promotions with consumer values and leveraging innovative tools, brands can transform one-off transactions into enduring relationships that drive growth and loyalty in the long term.

Conclusion

*The consumer: The unwavering north star
in retail's constantly shifting sky*

Retail today is faster, more furious, and undoubtedly more competitive than ever before. There are more entrants to the market, more ways to sell and more products available at the click of a button. As we've explored throughout this book, the landscape is flooded with options – from immediate delivery of everything from a designer dog outfit to a gourmet ice cube mould, to personalized shopping experiences that anticipate our needs before we even know them ourselves. Retail has evolved into a relentless 24/7 arena, and in this race, there is a tendency to believe that speed, data and convenience are the only factors that matter.

But the real story is more nuanced. As we've dissected retail's many logics and strategies, a single red thread has emerged, connecting every element of this fast-changing game: the consumer.

In many ways, the consumer remains the true constant in a sea of flux. Yet, how we understand, engage with and respond to consumers has fundamentally shifted. The old guard of retail has grown weary, frustrated by the pace and overwhelmed by a need to adapt. And on the other side, the all-digital, data-driven crowd has started to realize that, while data is invaluable, it is far from sufficient on its own. The next frontier – the one that will truly guide retail into the future – is a deeper focus on the consumer, one that goes beyond algorithms and numbers, and taps into something more profound: humanity.

In this new age, it is not enough to let the consumer lead. The belief that the customer should guide all decisions is flawed – how can the consumer lead when they too are unsure of what the future holds? As retailers, we are tasked with the responsibility to listen, to engage and to be ahead of the curve in ways that resonate deeply with the consumer's emotional intelligence. This is where empathy and authenticity become the most valuable assets a business can have.

The consumer connection: Building relationships beyond transactions

For years, the mantra of 'the customer is always right' ruled retail. Yet, as I've argued throughout, this simplistic adage no longer holds true in the complexity of today's environment. Consumers are not infallible. They don't always know what they want, nor should they be expected to. But what remains steadfast is their emotional intelligence – their gut sense of what feels right and what doesn't. The challenge for retailers is to meet consumers where they are emotionally, to ask the right questions, test assumptions, support and nurture the connection, and then ask again.

This isn't just about gathering data – it's about empathy-driven insight. It's about respecting the consumer enough to not only ask for their preferences but understand their deeper motivations and desires. In an era where everything is available, where choice is infinite, the brands that will stand out are the ones that stay connected to the human element.

This means showing patience, being clear and consistent in communication, and offering transparency at every stage of the customer journey. It is about showing respect through reliability – under-promising and over-delivering, being honest about what your product or service can do, and never overstating capabilities. The days of dressing things up to look better than they are have long passed. Today's consumer has an acute ability to discern authenticity from marketing fluff, and they will not hesitate to sever ties with brands that betray their trust.

Authenticity in the age of distrust: How to build and maintain trust

At a time when consumer scepticism is at an all-time high, authenticity has never been more critical. It is what separates enduring brands from fleeting trends. Retailers that lead with transparency and honesty will earn long-term loyalty. The truth is, no consumer expects businesses to be altruistic;

they understand that companies need to turn a profit. But what matters most is how that profit is made.

As I've always said: 'Make a profit with pride'. That means building a business model that prioritizes value for the consumer, not just short-term financial gain. It's about having the courage to say 'no' when the product isn't right, or to push back on practices that undermine trust or authenticity. Consumers can and will forgive mistakes – what they will not tolerate is repetitive dishonesty or manipulation.

To put it simply: be real. Be real in your communication, in your promises and in your delivery. Be real in every interaction, because consumers can sense when something is off. They may not be able to articulate it immediately, but there's an innate awareness that lets them know when a brand is out of alignment with its values. Once trust is broken, it's incredibly difficult to restore. This is why integrity must be at the heart of any retail strategy.

Keeping it human in an automated world

The future of retail will be driven by technology – there's no doubt about that. From AI to machine learning, from augmented reality to instant delivery, the possibilities are vast. Yet, for all the advancements that technology can offer, humanity will remain central to the retail experience. There is a growing understanding that while tech can streamline processes and enhance convenience, it can never replace the human touch.

As retailers rely increasingly on automation, it is essential not to lose sight of what makes a brand relatable. Human interaction, even in a digitally dominated world, will continue to be a key differentiator. Whether it's in personalized customer service, authentic storytelling or simple acts of kindness – retailers that remember to stay human will resonate most with their audience.

In many ways, the rise of technology provides an opportunity to enhance human connection, not diminish it. By automating routine tasks, retailers can free up time and resources to focus on what truly matters: building relationships. Imagine a world where most logistical issues are handled by AI, leaving humans to focus on creativity, empathy and emotional engagement. This is my hope for the balance that will define the next era of retail.

The power of emotional intelligence: Reading between the lines

The most successful retailers moving forward will be those that understand and prioritize emotional intelligence (EQ). In a world of data-driven decisions, it's easy to forget that consumers are not robots. They are emotional beings, driven by subconscious desires, social connections and personal values. Brands that can tap into this emotional depth – without being manipulative – will succeed where others fail.

This means moving beyond simply listening to what consumers say they want. It's about reading between the lines, understanding the emotions behind the preferences, and using that insight to anticipate needs before they're expressed. Retailers that can master this delicate dance – combining hard data with soft intuition – will not only stay relevant but become indispensable.

Consider the companies that consistently go beyond transactional relationships where customer experience is a relationship, not a momentary exchange. These brands understand that the emotional investment of their customers is just as important as their financial one, and they work to nurture that emotional loyalty with every interaction.

Profit with pride: A new ethos for retail success

Retail is, and always will be, a business. But the path to profitability need not come at the expense of values or integrity. In fact, the brands that will thrive in the coming years are those that understand the importance of profit with pride. This is about more than just a catchy slogan; it's a principle that should guide every decision a business makes. It's about running a business in a way that not only meets the bottom line but also creates real value for consumers and the world.

Consumers today are more discerning than ever. They know that businesses exist to make money, and they are not opposed to that – what they object to is profiteering at their expense. They want to support businesses that have a higher purpose, that contribute to society in meaningful ways, and that operate with integrity. Retailers that embody this ethos will not only earn customer loyalty – they will earn respect.

As the industry continues to evolve, those who make decisions rooted in pride and integrity will rise to the top. Consumers are looking for businesses that align with their values, that are transparent in their operations and that treat their customers with respect. And that is where the true value lies – both for the consumer and for the business.

Keeping it human: The ultimate competitive advantage

In conclusion, as we navigate the complexities and rapid changes in retail, one thing remains clear: keeping it human is the ultimate competitive advantage. Technology may change, trends may shift, but the fundamental principles of good business – honesty, authenticity and empathy – will never go out of style.

Retail is, at its heart, a human endeavour. It's about understanding people, anticipating their needs and creating experiences that resonate on a deep emotional level. As we move forward, the businesses that keep this in mind will not only survive – they will thrive.

The brands that succeed in the next era will be those that act with integrity, that put the consumer at the centre of everything they do, and that remain true to their values. Because at the end of the day, retail is about more than just selling products – it's about connecting with people.

And as long as we keep that human connection at the core of everything we do, we'll always be on the right path – and that is exactly what my grandparents did – making them (to me) some of the world's best at understanding the science of shopping. Good luck on your path and thank you for shopping with me.

INDEX

The index is filed in alphabetical, word-by-word order. Acronyms are filed as presented. Numbers within headings are filed as spelt out. Locators in italics denote information within a Figure.

Looking for another book?

Explore our award-winning
books from global business
experts in Marketing and Sales

Scan the code to browse

www.koganpage.com/marketing

More from Kogan Page

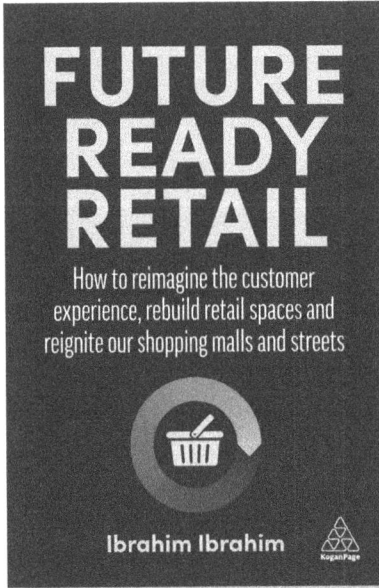

FUTURE READY RETAIL

How to reimagine the customer experience, rebuild retail spaces and reignite our shopping malls and streets

Ibrahim Ibrahim

ISBN: 9781398603349

2nd Edition

OMNICHANNEL RETAIL

HOW TO BUILD WINNING STORES IN A DIGITAL WORLD

Tim Mason and Sarah Jarvis

ISBN: 9781398612723

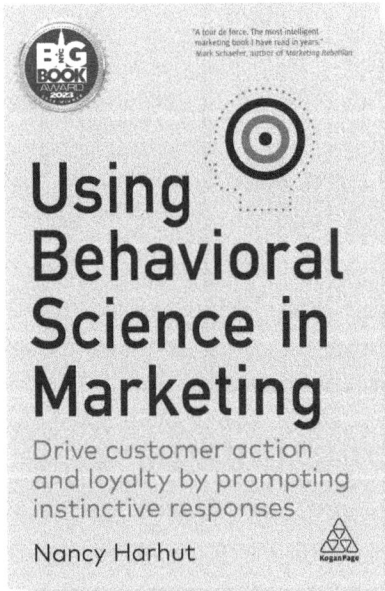

BIG BOOK AWARD 2023

"A tour de force. The most intelligent marketing book I have read in years." Mark Schaefer, author of 'Marketing Rebellion'

Using Behavioral Science in Marketing

Drive customer action and loyalty by prompting instinctive responses

Nancy Harhut

ISBN: 9781398606487

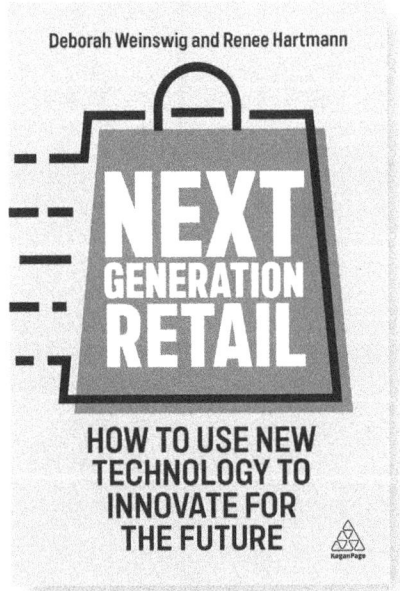

Deborah Weinswig and Renee Hartmann

NEXT GENERATION RETAIL

HOW TO USE NEW TECHNOLOGY TO INNOVATE FOR THE FUTURE

ISBN: 9781398609631

www.koganpage.com

From 4 December 2025 the EU Responsible Person (GPSR) is:
eucomply oÜ, Pärnu mnt. 139b – 14, 11317 Tallinn, Estonia
www.eucompliancepartner.com

www.ingramcontent.com/pod-product-compliance
Lightning Source LLC
Chambersburg PA
CBHW040915210326
41597CB00030B/5086

9 7 8 1 3 9 8 6 2 0 4 6 9